David Ker

O'er Tartar Deserts or English and Russian in Central Asia

David Ker

O'er Tartar Deserts or English and Russian in Central Asia

ISBN/EAN: 9783744750240

Printed in Europe, USA, Canada, Australia, Japan

Cover: Foto ©Andreas Hilbeck / pixelio.de

More available books at **www.hansebooks.com**

O'ER TARTAR DESERTS

OR

ENGLISH AND RUSSIAN
IN CENTRAL ASIA

BY

DAVID KER

AUTHOR OF 'SWEPT OUT TO SEA,' 'PRISONER AMONG PIRATES,'
'WIZARD KING,' 'COSSACK AND CZAR,' ETC.

WITH SIX ILLUSTRATIONS
BY
J. FINNEMORE

W. & R. CHAMBERS, LIMITED
LONDON AND EDINBURGH
1898

TO MY GODSON,

ROMNEY PATTISON MUIR, OF CAMBRIDGE,

THESE 'TALES OF A GODFATHER' ARE

AFFECTIONATELY DEDICATED.

CONTENTS.

CHAPTER	PAGE
I. A STRANGE COIN	1
II. BEFORE THE CZAR	9
III. SACKING A RAILWAY STATION	21
IV. BETWEEN WALLS OF FIRE	34
V. OVER THE BLACK SEA	43
VI. THROUGH THE GIANT MOUNTAINS	56
VII. A RUSSIAN GENERAL	63
VIII. HARRY MAKES TWO NEW ACQUAINTANCES	70
IX. NIKOLAIEVITCH THE FORESTER	84
X. INSIDE THE PALACE	89
XI. THE PERSIAN DAGGER	96
XII. AN UNEXPECTED SUMMONS	104
XIII. THE MIDNIGHT STORM	118
XIV. ON THE BRINK OF THE ABYSS	127
XV. MR ARCHER SEES A FACE	135
XVI. IN DARK WATERS	141
XVII. RIDING THE WHIRLWIND	153
XVIII. MOBBED BY MOHAMMEDANS	166
XIX. MEETING A HIGHLAND CHIEF	180
XX. THE PHANTOM CITY	187
XXI. ESCORTED BY THIEVES	195
XXII. THE BLACK MOUNTAINEERS	204
XXIII. BURIED IN THE SWAMP	214
XXIV. FAMINE	221
XXV. AMONG WILD BEASTS	228
XXVI. CAUGHT IN HIS OWN TRAP	233
XXVII. A TRIP THROUGH MONTENEGRO	241
XXVIII. MISSING	247
XXIX. BURIED WITHOUT A GRAVE	253
XXX. LOST ON THE MOUNTAINS	266
XXXI. NEWS FROM EUROPE	276
XXXII. DRIFTING TO THEIR DOOM	284
XXXIII. AN EASTERN ROB ROY	290
XXXIV. THE OLD MAN OF THE MOUNTAIN	298
XXXV. THE LAST NIGHT OF THE YEAR	307

LIST OF ILLUSTRATIONS.

	PAGE
The path was just a ledge along the brink of a precipice.	*Frontispiece*
Slowly and painfully . . . the obstructing tree was at length forced aside.	39
The fainting man sucked in the cool draught with a frightful eagerness.	99
Wavering for one terrible moment between the precipice and the cliff.	130
The eagle hung poised for an instant on its expanded wings.	257
Sprang upon them with a yell of ferocious triumph.	288

O'ER TARTAR DESERTS.

CHAPTER I.

A STRANGE COIN.

HERE was a stir in the crowd of Russian promenaders that eddied along the broad, white pavement of the 'Kooznetski Most' (Blacksmith's Bridge), the Regent Street of Moscow, on a bright, keen April afternoon; and all the way down the steep, curving incline of the famous street —from which the last snow of the six months' winter had just been cleared—heads were being turned round, fingers pointed, and excited whispers passed from man to man.

Even the light-haired, round-faced children (whose long, frock-like gray coats, reaching right down to their heels, made them look very much like animated flour-sacks) turned away from the glittering shop-windows to stare with the rest; and so marked and universal was this movement of curiosity that a stranger would certainly have thought that the Czar himself, or at least some member of the imperial family, must be passing at that moment.

A

At first sight, however, the man who was apparently the object of all this attention seemed to have nothing about him which could account for it. He was very simply dressed; his appearance was that of an ordinary Russian gentleman; and the only thing remarkable about his handsome though somewhat thin and worn-looking face (the thick, brown moustache of which was slightly sprinkled with gray) was the quietly-watchful expression of his keen blue eyes—an expression such as might be worn by a man who had for years been used to see danger or death start up to face him at any moment.

But if you had looked closer at him, you would have seen that every feature wore that tough, hardy, seasoned look which the English so aptly call 'hard-bitten,' and that his tall, wiry frame, spare and almost gaunt as it was, had all the sinewy strength of a wolf-hound; and as he lifted his right hand to draw his *shooba* (long overcoat) closer round him, it might have been noticed that the finger-tips were curiously cracked and seamed, and stained as if with some dark purple dye.

Altogether, any practised reader of faces would easily guess that this man must have dared and suffered far beyond the measure of his fellow-men; and that such was indeed the case was shown by the excited whisper that buzzed through the throng from mouth to mouth:

'*Vot nash znameneeti pooteshestvennik!*' (There is our famous traveller!)

A famous traveller he undoubtedly was, being no other than Count Feodor (Theodore) Alexandrovitch Bulatoff,[*] the

---

[*] All purely Russian names end in *off* or *in*, *ski* being a Polish and *ko* a Cossack termination. I need hardly say that all the names of my Russian characters in this story are, for obvious reasons, purely fictitious.

most daring and successful of Russian explorers, living or dead. Though still in the prime of life, he had already achieved journeys and researches for which three lives might well have seemed too short. He had penetrated into more than one region in which no white man had ever set foot till then, and had met with a series of deadly perils and hair-breadth escapes which had long since made his name a household word from the White Sea to the Black.

But, so far from being flattered by all this homage, the great explorer seemed to think it rather a bore than otherwise, and did his best to escape from his inconvenient popularity by making a sudden plunge down one of the narrow by-streets that led out of the fashionable thoroughfare.

This hurried exit, however, proved to be a case of 'Most haste, worst speed;' for hardly had he gone a dozen steps along the narrower street, when he was brought to a sudden stand-still by a sharp, ringing sound on the pavement at his feet, as if he had let drop a piece of money.

Money or not, the lost article had evidently some special value, for in another moment the count was down on his knees upon the wet pavement, hunting, as if his life depended on it, for what he had just let fall.

'Excuse me, is this what you are looking for?' said a deep voice behind him in good Russian, but with a slightly foreign accent, as a man who had just come up the street from the opposite direction held out a piece of metal that he had picked up from the ground, apparently a small coin or medal.

But ere the Russian's eagerly extended hand could close upon the prize, the man who had found it started visibly, and holding it up close to his eye, made a keen and careful inspection of it.

It was a small brass coin, a good deal battered, but still retaining some remnants of its original superscription. On one side of it was still visible the faint outline of a helmeted head, and beneath it appeared, in half-effaced Eastern letters, 'KAR... FEE... AN;' but the obverse of the coin, in startling contrast to these Oriental characters, was a genuine *Greek* chariot, worthy to have borne Achilles himself!

'May I be allowed to ask where you got this?' said the stranger politely. 'So far as I know, there is only *one* place in the world where such coins are to be found.'

'And it was there that I got this one,' replied the Russian quietly.

'I will ask your permission, then,' rejoined the other, with a courteous bow, 'to compare it with the specimen that I have here;' and opening a small locket that hung at his watch-chain, he took from it, to the manifest dismay of the count, a coin of exactly similar pattern, and in even better preservation; for, though the chariot on the obverse was all but effaced, the head itself was much plainer, and the inscription beneath it quite uninjured, running thus: 'KARA SUFFEE KHAN.'

'That is really a far finer example than mine,' cried the explorer, forgetting his passing chagrin in a movement of honest admiration. 'Well, I had thought that I was the first European who had reached that spot, but I find I must own myself mistaken. I remember now that the Mongols of the place *did* tell me that one " White-face from the West" had been there before me; but I took it for granted that they were lying, as they usually are whenever they tell one anything at all. It seems, though, they *did* tell the truth for once.'

'They did,' said his new friend; 'and I shall always be proud to think that, once in my life, I had the honour of equalling one of the achievements of Count Bulatoff.'

'You know me, then?' cried the count, looking fixedly at him, as if expecting to recognise an acquaintance.

'Nothing wonderful in that,' laughed the other, 'since your portrait is in the window of every photographer in Moscow and St Petersburg. But, apart from that, when one hears of a daring journey made into the wilds by a Russian explorer, it is an easy matter to guess *who* he must be.'

'You are very good,' said the Russian, evidently pleased with the compliment; 'but since you know *me*, may I not know, in my turn, the name of my successful rival?'

'Don't say *rival*, pray—say a fellow-labourer in the same field,' cried the stranger heartily. 'And as for my name, I am an Englishman, called Livingstone Archer.'

'Livingstone Archer!' echoed the count, eyeing with a new interest the short, square, sturdy frame and firm, sun-browned, bearded face of the man whose name was as famous in the world of travel as his own. 'I am indeed fortunate, then; for though I always hoped that we should meet some day, I never expected it to come so soon; and I have no cause to take shame to myself for having been beaten by such a worthy namesake of the great Dr Livingstone;' and he grasped the Englishman's strong, brown hand with a frank cordiality which there was no mistaking.

'There is no question of being *beaten* in the matter,' rejoined Archer, returning his grasp with equal energy; 'you did just as much as I did, only I happened to be a little earlier. After all, so long as a thing *is* done, and the world gets the good of it, what does it matter who gets the credit? Hollo!' he went on, glancing with an air of recognition at the scars on the hand that he held, 'I ought to know those marks! Was it the fire-torture?'

'Indeed it was,' said Count Bulatoff, with a grim smile; 'and if it had lasted only a few minutes longer, I should never have shaken hands with any one with this hand again!'

'Well, you beat me there,' cried the Englishman, 'for, though I have often seen it tried upon other men, I have never had a taste of it myself; although, as you see, I've had *my* right hand speared through (showing a deep scar, or rather trench, in his palm). Well, Feodor Alexandrovitch (Theodore, son of Alexander), we English sometimes say that it was "the toss of a halfpenny" that such-and-such a thing happened as it did, and not otherwise; and that has been literally the case with this meeting of ours.'

'And now that we *have* met,' cried the count, 'and met in such a way, we must not part again so soon. Where are you staying?'

'Billot's Hotel,' replied the Englishman, turning as if to move on again.

'Aha! the old place in the Loobianka?' said Bulatoff. 'Many a merry evening have I had there with my friend Professor Makaroff, who has just gone off to dig up some Persian kings at Persepolis. But where are we going now? I don't want to get back into that crowd again, and be stared at as if I were a newly-caught wild beast. Are *you* bound anywhere in particular just now, may I ask?'

'Not in the least. I am only out for a stroll.'

'Let us go to the Kremlin, then; there won't be many people on the promenade just now, and we can have a good long talk.'

Away they went, through the narrow, dingy lanes of the Gorodskaya Tchast, or city quarter, and across the wide, bare expanse of the Krasnaya Ploshtchad (Red Plain), over which the vast, red, many-turreted rampart of the Kremlin cast a lengthening shadow in the slanting sunlight; and then, leaving to their left the cluster of brightly-painted domes crowning the great church of St Vasili the Blessed—piously erected by Ivan the Terrible on the spot where he had put four hundred men to death—they entered the famous citadel by the Spasskaya Vorota, or Gate of Deliverance. Through this gate, in October 1612, the few Polish invaders who had survived one of the most desperate sieges on record filed out and left Moscow free, in memory of which great deliverance every one who now enters that gate must doff his hat in reverence.

As the count had foretold, there were but few promenaders on the pretty but still leafless walk that led up the smooth green slope within the walls toward the modern palace of the Czars; and our heroes, settling themselves on one of the seats, began their talk.

Whatever might be the subject of it, it seemed to be an interesting one to them both, for the talk lasted till the sun began to sink behind the Sparrow Hills, and the air grew so chilly as to warn them that it was time to depart.

'Well, then,' cried the Russian as they rose to go, 'if you are only on a rambling tour, and have no special journey in view, you had better just come south with me next Monday week, when I go back to my country-place at Borjom, in the Western Caucasus. If I am not mistaken, that part of the mountains is still new to you; and if I cannot offer you very princely accommodation, you can, at all events, be sure of a hearty welcome.'

'I can always be sure of that in Russia,' said the Englishman politely, 'and I would gladly accept your kindness if I were alone; but, you see, I have my son with me, and as he is a boy with a good deal of life in him, he might perhaps be a little too much for you.'

'Quite the contrary,' rejoined the count, 'for, as it happens, I have *my* son down at Borjom, and he, on the other hand, has not quite life enough in him; so perhaps your young fellow's superfluous vitality may be of use in stirring him up. I assure you I shall be most happy to receive you both. Come, is it a bargain?'

'Done!' said Archer. 'Next Monday week, then, we will all start together.'

Both men were famed for plunging at a moment's notice into the most adventurous and dangerous enterprises; but never in all their lives (if they had but known it) had they launched themselves more suddenly upon a more perilous train of adventures.

CHAPTER II.

BEFORE THE CZAR.

UT there is many a slip betwixt the cup and the lip; and, as if to give the two bold travellers a last chance of escape from the evil to come, the journey which was to be their first step towards the terrible experiences that were in store for them was unexpectedly delayed. Three days before the time fixed by Count Bulatoff for their start southward, it was suddenly noised abroad that the Czar was coming to Moscow from St Petersburg; and, sure enough, on the following evening he came.

Alexander II. (for at that time the 'Liberator-Czar' had not yet fallen a victim to the cruelty of his treacherous and cowardly murderers) had always been a zealous patron and friend of native travellers and men of science, and took an especial interest in the explorations of the adventurous count, who had more than once been his guest at the country palace of Tsarskoë-selo (Czar's village), the Russian Windsor, lying about sixteen miles from St Petersburg. Hence it was out of the question for Bulatoff to be guilty of such a disloyal rudeness as to bolt out of the city just as his imperial friend entered it. And, moreover, he could not have done so even if he would; for his presence in Moscow soon became known to the Czar, and he received a summons to the Kremlin Palace at the very time when he ought to have been rattling off to the railway station with his new English friends.

The English friends themselves, however, took this delay very coolly, especially Harry Archer, who, though he had shared three or four of his father's shorter trips through Western Europe, had never been in Russia before, and was hugely delighted with all that he saw and heard in the quaint old semi-Eastern city, which had been the capital of a great empire in days when marsh-frogs were croaking around a tiny Swedish fort on the future site of St Petersburg. The bright, lively, quick-witted boy found a never-failing source of enjoyment in the spectacle of the many-coloured wooden houses and painted metal roofs that made the whole town one vast flower-bed—the domes and church-towers plated with solid gold—the great white ramparts from which Moscow takes its popular nickname of 'Byelo-kâmennaya' (White-stoned)—the queer little *droshkies* (native cabs), consisting merely of a seat for the driver and another for the fare, and aptly likened by our hero to chairs with their backs knocked off — the quaintly-carved archways and narrow, crooked, uneven streets, swarming with bun-faced Tartars, handsome brigand-like Greeks, low-browed Russian peasants in greasy sheepskin frocks; sleek, dark-eyed, long-haired Jews; gray-coated native soldiers with hard, wooden faces; and bearded Russian priests in flowing robes and high, black, funnel-shaped caps. And when he at length climbed the Sparrow Hills, and looked down upon the forest of tall towers, shining cupolas, and painted houses below, from the very spot where Napoleon, catching his first glimpse of it in 1812, uttered, with grim significance, his famous

'It was *time!*' Harry Archer had good cause to exclaim admiringly:

'Well, if the old place looked half as grand when old Boney saw it, it was a burning shame to set it on fire!'

In a word, though our hero had been long enough in St Petersburg to take in fully the glittering perspective of the Nevski Prospect, the mighty expanse of the Admiralty Plain, and all the glories of the Isaac Cathedral, with its gold-plated dome and sixty-foot pillars of polished granite, he never altered his opinion that 'Moscow was worth two of it any day.' In truth, St Petersburg, with all its splendour, looks, and is, a town made to order; while Moscow, like Topsy, has 'kind o' growed.'

Nor was the language of this new region less interesting to the smart English lad than its outward aspect. Under the able guidance of his father (who spoke fluently every language of Europe, and many others as well), he had already picked up a smattering of Russian, and pronounced it, with schoolboy frankness, 'the queerest lingo he had ever come across.' He was greatly amused to learn that the Russian phrase for 'Thank you' was (as it sounded to *him*) 'Blackguard are you!' (*Blagodaryoo*), and declared that the native name of the national cabbage soup, or *shtchee*, would be best pronounced by giving a loud sneeze!

Thus it was that matters stood when, one afternoon about a week after the Czar's arrival, the count presented himself at Livingstone Archer's hotel, and announcing that he was on his way to the palace, asked his brother-explorer to go with him as far as the esplanade of the Kremlin, and to hang about it for a little while, as the Czar was likely to ask for him, and he might thus be ushered into the imperial presence without any delay.

Archer agreed, and the two set off at once, leaving Harry in the midst of a long letter to one of his late chums at Winchester, depicting in glowing colours all the wonders of 'Mâtushka Moskva' (Mother Moscow).

When his friend had gone into the palace, Mr Archer, thus left to himself, began to pace up and down the promenade like a sentry. But time went on, and the count did not come back; and at length the Englishman, getting tired of this monotonous walk to and fro, set off to make the round of the interior of the Kremlin, and survey once more its various marvels, which, though he already knew them well, had not lost one whit of their fascination for him.

He paced slowly by the long line of cannon left behind by Napoleon in the fatal retreat from Moscow, and the sentry planted in front of them—with a simple and poetical chivalry worthy of any knight of old romance—to keep any passer-by from halting to stare at them in idle curiosity, 'since it was God's hand, not ours, that took them from the enemies of Russia.' He went past the deep shadowy archway where a twelve-year-old boy called Peter the Great had once faced without flinching the armed and furious mob of the town, and had sternly asked 'how that rabble dared to come into the palace of the Czars!' He paused for a moment to look up at the tall dark-red spire that surmounted the Gate of Deliverance—through which, two centuries and a half before, had staggered forth the livid and ghastly survivors of the most terrible siege in the red chronicle of Russian history —and then he came round once more to the vast white bell-tower of Ivan Veliki (John the Great), the gold-plated cupola of which shone like a mighty helmet in the bright May sunshine.

Just at the foot of the tower, on a gun-carriage as massive as itself, stood, covered with quaint antique carvings, the huge, cumbrous mass of the renowned 'Tsar Pushka' (King Cannon), the 'Mons Meg' of Russia, cast in 1594 by the last of the old Ruric dynasty, the weak and worthless Feodor Ivanovitch, son of Ivan the Terrible; and beside it was the most striking of all these strange relics of Russia's past—the far-famed 'Tsar Kolokol,' or King Bell.

At this last relic the English traveller looked with visible interest; and, in truth, it was a spectacle which the most careless observer could hardly have passed unmoved. There stood the mightiest bell in the world, a dumb giant, whose voice had never been heard; for, cast by the Empress Anne in the eighteenth century, it was cracked in the casting, and after lying buried in the earth for one hundred and thirty-six years, was brought back to the light in our own time by the Emperor Nicholas, and placed where it now stands, planted on a low, massive pedestal of solid stone, beside which lies the chip of metal—*only* as large as an ordinary door—that parted from the bell's rim at the time of the disaster.

All at once the traveller's keen eyes espied some pencil-writing on the narrow space between the rim of the pedestal and that of the bell itself. Knowing well by *whom*, and for what purpose, these seemingly careless scribblings were often left in public places, he fully expected to see some Russian sentence which, couched by a secret conspirator in apparently harmless and even unmeaning language, would convey to his brother-plotters a message of deep and deadly import. But, to his no small surprise, the words were *English*, and ran as follows:

From thy darksome grave arisen,
    Thou stand'st on the holy ground
In thy grim, eternal silence,
    'Mid thy joyous brethren round.

The peal of their gladsome voices
    The living air doth thrill,
And earth in their joy rejoices—
    But *thou* art sad and still.

Gray relic of days departed!
    In the depths of thy cavern vast
Hast thou no tongue to tell us
    The secrets of the Past?

Did the wail of trampled millions
    Disquiet not thy long repose?
Did no shuddering thrill run through thee
    From the pangs of thy country's woes?

Didst thou quake when the Northern Monarch *
    O'er the land in his fury came,
And darted, and smote, and vanished,
    Like the rushing lightning's flame?

Didst thou quail when the tread of the Foeman †
    Clanged through the ancient town,
And the blast of the Western thunder
    Shook tower and temple down?

Once more to the golden sunlight
    Thou art risen from earth's dark breast,
Like the soul of thine own great nation,
    Long buried and sore distressed.

She too, in the earth down-trodden,
    For ages entombed hath lain;
She too for speech hath struggled,
    And struggled—how long!—in vain.

She too from her grave hath risen,
    By the hand of God up-stirred;
Ah! woe to her sceptred tyrants
    If once *her* voice be heard!

---

* Charles XII. of Sweden.   † Napoleon.

Archer had just got to the end of this precious effusion (the author of which had evidently forgotten that Charles XII.'s invasion took place long before the bell to which he was appealing for information about it had ever been cast at all), when a hoarse voice behind him said gruffly, 'What are you doing there?' and turning quickly, he saw a big Russian sentry, whose post was near the spot, eyeing him with a look of stern suspicion. The soldier had plainly caught sight of the writing, and, though of course unable to read it, seemed very much excited by his discovery.

'I was reading some verses which some one has written here,' said the traveller quietly.

'You lie!' cried the Russian fiercely. 'I saw you with my own eyes writing it yourself!'

At this coarse insult the Englishman's first feeling was a truly British impulse to knock the man down on the spot; but, happily for himself (for to resist authority of any kind, and military authority more especially, is a serious matter in Russia), he suddenly remembered that he had once or twice brushed aside with his hand the dust that obscured some of the words—an action which, seen from a little distance, might well convey to an unlettered Russian soldier the idea of actual writing.

The experienced traveller began to realise that he had got himself into a very awkward dilemma, which was doubly serious at that particular time. The famous plot of 1871, of which Sergi Netchaieff was the head, and Moscow itself the centre, had just startled all Russia into a fever of excitement, which, as usual, gave to every trifle a secret and formidable meaning.

'Look here, my good fellow,' said he; 'you see that this writing is in pencil, don't you? Well, I have not got such a thing as a pencil about me; you may search me if you like and see.'

The scornful laugh with which the big guardsman met this suggestion showed how much effect it had had upon him; and, in fact, one might as well read poetry to an oyster as try to convince one of these human machines by argument. But ere he could reply a gray-coated *gorodovoi* (constable), attracted by the dispute, came hurrying up to the spot, and a second was seen approaching.

'What is the matter here, brother?' called out the foremost policeman.

'I've caught one of those rogues that are plotting against our father, Alexander Nikolaievitch (the Czar), and, for all I know, he may be Netchaieff himself!'

'Netchaieff?' echoed the constable, with sparkling eyes, for a large reward had been offered for the arch-traitor's head. 'Is it really *he*?'

'Well, it's one of his gang, anyhow. I caught him just as he was writing some of their villainous signals. Besides, he's a foreigner by his tongue, and they are always up to some mischief or other. Catch hold of him.'

Constable No. 1 promptly seized the supposed conspirator by one arm, and No. 2 (who had come up just in time to hear the soldier's explanation) clutched him as briskly by the other; and so they dragged him away between them, giving him a good shake at every step, just as a nurse might do to a naughty child.

Archer, though his English blood boiled at this rough treatment, had the good sense to make no resistance; for he knew that the testimony of his friend the count, as a known intimate of the Czar himself, would suffice to clear him in a moment from this absurd charge, and a smile flickered over his grave face at the thought of the dismay of his guardians when they found out what they had been doing.

'See the rascal; he's actually laughing!' cried No. 1 indignantly to No. 2. 'What a hardened villain he must be!'

'He'll have something to laugh at,' grunted No. 2, 'when he goes tramping in irons along the Vladimir road' (the highway leading eastward out of Moscow toward Siberia).

But hardly had they gone twenty yards when a well-known voice called out suddenly, 'What! my friend Monsieur Archer under arrest?' and the prisoner, looking up, found himself face to face with Count Bulatoff, beside whom stood a tall man in the uniform of a colonel of the Russian Imperial Guard. But even had Archer never seen the latter before, any print-shop in Moscow or St Petersburg would have made him aware that the stately figure, handsome though rather worn face, and heavy brown moustache slightly tinged with gray, of this seeming colonel, belonged to no other than the Czar himself!

'Is this gentleman, then, Monsieur Livingstone Archer, the great English traveller of whom you have just been telling me, Feodor Alexandrovitch?' asked the Emperor, looking from Bulatoff to the captive Englishman.

'The same, at your Majesty's service,' replied Archer himself, doffing his hat with an easy bow; for his two guards, thunderstruck by this unexpected turning of the tables, had let go his arms in helpless dismay. 'But I little thought that I should make my first appearance before you in the character of a political criminal, accused of high treason.'

And then, in answer to the Czar's inquiring look, he briefly related the whole affair, and ended by reciting, at the Emperor's special request, the suspicious verses which his proverbially retentive memory had grasped in the course of one reading.

But just then two other men came bustling up to the group from the direction of the Great Bell, and the foremost (who was evidently one of those professional guides and interpreters that haunt every Moscow hotel) put a whispered query to one of the constables, and then translated the reply to his companion, an unmistakable English tourist.

The moment the latter heard it he pressed hastily forward, and called out to the two Russian policemen in English— seeming to forget, in his sudden excitement, that they could not possibly understand him:

'Let that man alone, will you? If you're taking him up for writing that poetry on the bell, he had nothing to do with it—I wrote it myself.'

The speaker was one of those Byronic young men with a pale face and long dark hair, and a chronic look of having lost their way, who are so unlucky as to mistake themselves for poets just because they are fit for nothing else. But if a fool, he was at least an honest and a brave one; and the manly impulse that had sent him forward to save another person at his own imminent risk shed over his usually silly and affected face a glow of real dignity.

'Mr Archer,' said the Czar courteously in very good English, 'I beg to offer you my best apologies for the rough behaviour into which these worthy fellows (with a sideglance at the terrified policemen, who looked ready to sink into the earth) have been betrayed by over-zeal in the discharge of their duty. As for this gentleman,' he added, bowing to the author of the unlucky verses, 'I hope he will not think so ill of me as to fear any punishment for so slight an imprudence; for, though I may be a "sceptred tyrant," I am not quite so tyrannical as that.'

At this sudden intimation that he was face to face with the Emperor himself, the would-be poet started, and was about to speak. But Archer, whose ready tact told him that the scene had gone far enough, whispered a few words to the young scribbler himself, and a few more to his guide, and had the satisfaction of seeing them at once march off together.

The very next day Mr Archer was invited to the palace, and (to Harry's great glee) specially requested to bring his son along with him. Their reception was marked by the frank and kindly courtesy for which Alexander II. was always noted; and the Czar took particular notice of Harry, whose outspoken admiration of all that he saw in the palace greatly amused the kind-hearted autocrat.

'And what occupation is this young gentleman going to follow?' asked the Emperor.

'I'm going to be a traveller, like my father!' cried Harry, whose secret ambition this had been ever since he was old enough to know what his father had done, and who, ere leaving Winchester, had fought a desperate single combat with a schoolfellow half a head taller than himself, who had dared to laugh irreverently at his assertion that his renowned parent was the greatest traveller that ever lived, 'except perhaps Robinson Crusoe.'

'You have set yourself a hard task, my young friend, if you mean to be a traveller like *him*,' said the Czar, smiling; 'but I am sure you will show yourself worthy of him, and I wish you all success.'

Harry was delighted with this friendly reception, and vowed that the Czar 'might almost have been an Englishman '—the highest praise that he could give to any foreigner. But the interview, however gratifying, still further delayed their journey; for the Czar was only too glad to get the opinion of an expert like Archer on the roads and railways, and artificial irrigation, which he was planning for the improvement of his new conquests in Central Asia, and the middle of May was already past ere our three friends at length got away from Moscow.

CHAPTER III.

SACKING A RAILWAY STATION.

'S all Russia as flat as this, Feodor Alexandrovitch?'

'No, Monsieur Harry; in some places it is a good deal flatter. We have a story of a peasant who, meeting a single horseman on the great southern steppe near the entrance of the Crimea, asked him to draw aside and let him see what the people were doing in *Moscow!*'

The three travellers were half-way through the first day of their long journey southward to the Black Sea, and Harry was in high glee at all the strange sights that met him at every turn, though he was somewhat startled to find that they were to be *three days* on the same railway ere they reached the coast; for at that time, and for many a day after, even the express-trains took seventy-three hours and a half to cover the 1027 miles between Moscow and Odessa.

Long as it was, however, this route was really their shortest way to Count Bulatoff's far-off mountain home; for the great south-eastern railway that now links Moscow to Vladikavkaz itself, on the northern slope of the Caucasus, was not yet half-finished, and their only way to avoid the multiplied horrors of travelling 'post' in Southern Russia was to go by the newly-completed line to Odessa *via* Kursk and Kieff, the last section of which had been opened only the year before.

To Harry's great regret (for he had as yet seen very little of the country, his journey from St Petersburg to Moscow having been made chiefly by night), they left by the evening mail-train, thus seeing little or nothing of the country immediately south of Moscow, and passing in the dark the tall chimneys and flaring furnaces of Tula, the Russian Sheffield.

But the train itself was no small amusement to our hero, with its unexpected passages, its doors leading nowhere, its seats collapsing into beds at a moment's notice, and its stuffed chairs cropping up in dark corners as if playing hide-and-seek. And when, after an unbroken nap of seven or eight hours, he stepped out upon a small platform at the end of the carriage in the freshness of early morning, and saw the great plain of Central Russia gliding past him like a dream, he had good cause to exclaim gleefully, as he expanded his chest with a long, deep breath of enjoyment:

'Well, come! this is better than being locked up with half-a-dozen other fellows in a stuffy compartment at home, just as if one was packed up in a hamper!'

'Others beside you have been of that opinion, Harry,' said his father, stepping out at his side. 'Do you remember that picture in the German paper that we picked up at Berlin, where the guard says furiously to a man who is complaining of being overcrowded, "If you don't hold your tongue this minute, I'll lock you up in a compartment all by yourself!"'

But Harry's admiration rose to a height when, at a chance knock of his elbow against the woodwork of one of the doors, a small table, or rather desk, sprang forth beside him, just in front of the window-seat.

'Well, that *is* a knowing dodge, and no mistake!' cried the boy. 'Why, if one were writing a book or had a lot of letters to knock off, one might do it here quite comfortably, with the train going all the time.'

'I am afraid, though, Monsieur Harry,' said the count, smiling, 'that the makers of that contrivance did not concern themselves much about the interests of literature. That table is meant for playing cards.'

'Cards!' echoed Harry in amazement. 'What! are they so keen on gambling as all that out here?'

'They are indeed—more's the pity!' said his father gravely. 'On this very line, I've seen four young lads play for eight hours on end, and win or lose several thousand roubles; and I suppose the poor little fools thought that *manly!* But here we are at Orel; let us get out and have a snack.'

The 'snack' in question lasted nearly half-an-hour, for the time given for refreshment on a Russian railway would suffice to make the whole journey by an English express. But it must be owned that the meals are as good as they are long, and contrast very strikingly with the sawdust sandwiches and quarry-like pies of English 'Mugby Junctions.'

The young Wintonian, though he ate as much as both his companions together, contrived to finish before them, and instantly rushed off to help down his food by tramping up and down the long platform as if for a wager, in order to work off the stiffness of this endless journey, which made him feel (in his own graphic phrase) 'as if he had been born with his boots on.'

He was just taking his sixth turn up and down, when the up-train for Moscow came creaking and groaning into the station; and three or four peasants who had come from Moscow like our heroes (evidently new to railway-travel) were just getting into the *return*-train by mistake, when a charitable guard warned them of their error.

At sight of these stray sheep the count, who had just come out again, burst into a laugh so loud and hearty that Harry was beginning to laugh too, without knowing why, when the Russian checked himself, and said, as they got back into the train:

'I beg your pardon, Monsieur Henri; I was just reminded of a curious thing that happened not long after the Nikolaievski line was opened. It was only the second railway ever opened in Russia (that little bit from St Petersburg to Peterhof being the first), and of course it seemed very strange and terrible to the peasants, as all new inventions do. Some of them took it for a monster or fire-breathing dragon, and when the whistle sounded, whispered tremblingly to each other, "Hear how he screams!" Others thought it a direct invention of the Evil One, and preferred to walk, till they saw the priests go by it, and *then* they felt sure that it must be all right.

'Well, there was an old peasant of Ostashkovo (a village on that line) who, having saved a little money, made up his mind to treat himself to a trip by this wonderful machine, and have a look at St Petersburg, which he had never seen in his life; and so he did.

'Now, at that time (for it's altered now) the up-train and the down-train reached Bologoë, the half-way station, just at the same time; and in the refreshment-room old Ivan met a chum who was going the other way. So they got into talk, and had some tea together; and in the end Ivan got into his friend's train instead of his own, and was soon rattling merrily back, without knowing it, toward the place from which he had started. But after a time he began to get silent and thoughtful, and then broke out suddenly:

'"Ah, Pavel Petrôvitch! (Paul, son of Peter) what a wonderful thing these railways are, to be sure! You're going to Moscow and I'm going to St Petersburg, and yet here we are in the same carriage!"'

And so, mile after mile and hour after hour, the never-ending journey dragged on. Even Harry's buoyant spirits were somewhat damped by the grim sameness and utter desolation of these bare and boundless plains, especially when a cold white mist gathered over them and a drizzling rain began to fall. A sky as dreary as a comic paper overhung a vast expanse of thick, brown, greasy mud (on which no living thing was to be seen), suggesting to our hero the idea of a deluge of treacle that had drowned the whole land. In the midst of this mess lay something which the boy took for a small stream, till the sight of a wagon crawling along it showed it to be a high-road!

'I don't wonder *now*,' muttered Harry, 'that, in these Russian famines, it's such a job to bring food from one place to another!'

At Kursk they changed trains, and the prudent count, remembering that this second stage of their journey, from Kursk to Kieff, was a pretty long one, advised his friends to make a good meal before setting off again—a motion warmly seconded by the ever-hungry Wintonian.

They were just at the door of the refreshment-room, when a stout, red-faced man of unmistakably British aspect, in a rather 'loud' check suit, hearing Archer speak to his son in English, stepped hastily up to him and said:

'I want to get a raw egg—can you tell me what's the Russian for "raw"?'

'*Ne varyonni*' (Not cooked), replied Archer.

'Thank 'ee, thank 'ee,' said the red-faced man eagerly; and he bustled forward into the room.

When he got there it suddenly flashed upon the bold Briton that he did not know the word for 'egg' either; but his English courage rose to meet the emergency. Snatching a *boiled* egg from a dish beside him, he thrust it full in the face of the amazed Russian manager, and—true to John Bull's traditional conviction that the best way to make a foreigner understand him is to roar at the top of his voice—let fly, in tones of thunder, all the Russian that he knew:

'Raw!'

'Raw, do you say?' cried the Russian indignantly. 'It's *not* raw; it's properly cooked! See for yourself!' and, snatching the egg, he broke its shell, and handed it back to the chafing Englishman.

'Raw! raw!' yelled Red-face, louder than before, as he brandished the egg like a cricket-ball within an inch of the Russian's nose.

'Are you out of your mind, you blockhead?' bellowed the manager, waxing enraged in his turn. 'Look here, gentlemen—look here, all of you—that fellow *will* have it that this egg is raw!'

The noise of the dispute had already drawn every one in the room to the spot; and, unluckily, the red-faced hero, in one of his wild flourishes of his egg of discord, brought it with such force against the broad chest of a big Russian merchant who had pressed too eagerly forward that the whole breadth of the unfortunate man's coat-front was instantly lighted up with a wide blaze of yellow, suggestive of one of Claude's sunsets.

The man who had been thus *egged-on* vented his feelings in a series of remarks too vigorous and pointed for translation. Several of his friends warmly took up his cause. The sturdy Briton, hemmed in by a ring of angry faces, clenched his fists and squared himself for action; and one moment more would have witnessed the outbreak of a 'free fight' worthy of Bret Harte himself, had not Mr Archer (who had till then been too helpless with laughter to interfere) stepped forward and briefly explained matters to the fuming manager.

The good-natured Russian laughed heartily at the mistake, and insisted on giving the outraged Briton an egg gratis, as some amends for the trouble caused him. The merchant, having been scraped clean, became pacified, and shook hands with his aggressor; and the crowd ebbed back to the train, Harry remarking, with a grin, that that merchant was 'not the only Russian who had been impatient under the *yolk*.'

Our travellers were so lucky as to have daylight for their approach to Kieff, and the crossing of its splendid bridge of stone and iron over the Dnieper, which would alone suffice to make the name of Vignoles famous had he done nothing else. Harry was greatly pleased with the picturesque old city, one of the finest as well as most ancient of Russian towns, and the capital of a heathen Muscovy before the Norman Conquest; but, as I have already described it fully elsewhere,* I must not inflict it again upon my long-suffering readers.

'Do you see that black marble statue yonder, Harry, with the big cross in its hand?' said his father. 'Well, it was just there that, in the year 988, Prince Vladimir, the man under whom Russia became Christian, hurled down the hillside into the Dnieper the idol of Peroon the thunder-god, which he and his men had worshipped; and at that same spot they were all baptised in the river that very day by a Greek monk from Constantinople.'

It was just about sunset on the second evening of their journey that the train at length came in sight of Jmerinka Junction, the point at which the south-western line from Moscow meets the railway running north-west from Odessa to the Austrian frontier.

They ran into the station just as Mr Archer was trying to divert his son (who was manifestly getting rather 'used-up') by telling him the history of the curious coin which had been the means of his strange introduction to Count Bulatoff.

'It's a queer tale,' said he; 'very much as if some one had just brought out the second volume of a story, the first volume of which appeared more than two thousand years ago. The chroniclers who wrote of Alexander the Great's campaigns in Central Asia (some of whom had been through the whole business themselves) say that when Alexander finally turned back from his advance eastward—which he did not far from where the town of Khojend now stands—a certain Cheirisophos, who was one of his *chiliarchs* or colonels, was somehow left behind in the hills with a small detachment of Macedonian infantry, and was always supposed to have perished.'

* See *Cossack and Czar*, chapter iv.

'And didn't he, then?' asked Harry, who began to look interested.

'I think not; for when I was in those parts a few years ago, I heard from the natives (and our friend Count Bulatoff heard it too, when he went out there) a strange legend of a great chief from the setting sun, who came among them in the days of Sultan Sekundur (they always call Alexander "Sekundur Roomi," you know), and this chief had a skin made of brass, which no arrow could pierce; and he and the other brazen-skinned men who were with him built a strong castle among the hills, and when the tribes of the mountain came to attack it, he made stones fall upon them from the sky by the power of his magic, and slew many of them (some stone-hurling engine that he constructed, I suppose); and those that escaped were terrified, and became his vassals—and so at last he made himself a king!'

'Well done he!' cried the boy, who was listening with marked interest. 'He must have been a very 'cute fellow, whoever he was.'

'Well, I'll tell you who *I* think he was—no other than the lost Cheirisophos himself; and he must have got the place finely civilised, to be able to strike coins of his own. But that these coins *were* struck by him I think there can be no doubt whatever. In the first place, the spot in which they were found and the manner of finding them point to their having been there at least since the time of the early Cæsars—since the birth of our Lord, in fact; and, moreover, the helmet and chariot on the coins themselves are both distinctively Greek, and Greek, too, of a pattern that was not much used after Alexander's time. Then, too, the king's title, Kara Suffee (which means 'Black Devotee'), is just the sort of corruption that these Eastern barbarians, who knew no Greek, would make of the sound of "Cheirisophos;" and all that tallies exactly with the native traditions.'

'But I say, daddy, are those traditions of theirs any good? I've heard you say yourself that those Eastern fellows never open their mouths without telling as many crams as Baron Munchausen.'

'Well, that's only too true as to their own every-day life; but it's wonderful how exactly they hand down their old national traditions from father to son without altering them a bit. The first time I was in Western Tartary I met an old Kirghiz (a fellow who could not read or write, and had never been out of his own country) that talked as glibly of "Aleksandr Makedonski" as if he had been a special correspondent with the Macedonian army, and told me some facts about Alexander's crossing of the Oxus and his march through Bactria (evidently handed down by verbal tradition) for which Grote would have given any money for his History of Greece. But here we are at Jmerinka.'

And as he spoke the train came to a stand-still, with a long creaking groan, beside the low, brick-paved, far-extending platform of the junction.

'Now then,' cried Archer, 'we'll just get out here and have some tea, and then we'll be set up for the night.'

'If you take *my* advice, Monsieur Archer, you will do nothing of the kind,' said the count; 'for this *buffetchik* (refreshment-room keeper) is a sly fellow, who has a trick of heating his tea scalding hot, so that you can't drink a drop of it, and it usually remains to be sold over again to the up-train passengers half-an-hour later.'

'Oh, that's his little game, is it?' replied the Englishman quietly. 'Well, two can play at that game, and we'll see which can play it best;' and, bidding Harry stay where he was, Mr Archer got out and went straight to the refreshment-room, which was all but full already.

Looking round him as he entered, the traveller saw that most of the steaming *tumblers* of tea (the usual way of drinking it in Russia) were already appropriated; and he could easily perceive, by the dissatisfied faces of the customers, that they were fully aware of this trick of over-heating the tea, and that it was not at all to their liking; though, with true Russian resignation, they made no resistance, and gulped down the scalding liquid as best they might.

Having waited a minute or two to satisfy himself on these points, Archer stepped forward and took up one of the few tea-glasses left on the table in front of the fat, red-faced *buffetchik*, who, standing behind his huge *samovar* (urn), looked like some over-fed native saint, with the steam forming a kind of 'glory' around his great shaggy head.

'Look here, my friend,' cried Archer, with an admirably assumed air of angry surprise, 'what on earth do you make your tea so hot for? How do you think any one is going to swallow such scalding stuff as this? One might as well drink out of a boiling kettle!'

'If it's not good enough for you, you're not forced to drink it,' said the man insolently; 'it don't matter a bit whether you do or not, so long as you pay. If you don't like it, let it be.'

'No, I won't do that,' said the Englishman, raising his voice so as to be heard by all around him; 'I'll take it into the train and drink it there;' and suiting the action to the word, he vanished through the door, tea and all.

This struck every one as such a good idea that in a trice every glass, saucer, and spoon had disappeared from the table, and a general rush to the train left the room almost empty.

For one instant the old rogue stood petrified at this sudden turning of the tables; and then, shouting wildly to his two assistants, he rushed in frantic pursuit of his vanishing crockery.

Meanwhile Count Bulatoff, who was watching eagerly to see what his friend would do, wondered much to see him come dashing out of the refreshment-room as if flying for his life, with an excited crowd at his heels. Bulatoff's first idea was that Archer had got into a quarrel with the native passengers; and so, too, thought Harry, who jumped up at once to go to his father's assistance.

But the count stopped him short; for the exclamations of the throng, and the brimming tea-glasses in their hands, had already given the shrewd Russian a good guess at the truth, which was amply confirmed by the bursting out of the *buffetchik* like a raving madman, abusing by turns his own heavy-heeled assistants and the grinning spectators at the carriage-windows. The latter, feigning great zeal to help him, held out their glasses and saucers for him to snatch as he went by; but the moment he passed, others *behind* put forth their glasses, and shrieked to him to come and take them ere the train started. Back flew this new Orestes, goaded by tea-drinking Furies, and came bump against the laden assistants at his heels, each collision smashing on the pavement half-a-dozen saucers and glasses, every crash of which sent a throb of anguish through the heart of the *buffetchik*, who knew too well that the cost of all these breakages must come out of his own pocket. This harrowing consciousness, and the loud laughter of the lookers-on (most of whom had suffered by his tricks before) goaded the baited rogue to such a pitch of desperation that he looked like nothing but a lunatic juggler trying to play ball with ten tumblers at once.

But his punishment was not at its height even now. He and his men had gradually piled the accumulating crockery in a heap on the platform, and as he came yelling back to his pile for the sixth time, his feet slipped, and he fell right on the top of it, with a crash that echoed through the whole station; and there he lay sprawling, as if indulging in a swimming-bath of broken crockery, while the whistle of the departing train seemed to shriek despairingly over his fall.

And then a venerable old Russian monk who had just got into Archer's carriage, and had watched the knavish *buffetchik's* agonies with an enjoyment too deep and heartfelt for words, bent toward Archer and said, with a fervour that could not be mistaken:

'Bless thee, my son, bless thee! thou art worthy to have been a Russian!'

CHAPTER IV.

BETWEEN WALLS OF FIRE.

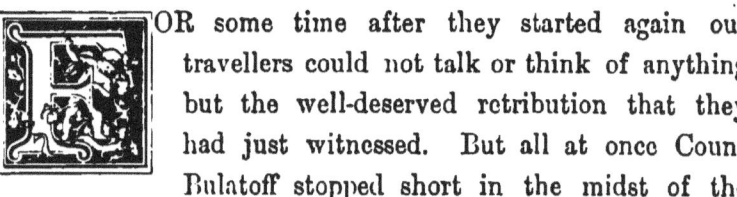OR some time after they started again our travellers could not talk or think of anything but the well-deserved retribution that they had just witnessed. But all at once Count Bulatoff stopped short in the midst of the chat, as if a new idea had just struck him, and thrusting his face out of the window, gazed fixedly ahead for some time, looking graver and graver as he did so.

'Monsieur Archer,' cried he to his comrade, 'come here and see what you think of this sky; *you* ought to be a sure weather-prophet.'

The English explorer's quick wit divined at once that his companion had some secret purpose in this summons. He obeyed it instantly, and the count, bending close to him, said in a low whisper:

'I know our friend Monsieur Harry is not easily scared; but still he is a young traveller, and it might not be well to let him learn too suddenly that we may all risk losing our lives ere this night is over.'

'Indeed? How is that?' asked the Englishman in an equally cautious tone.

'Well, I've just learned that, although the summer has

been so late in Moscow, it began unusually early down here; and, as you can see for yourself, a month's heat, without a drop of rain, has dried all the trees to tinder. Now, after we get into the last-opened section of this line (as we shall do in about half-an-hour), we run for a good many miles through the heart of a forest so thick that the train brushes the boughs every here and there in passing.'

'Ah, I see,' said Archer quietly; 'you think we may have to run the gauntlet of a forest-fire.'

'That's just it. I dare say you know that a spark from some passing train is often enough to set one of these pine-woods of ours in a blaze for miles; and if such a thing were to happen before we came through, I need not tell you what might be the result.'

Meanwhile Harry, luckily quite unsuspicious of this fatal secret, was doing his best to keep up a talk in Russian with the old monk opposite, whose pleasant, kindly face had taken his fancy at first sight, and who seemed quite as much pleased with the bright, fresh, high-spirited English boy as the latter was with him.

Harry's ideas of the manners and customs of monks being drawn chiefly from Sir Walter Scott, some of his questions about them amused his new friend not a little; and the latter had hard work to keep from laughing outright when the young Wintonian gravely asked if he had ever seen any one buried alive in the wall of the monastery! But Brother Aphanassi (Athanasius) answered all his queries very good-naturedly; and it was with no small regret that our hero saw the friendly old man get out and disappear at the next station.

As soon as he was gone, Mr Archer seated himself beside

his son once more, and told him, as gently and kindly as possible, what he had just learned from the count.

No boy on earth could be expected to hear such a communication wholly unmoved, and Harry was visibly startled; but the flush on his cheek and the gleam in his clear, bright eye showed that his bold English spirit, so far from being overwhelmed by this sudden and horrible peril, was only roused to face it manfully.

'You'll tell me what to do when the time comes, won't you, daddy?' said he; 'and *I'll do it*, whatever it is!'

'You need not tell me *that*, my boy,' replied his father, clapping him affectionately on the shoulder.

Night came on, and Harry, in spite of this new excitement, gradually dozed off to sleep. But his slumbers, though sound, were not undisturbed; for all the strange experiences of the last two days seemed to mix themselves up together in his wild and troubled dreams.

He dreamed that he was the Emperor Nero, hemmed in by a band of mutinous guards, who menaced him with instant death, which he could only escape (as it seemed) by drinking at one draught a cup of scalding tea; but the moment he raised it to his lips the tea shrank away from them like the water from those of Tantalus, and at length the cup itself slipped from his hold and fell broken on the ground. Closer and closer round him pressed the brandished swords and flaming torches of the savage soldiers; and in vain did he shower among them handfuls of money, for they all shouted fiercely that these were Greek coins of Cheirisophos the Macedonian, and would not pass current in Rome. At last, driven to desperation, the dreamer cried out, 'Set fire to Rome, then; it is my only chance!' and instantly a fierce red glare and a wave of stifling heat surged up around him, and, with shrieks of horror and agony ringing in his ears, he started and awoke.

But he might well think himself dreaming still; for the cries and screams of his vision were still in his ears, and all around him was a whirlpool of leaping flames, to which even the conflagration of which he had dreamed was nothing.

The count's gloomy forebodings had proved but too true. The flying sparks from a passing train had fired the pine-wood just before they entered it, and they were now rushing between two quivering walls of fire, the scorching heat of which made itself felt right through the closed windows with almost unbearable intensity; while the hoarse shouts of men, the screaming and crying of frightened women and children, the clank and rattle of the flying train, the deep, unslackening roar of the flames, the crash of falling trees, and the sharp crackle of the dry boughs as the advancing fire caught branch after branch, startled the ghostly silence of midnight with a maddening din.

The moon had not yet risen, and the utter blackness of the night made the fearful grandeur of this wild scene tenfold more striking and terrific. So close on either side were those fiery walls that the jets of flame which darted out from them actually licked the sides of the passing carriages, blistering into huge boils the paint and varnish that covered them, cracking the glass of the closed windows, and threatening to set the train itself on fire. Beneath that infernal splendour the reddened stems of the pine-trees stood out against the surrounding blackness like pillars of red-hot iron, and the great drops of rosin that oozed from the burning timber wore a hideous semblance of trickling blood; while the scared faces at the carriage-windows, appearing and vanishing by turns as the flames leaped or fell, looked wan and ghastly as the faces of the dead; and the spectacle of this caravan of seeming corpses, bursting from the gloom of midnight to plunge into that sea of fire, formed a picture worthy of Dante himself.

When the first alarm was given, the terrified passengers had cried to the engine-driver to run them *back* out of the peril; but the brave man knew better than do anything of the sort. He had noticed already that the wind was driving the flames right *toward* them, and he saw plainly that thus (apart from the imminent risk of a collision which must attend any sudden backward movement on a single line) they would, by attempting to retreat, be simply travelling *with* the fire instead of escaping from it; whereas if they pressed straight on, the blaze, at the rate at which it was then moving, must soon be left behind.

To do this, however—exposed as he was to the full blast of a heat which even those in the closed carriages behind him could hardly sustain—was a feat of daring which equalled that of the sturdy seamen who kept the deck of Nelson's flag-ship under the hottest fire of Trafalgar. Scorched and almost blinded by the furnace through which they were passing, choked with thick gusts of hot stifling smoke, and parched with maddening thirst, he and his mate could only keep themselves from fainting outright by dashing water over each other every few seconds. But the brave fellows—two of those nameless heroes whose true worth is never known in this world—stood to their terrible work with all the stubborn courage of their gallant race, and never flinched for a moment.

Little by little the smoke began to grow thinner, the blaze less fierce, the heat less intense; and a background of smouldering ashes and half-burned stems, glimmering redly through the deepening shadows as the glare faded, told that the fury of the fire had swept past, and that the worst was now over. Though it was still impossible to open any of the windows, the imprisoned passengers could see that their trial was almost at an end, and were just beginning to rejoice, when all at once the train 'slowed down,' and then came to a dead halt!

Count Bulatoff flung open the window beside him, and looking out, saw that a huge pine, still burning, had fallen right across the rails, completely blocking their way.

'Follow me, whoever is a man!' shouted the count, in a voice like a trumpet-call, as he sprang to the door and leaped out.

Mr Archer and Harry were already at his heels, and instantly all three were dashing at full speed toward the spot where the burning tree lay smoking and crackling across the line.

But they had no lack of assistants, for Bulatoff's stirring call had drawn to the spot every man who heard it; and though the first plunge into that furnace was like the clutch of a strangling hand upon their throats, this stifling oppression was hardly felt in the overwhelming excitement of that supreme moment. In a trice a score of strong hands were grasping the still unburned part of the pine-stem, and tugging, pushing, or heaving at it with all their might; and most energetic of all was a tall, gaunt, swarthy man who stood shoulder to shoulder with Archer himself, with the aquiline features and high, black sheepskin cap of a Persian.

Slowly and painfully, and not without several severe burns to the daring volunteers, the obstructing tree was at length forced aside and the line left clear; but just as the crowd of amateur labourers began to disperse, a second pine-trunk, slighter but much taller than the first, fell blazing and crashing across the very spot where Archer and his comrades were standing!

The count's quick eye caught the coming peril, and seizing Harry by the shoulders, he whisked him out of the way just in time to save the boy and himself. But the man in the Persian cap, who had his back to the falling tree, would certainly have been crushed to death on the spot had not the ever-ready Archer clutched his arm and dragged him aside.

Even as it was, the brave Persian did not wholly escape; for a huge fragment of burning wood, broken off in the fall, flew up against his head with such force that, in spite of his thick sheepskin cap, he was felled to the ground, stunned and senseless.

Archer and Count Bulatoff had just time to lift the helpless man into their own carriage ere the train moved on again, not a whit too soon; for more than one of the passengers had been already overpowered by the heat and smoke, and even the courageous driver and stoker—who had till then borne up like heroes—were at last beginning to show ominous signs of giving way altogether.

And then the count, turning to the crowd that pressed around him with thanks and praises, said with his wonted air of easy and natural command:

'Gentlemen, I think you will all agree with me that we owe some gratitude to our brave engine-driver and his mate, but for whose courage and coolness we should certainly have lost our lives; and I am going to make the round of the train in order to invite contributions for their benefit, I and my friend here having the honour of giving the first.

Slowly and painfully . . . the obstructing tree forced aside.

Perhaps some of you may know me by name—I am Feodor Bulatoff.'

This sudden disclosure that the man who had taken the lead among them so boldly in that perilous crisis was no other than the famous explorer whose name had so long been a household word to them all, raised the general enthusiasm to the highest pitch. The great news flew through the train like wildfire; and when the count started on his collecting round, his appeal was so warmly responded to that he was able to hand over to the brave engine-driver and his mate, at the end of the journey, more money than the two good fellows had ever seen at once in their lives, much less possessed.

Meanwhile Archer had taken charge of the injured Persian, whose thick cap had luckily saved him from any serious hurt, though it was some time ere he came to himself. As he at length sat up and began to look about him, a Russian merchant, who had just come up to see how he was, called out suddenly:

'Ha, Barak-Ali! is this you?'

'Barak-Ali!' echoed the count, who had come back with the money that he had collected, just in time to hear the last words. 'I thought I knew your face—well met!'

The stunned man was indeed the great Persian merchant-prince himself, owner of one of the largest petroleum factories in Baku, from whom the count, passing through that town in one of his Eastern journeys, had got some valuable information as to the border-line of Northern Persia and its wild inhabitants. Barak-Ali greeted him courteously; and then, recognising Archer as his preserver, thanked *him* in a very simple and manly fashion, wholly free from those extravagant flourishes with which his countrymen are wont to say much and mean nothing. Then, tearing a leaf from his pocket-book, he wrote a few lines on it and handed it to Archer, saying in very tolerable Russian:

'If either of you gentlemen ever go to Meshid (the chief town of North-east Persia) give this letter to my brother, Ahmed Mirza, who is well known there. He may be of use to you.'

But in *what* way he was destined to be 'of use' to them neither they nor the Persian himself, nor any man living, could then have foreseen.

CHAPTER V.

OVER THE BLACK SEA.

'S that really the coast of the Crimea over there, daddy?'

'It is indeed; and that dark hill yonder, just coming out on our port bow, is the ridge of the Alma, up which our men charged in '54 to storm the Russian batteries.'

And Harry Archer, leaning over the quarter-rail of the Black Sea mail-steamer, devoured with his eyes the famous spot which had been a familiar name to him ever since he was old enough to understand anything.

Our three travellers were already well on their way over the Black Sea to the Western Caucasus, having wisely made their stay in Odessa as short as possible. In truth, the great corn-port of Southern Russia could hardly be transformed by the most imaginative guide-book into 'a spot where the passing traveller may while away a pleasant hour.' A very dirty semi-Italian town, with a still dirtier Greek and Russian population; three or four tall, scraggy churches, very much like overgrown coffee-pots; a number of straight, wide streets, which, coupled with the greasy yellow of the houses, are strongly suggestive of knife-strokes through a pat of butter; half-a-dozen hideous statues 'after the antique,' and a long way after it, too; a vast, bare boulevard (with a few shabby little trees shivering along it) facing the horrified sea in all its unabashed ugliness, where you are choked with dust in summer, smothered with mud in autumn, frozen to death in winter, and blown off your feet in spring—such is Odessa!

The passengers on board were of the usual type. The inevitable British tourist in the inevitable plaid suit, whose constant efforts to arrange the strap of his telescope gave him the look of an over-fed Laocoön struggling with a peculiarly thin snake; a bronzed and bearded 'inspector of telegraphs' from St Petersburg, on his way to some unpronounceable place in No-Man's-Land, a little to the south of the Oxus; an enormous Odessa merchant, whose ruddy face and fiery red beard, flaming out between the fur-cap above and the fur-collar below, reminded Harry of the fire in the pine-wood; an ill-fated lady, who 'had so many children that she didn't know what to do;' a Russian cavalry officer, home on leave from the 'Army of Central Asia,' on whose dark, firm face (stamped with that indescribable *something* which always marks the man who has commanded men) Count Bulatoff's experienced eye recognised at a glance the genuine rusty tan of the great Tartar desert. Then there was a plump, placid, German Fräulein, with the China-blue eyes and treacle-coloured hair which characterise Dorothea as infallibly as the rakish cap, thick turnip-hued moustache, and huge blunderbuss pipe mark her brother Hermann who sits by her side; two or three jaunty young cadets, oppressively conscious of their gilt buttons, and discussing, with all the boldness and fluency of utter ignorance, every topic of the day, from the anti-Turkish revolt in Arabia to the last new opera at St Petersburg.

But to the count and his friends (more especially Harry) by far the most interesting figure in this motley crowd was the young English wife of a Russian custom-house officer— on her way to join her husband at Lencoran on the Caspian Sea—who had lived nearly ten years in the Caucasus, and had met with not a few adventures worthy of the most sensational 'Christmas story.' Even the cool Archer was somewhat startled to hear this quiet, slender, pleasant-faced young woman relate, in the most matter-of-fact way, how, in the previous summer, she had been twice fired at while sitting at her window, the bullets missing her only by a few inches; and how, that very spring, she had been aroused from sleep by the bursting in of a gang of sixteen armed robbers, and had felt her shoulder clutched by the gory hand of the chief, a gigantic mountaineer, who, brandishing his dripping sword before her eyes, threatened her with instant death if she dared to utter a sound, while the life-blood of an ill-fated servant, cut down by the ruffians in a gallant but hopeless attempt to defend his mistress's door against them, splashed her night-dress and besprinkled her hands and face.

Harry, to whom such experiences were still new, listened in open-mouthed amazement to this 'page from real life,' equally startled by the frightful story and by the perfect composure with which it was told.

'Have any of the rascals ever been caught?' asked Mr Archer.

'All of them have, I believe, except *one*,' said the lady as quietly as ever, 'and it is a great pity they did not catch *him* too, for, by all accounts, he was the worst of the whole gang, though hardly older than a boy. I never heard what his real name was, but he was a perfect wild beast for fighting, and so cruel and merciless to all who fell into his hands that every one called him "Krovolil"' (the Bloodshedder).

Many a time in after-days did Mr Archer recall, with only too good reason, the unaccountable thrill sent through his strong nerves by the first mention of this ominous name, utterly unknown to him though it was; but at the time he paid little or no attention to it.

Meanwhile the count (to whom this bandit's grim nickname appeared to be not wholly unknown) proceeded to question Madame Dmitrieff about him; and she, in reply to his queries, related various instances of the brigand's beast-like ferocity, some of which were so horrible that even Harry Archer, with all his schoolboy love of startling stories, found them a little too strong for him.

But he soon had something else to think of; for just then one of those sudden squalls that make the Black Sea so dangerous set the light steamer rocking like a cradle; and as the motion grew more violent, the legible impress of the dreaded 'minister of the *interior*' began to show itself on the livid faces of not a few of the passengers.

The behaviour of the various races under this trial was a curious study. The Turk pulled his turban over his broad, patient, wooden face, and nestled closer into his warm corner beside the funnel. The Tartar coiled himself up and went snugly to sleep with his bare feet in a basket of oranges and his head in a pool of dirty water. The Englishman, thrusting his hands deeper into his pockets, tramped doggedly up and down the dripping deck with that look of stern resolution worn by John Bull when dancing a quadrille, making a speech, or performing any other act of painful duty. The Frenchman tripped to and fro for a few seconds with a jaunty step, ostentatiously humming an opera air, and then suddenly disappeared below. The Russian merchant made all his preparations for being comfortably sick with a quiet dignity suggestive of the 'suicide scene' in Addison's *Cato*, and turned up after every paroxysm a vast, harvest-moon visage of unruffled placidity. The little German Fräulein assumed a pose of charming helplessness, and swallowed sticky prunes by the dozen; and the jaunty cadets hung limply over the side, too miserable to care about keeping up appearances any longer.

Upon such veterans as the count and Mr Archer all this had not the slightest effect; but the less seasoned Harry began to feel, in his own graphic words, 'like a bottle of well up gingerbeer,' and he was not at all sorry to see the land closing in upon them at last, and to catch the loom of the huge gray stone forts which, like Bunyan's twin giants at the mouth of the gloomy valley, guard the entrance of the harbour of Sebastopol.

Here, to the young Wintonian's great joy, the steamer remained long enough to give him time for a hasty survey, under his father's guidance, of the famous spots of which he had heard and read so much. He looked down upon the city from the Lazareff Boulevard, and noted with an appreciative eye the gapped walls and roofless houses on which the great siege had set its deadly mark. From the crest of the ridge overhanging the Vorontzoff Ravine he saw the quiet little harbour of Balaklava nestling between its rocky walls, and the fatal valley of the death-ride lying outspread beneath the bright afternoon sunshine, green and beautiful and peaceful, as if no sight or sound of war had disturbed it since the world began. He wandered over the heights of Inkermann, and beheld all round the crumbling ruins of the famous

'Sand-bag Battery,' the soil which thousands of corpses had fertilised covered with a vast sheet of scarlet poppies, as if all the blood shed on that day of slaughter had risen to the surface once more. He stood beside the small white pillar of hewn stone raised on the site of the terrible Redan in memory of the British heroes who perished in that long martyrdom, and heard, with a hot flush of manly shame, that the Russians themselves had placed a sentry to guard the hallowed monument of the English dead from the defacing pocket-knives of their own countrymen. And then, in the stillness of evening, he and his father sat silently on the crumbling breastwork of green turf across which, on the eve of the great city's fall, the men who were to fly at each other's throats like tigers with the first gleam of sunrise, exchanged brotherly hand-clasps, and gifts of bread and tobacco, during their last night on earth.

'I quite agree,' said Mr Archer, looking meaningly around him, ' with what my friend Thomas Carlyle once said to me : "If war is, as people say, only a misunderstanding, what a thing a right understanding must be!"'

When they got back to the steamer Count Bulatoff met them with a somewhat troubled face.

'I have news for you, Mr Archer,' said he. 'I have just learned that that worthy gentleman, Krovolil the Bloodshedder, about whom Madame Dmitrieff has just been telling us, has got together another gang of rogues like himself, and has actually stopped and robbed a train on the Poti-Tiflis Railway.'

'The Poti-Tiflis Railway?' echoed Archer. 'I thought it was not open yet.'

'It's not open all the way, but a good part of it is; and it is along that very part (where this fellow has just been playing his tricks) that *we* must go to get to my *datcha* (country-house) at Borjom. So, you see, it concerns us all alike; and the question is, What is to be done?'

'Let us get a lot of men and hunt the fellow down!' cried Harry, with sparkling eyes.

'You speak like a brave Englishman, Monsieur Henri,' said the count, with a subdued smile; 'but you will pardon my hinting to you that the hunting down of a robber among the mountains of the Caucasus is not *quite* such an easy matter as you seem to think. We have at this moment 167,000 soldiers in the Caucasus, and yet you see what things are done there every now and then.'

'Well, in my opinion,' said Archer, after a moment's silence, 'our best plan is just to push right on to Borjom at once. It seems to me that we shall run less risk immediately *after* such an outrage as that, both because the news of it will stir up the whole district against the thieves, and because the thieves themselves will probably make for the hills at once with their booty, in order to put it in a place of safety.'

'You talk like an old soldier, Monsieur Archer,' replied the count, with an approving nod; 'but I must warn you that it is very hard to make any calculation as to what such fellows as these brigands may or may not do. That rascal Krovolil, by all accounts, has not even the sense to be afraid, and runs headlong into every danger that he meets; and as for his men, most of them are sure to be Mohammedan fatalists, who think that, if it is their destiny to escape, they *will* escape whatever happens; and if not, not. However, if you wish to go straight on, I am not the man to hinder you.'

The sun was just setting as they came in sight of Yalta,

the most perfect of all the Southern Crimea's beautiful landscapes. Already the smooth green sward of the lower slopes, the clustering vineyards around the dainty little toy-village, and the white, balconied houses, ranged like chessmen along the curving shore, were fast melting into the rich purple twilight that brooded over the slumbering sea; and the golden splendour of sunset was fading from the dark woods above, the red light dying away from tree-top after tree-top as the deepening shadows crept slowly up the hillside. But a last gleam of brightness still lingered lovingly on the great towers of castellated rock overhead, and falling athwart the broad white front of the Czar's palace of Livadia, high on its lonely hill-top, kindled all its many windows into one blaze of living fire.

The night set in wet and chilly—for one of the Black Sea's most striking characteristics is the strange difference between its temperature and that of the land around it—and Harry Archer, finding no great amusement in standing still to be rained upon, without having anything to look at, went below not very long after dark.

But though he turned in early, it was long ere he could sleep; for the exciting thoughts that filled his mind were more than enough to keep any one awake. Less than half a year before, his life had been still flowing in the quiet and even routine of an English public school, its greatest excitement being a football-match or a hamper from home; and now, in the space of one short month, he had spoken face-to-face with a man whose nod was obeyed by one-seventh of the whole world. He had crossed the entire continent of Europe, first from west to east, and then from north to south; he had had a hairsbreadth escape of being burned alive; and last, but certainly not least, he was at present, to all appearance, in a fair way to fall in with a robber-captain who had never shown mercy in his life!

With such thoughts to occupy him, it was no wonder that our hero did not go to sleep till it was long past midnight; and when he came on deck again, it was to see the ruined temple of Mithridates looking down from the crest of its bold ridge upon the wide, crescent-shaped bay and white, dusty, tawdry town of Kertch.

Here, to Harry's great amusement, the mail was brought on board tied up in an old towel; and as there happened to be a pretty large hole in it, not a few of the letters fell overboard and drifted away, no one seeming to feel moved to pick them up.

'There, Harry,' cried Mr Archer, pointing to the floating papers; 'that's what you may call a *fluctuating correspondence.*'

'Well, I don't know,' said our hero, with a schoolboy grin; 'I should rather call it a *current story!*'

'And as for me,' chimed in Count Bulatoff, who was a wonderful master of English, though he very seldom spoke it from choice, 'I should call it a *floating report.*'

'Well done!' cried Harry, laughing; 'it's just gone round. That's how we used to do last half at Winchester in the long winter evenings; every one had to make a joke of some sort, or else have a jug of water emptied over his head. And precious bad jokes some of 'em were, I can tell you!'

'I am sorry to hear you give such a poor account of the wit of Winchester College, Monsieur Henri,' said the count, with commendable gravity; 'but I trust that the degeneracy of which you speak was not universal.'

'Well,' cried Harry, 'out and out, the best joke I heard

there that year was made by our second master, old Bookham, who was a dry old chap, with more fun in him than you'd think. You see, there was a fellow, Crawley Meggott—"Crawling Maggot" we used to call him, because he was such a long, thin, white-looking beggar—who was always scribbling what *he* called poetry, like that duffer who got us into that row with the Czar at Moscow. Well, what does he do one day but go to work to write a *valentine* in school, and he had just got as far as—

> The tender blush upon the rose
> Is like your blooming cheek,

when old Bookham peeps over his shoulder and says quietly, "It's like your *blooming cheek* to say so, Mr Meggott." *Didn't* we all yell, just! And all the rest of that half we called Meggott nothing but "Blooming Cheek."'

This being one of the places where the steamer halted for some time, our three voyagers went ashore to look about them; and as they climbed the hill toward the ruins of the ancient temple Harry said earnestly:

'Now, daddy, tell us all about Mithridates. This was where he lived, wasn't it?'

And his father, nothing loth, told as briefly and simply as he could the stirring tale of this classic Cetywayo's adventurous career, his long and valiant resistance to Rome, and his tragic end, to which the boy listened eagerly; for though, when served up as a lesson, the grim despot of Pontus had been to him one of those 'bothering old kings' whom Harry regarded with true schoolboy aversion, the story of the great warrior's exploits sounded widely different when told in words of fire on the very spot that had witnessed them.

The town itself was not very attractive, though hardly

meriting the sweeping verdict passed upon it by a plain-spoken Scottish grenadier during the Crimean war: 'A Glasgow beggar wadna tak' it at a gift!' But it had a certain picturesqueness of its own from the motley mingling of races natural to a place which forms the gateway between the Black Sea itself and the Sea of Azov—the shaggy, thick-set, beetle-browed Russian; the gaunt, sinewy Cossack; the bullet-headed, onion-complexioned Tartar; the hook-nosed, keen-eyed, sad-looking Jew; the burly, stolid Turk, and the swarthy, high-cheeked Persian; the handsome, knavish Greek, with the intense vitality of his race betraying itself in every line of his supple frame; the black-haired, aquiline Georgian, and smooth, voluptuous Imeritine; the brawny English sailor, looking down with a grand, indulgent British contempt upon those unhappy beings whom an inscrutable Providence has doomed to be foreigners; and, more striking than all, the fierce, panther-like beauty of the Circassian highlander, glittering in all the barbaric pomp of his mountain finery.

And now, as they ran down the eastern coast of the Black Sea, and drew closer and closer to the base of that mighty mountain rampart which, stretching eastward to the Caspian in one unbroken wall, shuts off Europe from Asia, the soft Italian beauty of the Crimea gave place to a rugged grandeur worthy of the Alps at their best. In fact, the scenery from this point onward was a mingling of all countries and all latitudes—Swiss precipices overhanging French vineyards, dainty little Spanish towns nestling in the skirts of dark Russian moorlands, and Persian gardens springing up beneath the shadow of Swedish forests; and, high over all, the vast snow-peak of Elburz—the highest point of the Caucasus—hung like a white summer cloud on the eastern sky.

And so, hour after hour, the great panorama rolled by. Novorossisk, Tuapsé, and Sotcha slipped past one by one, each with its tiny zigzag of quaint little toy-houses, dotted, like a half-finished game of chess, over the vast purple ridges that rose terrace beyond terrace into the very sky. And then came dainty Sukhum Kale, a charming little nook of Italian scenery nestling in the shadow of the everlasting hills, which stood over it like some war-worn soldier with his children playing around his feet.

'Look here, my boy,' said Mr Archer to his son; 'do you see a sort of shrubbery about half-way up that hillside yonder? That's one of the tea-plantations that have been started here lately—Russia's first attempt, in fact, to grow her own tea within her own borders.'

'An attempt which, unluckily, has not met with any very dazzling success as yet,' put in the count, smiling. 'We Russians are certainly the greatest nation in the world for drinking tea, but somehow or other we don't seem to be exactly the greatest at growing it. In fact—though it is a sad confession for a Russian to make—the Turks have done much better with it down in Anatolia, away yonder to the south.'

Archer was about to make some polite reply, when he suddenly stopped short, and surprised his companions by darting off in hot pursuit of the captain of the steamer, who happened to pass at that moment—the fact being that he had just heard several emphatic sentences exchanged between the captain and a Russian officer who had just come on board, in the course of which the Englishman's quick ear caught more than once the dreaded name of Krovolil the Bloodshedder.

A few moments later, however, back he came again as

suddenly as he had gone, with an air of very unwonted excitement.

'Do you hear this, Feodor Alexandrovitch?' cried he. 'General Naprashkin, the Governor of the Rion district, has got in between Krovolil's gang and the hills with a detachment of Tcherne-Morskoi Cossacks, and fairly cut off their retreat; and he hopes to capture the whole band in a few days' time.'

'Yes, Naprashkin generally does his work pretty promptly,' said the count, with a quiet smile. 'You know, I suppose, that he is my brother-in-law?'

'Indeed? Well, then, I have less cause to wonder at his energy, if he is related to *you*. Shall we see him at Borjom?'

'I have no doubt you will, for he usually takes charge of my boy Yury (George) in my absence; and if by any chance he should not be there, I'll take you to visit him at his own house. I think you'll like him, and I am sure he will be very glad to meet *you*.'

'And I shall be very glad to meet *him*,' said the Englishman courteously.

But he might have spoken less lightly and carelessly had he known how strangely this same Naprashkin (whose name he now heard for the first time) was destined to figure ere long in the story of his own life, and that of his son likewise.

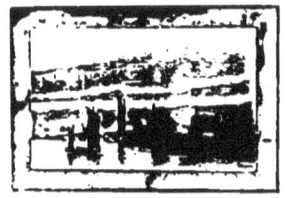

CHAPTER VI.

THROUGH THE GIANT MOUNTAINS.

UKHUM KALE was the steamer's last stopping-place before reaching the end of its voyage at Poti; but these long halts at so many ports in succession took up nearly as much time as the actual voyage itself, and it was not till the fifth evening after leaving Odessa that our travellers at length saw the white peaks of the Armenian mountains glimmering faintly along the southern sky through the fast-falling shadows of night, and the long, low bank of the Rion rising like a brooding mist above the sea, as they steamed toward the mouth of the overgrown gutter on which lies Poti, the dirtiest and most unhealthy port (which is saying a great deal) in all Russia.

'What sort of place *is* Poti, daddy?' asked Harry Archer.

'Well,' said his father, laughing, 'if I were writing an official report upon it, I should be apt to sum it up in this style: Local products, fever and cholera; population, frogs and mosquitoes; principal exports, malaria, boils, and fleas; principal imports, quinine and Florida water; manners, none; customs, very hard to pass with luggage; revenue, varying according to the success of the overcharges; internal communication, jumping from one stepping-stone to another; climate, a compromise between West Africa and the Bog of Allen; chief local industry, sending strangers to the wrong hotel; government, every man for himself, and the nearest policeman for all.'

'You are rather hard on our poor little seaport, Monsieur Archer,' said the count, who had listened to this tirade with a smile of quiet amusement.

'And well I may be,' retorted the other; 'for, the last time I was here, *it* was very hard upon *me !*'

'Well,' said the Russian more gravely, 'perhaps the next time you come this way you may land at Batoum instead of Poti, and travel by rail, not along the Rion, but through Anatolia.'

The count spoke truly; but even *he* could not foresee how soon his prophecy would be made good. Even then the suggestive contrast between the shallow, unsheltered roadstead and deadly swamps of Poti on the one hand, and the fine harbour and breezy hills of the adjacent Turkish port of Batoum on the other, had long since forced itself upon the attention of Russia's leading statesmen; and the official journals of St Petersburg had already begun to declare, with ominous unanimity, that 'Batoum was manifestly intended by nature to belong to Russia'—which must, no doubt, have been a great consolation to the Turks seven years later, when Russia had succeeded in impressing the same conviction upon *them*, at a cost of several millions of roubles and ninety thousand Russian lives.[*] Anyhow, right or wrong, the thing was done; and to-day the traveller *does* land at Batoum, and journeys eastward from it by a

[*] Batoum was one of the places ceded to Russia by the Sultan after the war of 1877-78.

branch railroad joining the main line to Tiflis at Samtredi, and ignoring the swampy Rion basin altogether.

Unlike most things in this world, the Poti-Tiflis Railway shows all its worst points at the outset; and when they set off along it next day, at the convenient hour of five in the morning, Harry Archer saw around him through the drizzling rain, look where he would, one vast drowned jungle, which seemed to cover the whole face of the country right up to Tcheladid, and was enlivened by a chorus of frogs which (as our young hero remarked with a grin) would have been 'just the thing for Aristophanes.' But as they advanced eastward the ground on either side became gradually firmer and higher; long ranges of wood-crowned hills began to lift themselves against the brightening sky; the cloudless sunshine of the warm south replaced the damp white mist that brooded over the fatal morasses of the Rion, and the genuine 'Kavkaz' (Caucasus) was before them in all its splendour.

And now, for the first time, Harry began to understand the savage wars of these famous mountains, and the desperate resistance of the fierce highlanders who had held them so long against all the armies of Russia. Till he actually got right in among the hills, the young Wintonian, after all that he had heard of Caucasian hotels, and Caucasian post-roads, and Caucasian railways, naturally found it hard to believe that in this quiet and orderly region—which seemed to be as safe and accessible as Saxony or the Tyrol—one of the bloodiest and most merciless conflicts of modern times had been raging barely twelve years before.

But here, in the very heart of this great natural fortress—shut in on either side by black, overhanging cliffs of immeasurable height, with the furious river lashing itself into foam far below, and just space enough for the train to slide past between the precipice above and the precipice beneath— the observant lad began to realise what the conquest of such a region must have been. The march of an army through such defiles as these (and even these are nothing to the terrific ravines of Northern Daghestan, where the bones of a hundred thousand men whiten amid tangled thickets and moss-grown rocks) would be grim work indeed, encumbered with sick and wounded, and pursued by a merciless enemy, with a fire-flash from behind every bush and crag, and the whole mountain-side alive with the crackle of the fatal rifles.

In truth, to all who question the fighting power of the Russian soldier, there is one sufficient answer: 'He conquered the Caucasus.' For in the days when he did so, the whole might of the wild Circassian tribes was in the hands of Shamyl himself, and Shamyl was still the dashing warrior and able general of Darga and Achulgo, not the aged, broken, white-haired man, grand even in his decay, whom I saw amid a circle of wondering guests at the wedding of Alexander III. and Princess Dagmar.

'It *must* have been tough work, and no mistake!' said Harry half-aloud.

'It was indeed,' replied the count, who easily guessed his meaning; 'and I can assure you that we were all very glad to see the end of it. I know *I* was!'

'You!' cried the boy, staring. 'Were *you* in it too, Feodor Alexandrovitch? Why, you never told me you had been a soldier!'

'Nor have I—not a regular soldier, at least; but I was with my friend Prince Bariatinski, as a volunteer, in that last campaign by which he ended the war and captured Shamyl himself; and it was then that I saw the old chief for the first time.'

'You *saw* him yourself, then?' cried Harry eagerly. 'What was he like? He must have been terribly chop-fallen at being taken *alive!*'

'He was indeed; and I'm very glad that all our officers were so kind to him, and did their utmost to lessen the bitterness of his defeat. As for him, though his face showed how deeply he felt it, he never uttered a murmur, and only said, in his fatalist Mohammedan way: "It was my destiny, and who can avert fate? It is the will of Allah that my mountains should belong to the Grecian Czar."'*

'Poor old chap!' said the brave boy pityingly; 'and what became of him after that?'

'Why, then they took him away, and brought him to St Petersburg; and there the Czar (the same one that is reigning now, you know, whom you saw in Moscow) received him very kindly, and presented him to the Empress, who was then the most beautiful woman in all Europe. And when the old warrior saw her he bowed his noble gray head courteously, and said, in that grand way which all Eastern chiefs seem to have by nature: "Lady, had I known against *whom* I was fighting, Allah would have taken away the edge of my sword in battle!" And the Empress has always said (and so has the Emperor too) that that was the highest compliment ever paid her.'

'I should think so!' cried Harry enthusiastically. 'What an old brick he must be! I say, is he alive yet? I should like to meet him.'

* Whether this curious title arose from the prevalence of the Greek Church in Russia, or from some vague idea of the Czars being the successors of the Greek Emperors of Constantinople, I have never been able to learn.

'No; he died just the other day, more's the pity. When he felt that he was beginning to break down, he begged the Czar to let him go on a pilgrimage to Mecca; for he was forbidden to leave Russia, lest he should kindle a fresh war.'

'And the Czar let him go, of course?'

'Of course he did; and Shamyl went, and died in the Holy City itself, with several of his old brothers-in-arms around him; and with his last breath he charged them to be true to the great Emperor, for it was the will of God that *he* should be lord of the Caucasus.'

'Well done!' cried the young Wykehamist warmly; 'he must have been a fine old fellow! Tell me some more about him, please.'

The Russian did so very readily, and Harry was so completely absorbed in the story that he hardly noticed a voice saying behind him, in Russian:

'Sir, is it *your* coat that that dog has got hold of?'

But the more observant count looked up at the warning, and beheld a very unexpected tableau.

At one of the larger stations a native hawker had paraded along the train a smoking batch of *piroshki* (small pies of chopped meat), and Harry had bought half-a-dozen of them; and, not feeling in the humour to eat them at once, had wrapped the dainties in paper, and thrust them into the pocket of his overcoat, which he had left hanging over the elbow-rest of the seat when he went across the carriage to talk to Count Bulatoff.

Little by little the jolting of the train shook down the coat on to the floor; and a few moments later the half-closed door leading into the other division of the carriage was pushed wide open, and a splendid English mastiff, drawn by the savoury odour of the pastry, pounced upon the fallen overcoat, and ferreting out the paper of pies, was just despatching them when a friendly fellow-passenger gave our hero the warning quoted above.

But this warning came too late to be of any use; for Harry sprang up just in time to see the last of his cherished pies vanish down the dog's capacious throat.

Indignant at this wholesale plundering of his stores, the bold English boy, who knew as little of fear as Nelson himself, darted to the spot, and, unchecked by the four-footed robber's menacing display of his terrible fangs, was just about to fall upon the huge beast tooth and nail, when—very luckily indeed for *him*—the impending fray was suddenly interrupted.

CHAPTER VII.

A RUSSIAN GENERAL.

'DOWN, Ruslan, down!' said a deep voice in Russian just behind the dog; and in the doorway stood a stalwart figure in the uniform of a Russian general.

'I fear my dog has been trespassing'—— began the stranger, whose keen eye had taken in the whole situation at a glance; but ere he could finish the sentence Count Bulatoff, who had started up at the first sound of his voice, sprang forward and caught him by both hands, calling out joyfully:

'What, Meetya (Dmitri), is this *you?* Whence has God sent you to us?'

And then, to Harry's no small surprise and amusement, the two big men embraced like children, and kissed each other on both cheeks; for Bulatoff, traveller and man of the world as he was, was a zealous observer of all old national customs. Then the count, turning to Mr Archer and his son, introduced the new-comer as 'My brother-in-law, General Naprashkin.'

Both father and son were naturally pleased at this unexpected meeting with a man of whose exploits they had lately been hearing so much, and who had just been employed in sweeping from their path the formidable brigand whom they had such cause to fear. In a trice the renowned general was on intimate terms with them both; and the first thing that he did was to make his dog Ruslan give its paw to Harry, by way of an apology for the theft of the pies.

The young Wykehamist, who had all the love of a true Englishman for fine dogs and horses, made friends with the noble creature at once; and the mastiff, as if wishing to atone for its past misdeed by special friendliness, laid its massive head caressingly on the boy's knee, and flapped its huge tail against the floor with a noise like the stroke of a heavy stick.

Meanwhile Archer made a close but unobserved survey of the veteran general himself, who, though rather younger, if anything, than his famous brother-in-law, looked several years older, his dark face being very deeply furrowed, and his short, crisp, black hair thickly streaked with gray. His large proportions and solid muscle contrasted very strikingly with the spare, wiry frame of the count; but both men alike had the same firm, self-reliant air, and the same quietly-watchful look, taught them by the constant presence of danger and of death.

'It seems, then, Fyodka,' said the general, 'that I have been next door to you, all this time, without knowing it; but though I knew you were on your way home, I never thought of your being upon this train. I only got down to Kutaïs late last night, and came this morning along the branch-line to Rion, where I caught this train of yours; and if I had happened to get in at this end of the carriage instead of the other, I should just have come right upon you.'

'And what have you done with my boy Yury?' asked the count.

'Sent him to his aunt at Tiflis; and she was to send him

back yesterday, under the care of one of my officers, who is to join me at Borjom; so I think you will find your young man safe at home when you get there.'

'And I hope, Dmitri Ivânovitch,' said Mr Archer, addressing Naprashkin in French for Harry's benefit, 'that we may take your own presence here as a sign that your expedition against Krovolil and his gang of rogues has been brought to a successful issue.'

'Yes, we have made pretty short work of them,' said the general, with a smile of quiet satisfaction; 'I don't think *they* will trouble any one again. It was a great piece of good luck for us to be in time to get between them and the mountains, so as to cut off their retreat; for by that means we drove them into a part of the country where the peasantry were hostile to them, and would give them no food, so that a good many of them were *fortunately* starved to death, which saved us a great deal of trouble.'

The English boy started (as he well might) to hear this kindly and pleasant man, with whom he had been so friendly, talk with such cold and cruel satisfaction of having destroyed so many of his fellow-men by the slow torture of famine; for this was Harry's first experience (though unhappily not his last) of the absolute indifference with which, in Eastern Europe as well as in Asia, the best and most kind-hearted men are wont to speak of human suffering and human destruction.

'My Cossacks shot a good many more,' went on the general, as coolly as ever, 'who were straggling among the hills to try and pick up something to eat; for by that time they had grown so desperate with hunger that they would have run any risk to get just one morsel of food to keep them alive. This brave old dog of mine pulled down two more—good old fellow! (and he fondled the destroyer's huge head affectionately as he spoke). As to the chief himself—the Bloodshedder, as they called him—I and four or five of my best men got right round him, and drove him back to the edge of a high cliff; and then, rather than be taken alive, the idiot threw himself over the precipice.'

'So that now there's an end of the whole gang?' cried the count briskly, while Harry sat speechless with mingled horror and disgust.

'Yes, I think they are all pretty satisfactorily accounted for,' replied Naprashkin as composedly as if he had been only counting teaspoons. 'Two or three of the wounded, who fell into my hands alive, begged me to kill them and put them out of their misery; but I had no orders to that effect, so I handed them over to the authorities for transmission to Siberia. Would you like to try one of these cigars, Fyodka? They have rather a good flavour.'

It was some time ere Harry Archer regained his usual composure, which had been a good deal shaken by this startling sample of what discipline and habit can do to harden the kindest and most feeling heart. Being in no mood for further talk just then, our hero took his seat close by the farther window, and set himself to watch the passing scenery.

And, in truth, it was well worth looking at. At one moment the train was gliding beneath the shadow of mighty cliffs, which seemed already toppling over to crush it; and an instant later it was rattling through a quiet little green valley, dotted with tiny log-huts. Now the wondering boy looked down into the black depths of a yawning chasm, and the next moment he caught a glimpse of some ruined castle perched high among the clouds; while all around him, mass on mass, surged up great billows of wooded mountain, as if all the waves of the Deluge had been suddenly frozen into forests.

Evening was already darkening into night when our party got out at Mikhailovo, close to the foot of the famous Suram Pass, and transferred themselves and their luggage to a nondescript vehicle (a kind of cross between a gig and a carriage, drawn by four horses *abreast*), which at once darted off across the great plain at a pace worthy of an Irish jaunting-car.

'You see, Monsieur Henri,' explained Count Bulatoff to the wondering Harry, 'we have only one or two railways in the Caucasus as yet, and so most of our travelling has to be done by post; and this is how we are going all the way to Borjom.'

This was, in fact, our hero's first experience of 'posting' in Russia; and a very strange experience he found it. For a time, indeed, the ghostly twilight was enlivened by human faces and human voices—Mingrelian carts rumbling and jolting along the highway, Georgian peasants trudging off toward the mountains with their long sticks in their hands, and a few Russian officers riding back to the great camp at Suram. But gradually all these sights and sounds of life melted away, and nothing broke the silence of night save the monotonous beat of the horse-hoofs, and the dull roar which told our travellers that they were nearing the bank of the Kura River (now in the second stage of its long journey eastward down to the Caspian Sea), with now and then a joyous bark from the general's mastiff, Ruslan, which—wild with delight at finding itself free once more, after being cooped up all day in a train—was galloping along beside the car, darting ahead of it and then frolicking back again, and at times leaping up almost into its master's lap.

Little by little the road grew steeper, narrower, and more zigzag, as the dark hills closed in on either side; and as the night went on, and the travellers mounted higher and higher, the piercing cold of the keen mountain air, coming so soon after the heat of the sun-scorched plains below, seemed to bite them to the very bone.

Harry, less seasoned than his comrades, felt the change severely; and though he would have been very loth to own it, he experienced no small inward satisfaction at feeling his neighbour, General Naprashkin—the very man who had just been destroying scores of human beings by famine and sword —wrapping a warm rug carefully around him.

'Thank you, Dmitri Ivânovitch,' said our hero, who, like a well-bred boy as he was, felt bound to acknowledge the Russian's kindness, and who knew instinctively that such a man could never be made to understand his own English horror of the general's cold-blooded severity. 'Hadn't we better take your dog up into the car? He must be tired with running so long.'

'Not he! He'll run beside my horse for hours when I'm up in the mountains; and after being in the train all day, a good run is just what he enjoys.'

'Why did you call him "Ruslan"? Was it after some friend of yours?'

'Hardly; for that gentleman, if he ever lived at all, must have lived a good many centuries ago. He was a Russian legendary hero, named Ruslan or Yeruslan Lazarevitch, who is said to have once routed a whole army single-handed; and I only wish he had left the recipe behind him, for we poor modern soldiers usually find one man at a time quite enough.'

A sudden halt, a hasty unharnessing and harnessing of horses, a dim vision of dark, bearded faces flitting to and fro in fitful lamplight, and then they were off again, up and down shadowy slopes, over half-seen bridges, past tiny specks of light glimmering amid dark trees, till all at once they found themselves rattling through a long, straggling street, and Mr Archer and his son began to realise that they were actually in Borjom at last.

CHAPTER VIII.

HARRY MAKES TWO NEW ACQUAINTANCES.

Y the time they reached Count Bulatoff's house Harry Archer was so drowsy that he had only a vague impression of a large, bare entrance-hall hung with the skins of various wild beasts, and a long winding stair of dark wood, up which he stumbled, half-asleep, to his snug little room on the first floor, where he slept till morning as soundly as a night-watchman. But the first ray of sunrise awoke him at once, and up he jumped, and flew to the window, eager for a sight of his new surroundings.

There are few things more delightful than seeing for the first time, in the brightness of early morning, a new place at which one has arrived after dark on the previous night; and our hero now enjoyed this pleasure to the utmost.

The house—which, being placed on a somewhat higher elevation than those around it, commanded a pretty extensive view—stood in the midst of a large garden, evidently cultivated with no ordinary care, and presenting a goodly show of flowers even at this early stage of the summer. On either side of the deep, narrow valley, or rather gorge, through which the rushing river foamed and roared among its obstructing rocks, towered up vast limestone cliffs, so thickly clad with firs and undergrowth that only now and then could a passing glimpse of the stern, gray rocks behind be caught through the endless mass of clustering leaves; but high above the dark precipices and shadowy woods, the warm, rich blue of the southern sky lay outspread in all the cloudless splendour of a true Caucasian sunrise. Here and there, however, these mighty battlements of rock melted away into smooth grassy slopes—the fresh green of which contrasted very prettily with the sombre hue of the encircling fir-woods—upon one of which, like a child in its mother's lap, lay the charming little semi-Eastern town of Borjom, the Cheltenham of Russia ; and just opposite it, on the right bank of the river, a large, quaint-looking, many-turreted building, not unlike a greatly magnified version of the ordinary Swiss chalet, rose, like the Sleeping Beauty's Palace, above the dark, shaggy woods that covered the whole hillside.

'I suppose that must be the palace of the Grand-Duke Michael, the Viceroy of the Caucasus, about whom the old general spun us such a lot of yarns last night,' muttered Harry, eyeing this woodland hermitage with no small interest. 'I wonder if they'd let one go over it; it looks just the sort of place that ought to be worth seeing.'

Early as it was, the neighbourhood was already awake and astir. Two or three barefooted peasant women were seen coming up from the river, with pails of water poised on their heads. Half-a-dozen sturdy fellows were tramping off, pick and shovel in hand, to their work on one of the many new roads that were now seaming the encircling hills in all directions. The shrill note of a cavalry bugle suddenly awoke every echo of the surrounding cliffs, and a few moments later a detachment of Russian dragoons came riding gallantly along the base of the ridge on which our hero stood, their silver-laced jackets and drawn sabres glittering in the rising sun, as they appeared and vanished by turns round the curves of the winding road.

'Hollo!' cried Harry; 'I must go down and have a look at those fellows. I wonder what time they have breakfast here; but it doesn't much matter—they won't be having it *yet* anyhow!' and, hurrying on his clothes as if for a wager, the young Wykehamist darted down the stair as though he were once more running to be in time for school at Winchester.

But, as usual, most haste proved worst speed; for, not meeting any one of whom he might ask his way, our hero took a wrong turn, and left the house by a side-entrance instead of the front-door. This at once involved him in a maze of garden-paths, ending at last in a high boundary-wall.

Not having patience to look for a door, Harry got clear of the garden by the simple method of climbing over the wall; and then, regardless of his torn trousers and his blackened hands and face, he flew down the hill as if running for his life. But, with all his haste, he came too late; for by the time he reached the foot of the ridge the soldiers were nowhere to be seen.

While the boy was standing irresolute, at a loss which way to go, his attention (which was never easy to hold for five minutes at a time) was suddenly diverted by a strange, booming, rumbling sound, which seemed to issue from the thickets that covered the face of a steep slope a little way beyond him.

'What on earth can that be?' cried he. 'It's not thunder, and it don't sound quite like a cannon either. I should have said it was a waterfall, only it leaves off every now and then. But, whatever it is, here goes to find out all about it!'

And in a moment more he was hurrying at his best speed in the direction of the sound, which grew louder and plainer as he advanced, till, coming suddenly round the border of a mass of tangled thickets, he found himself confronted with a very unlooked-for spectacle.

Beyond the thickets lay a broad, steep incline of several hundred feet, quite clear of wooding, and covered with short, crisp, dry grass. Right down the middle of this slope, from the crest to the very foot, ran a straight, narrow, dusty cleft or groove, not unlike a dry ditch, save that its sides were perfectly even, and that it had absolutely no bend from first to last. But Harry had seen such things more than once in the Higher Alps, and did not need the sight of the group of red-shirted woodmen on the brow of the ridge, or the huge pile of massive logs at its foot, to tell him that this curious funnel was nothing else than a 'log-slide.'

Sure enough, as he stood gazing upward, three or four huge fir-trunks and pine-stems came flying down the slide with the same hollow, booming rumble (repeated far and wide by a thousand echoes) which had so greatly puzzled our hero.

But poor Harry seemed fated to pay dear for his curiosity; for as he stood watching the downward rush of the ponderous tree-trunks, the largest of them, striking its smaller end violently against the side of the 'shoot,' whirled round suddenly, leaped clear out of the trench, and swept like a scythe right across the very spot where the boy was standing.

Happily the latter had seen the coming peril just in time

to throw himself flat on his face, and thus escaped by a hairsbreadth from being killed on the spot; but so tremendous was the force of the blow that a young tree on which it fell was snapped short off close to the root like a stick of sealing-wax.

'Close shave, that!' muttered Harry, drawing a long breath as he picked himself up. 'On the whole, it seems to me that I may just as well sheer a little farther off, for I shouldn't exactly care to try that game twice.'

And, drawing aside to a safe distance, our hero continued to watch with no small interest the rush of the great logs down the shoot, till at length, happening to glance at his watch, he saw, to his great surprise, that it was getting on for eight o'clock.

'I say,' cried he, 'this won't do! I shall be running myself late for breakfast, and I always hate to be late in another fellow's house; it seems so jolly unmannerly. Here goes for a spurt!' and away he flew up the hill like a hunted deer.

This time Harry was lucky enough to find the right entrance to the garden, and the right path through it, along which he hastened at a brisk pace, spurred not only by the fear of keeping his kind host waiting for breakfast, but also by a natural curiosity to see Bulatoff's son, the young Count Yury, of whom he had seen nothing yet.

But all at once he was brought to a halt by the sight of a lad about his own age, lying at full length under a tree, with his head propped on his hands, and seemingly deep in a large book; and our hero guessed at once that this young student must be the very person whom he wished to meet.

'Too fond of reading by half. *He* won't be good for much!' was the British schoolboy's characteristic comment.

'I should not wonder, now, if he didn't even know how to play cricket, poor little beggar! But, anyhow, let us see what he's made of.'

At the sound of Harry's advancing steps the boy-count (for it was indeed he) looked up, and rising to his feet, held out his hand, and said in very fair English, with quite the air of a grown-up man :

'Mr Henry Archer, I believe?'

Harry was somewhat taken aback by this ceremonious address, which seemed to him (as he afterwards said) 'as stiff as the head-master's speech at a prize-giving.' But he gave the proffered hand a hearty shake, and as he did so, made a hasty survey of his new friend; for, though far from guessing how strangely this lad was destined to be mixed up with his own fortunes, he was naturally interested in the first Russian boy whose acquaintance he had yet made.

Yury Feodorovitch Bulatoff, though slightly younger than Harry, was somewhat the taller of the two (for our hero had inherited the short, square build of his renowned father), but he lacked the latter's strong make and solid muscle, as well as the perfect training that showed itself in every motion of the Wintonian's active, sinewy frame. His face, which would otherwise have been very handsome, had a sickly, pallid, sodden look that told its own story; and his movements, so far from having anything of the elastic spring given by constant exercise and overbrimming vitality to the English boy, were heavy and languid, as if any exertion were an effort to him.

But more unbearable than all to our bold Harry was the air of quiet amusement with which his new acquaintance (whose whole exterior was a model of neatness and even of elegance) eyed the torn and dusty clothes, muddy boots, and grimy hands and face of the wild figure before him. At that look a sudden and overwhelming consciousness of his own superlative untidiness rushed upon poor Harry like a wave; and when he saw, or thought he saw, a lurking smile on the young Russian's face, the one feeling in his mind was a frantic longing to 'punch the fellow's head.'

But just then the young count addressed him again, as politely as ever.

'Have you had your breakfast? If not, I'll order you some in a moment,' said he, still with the same 'grown-up' air; for, having no companions of his own age, and mixing constantly with the generals, statesmen, and travellers who were his father's chosen friends, this poor lad had almost become a man without having ever been really a boy.

'Had my breakfast?' echoed Harry. 'Well, I hope you don't think I'm such a greedy fellow as to go and have it all by myself, without waiting for the rest of you!'

'Ah, you don't know our ways yet, I see,' said Yury, smiling. 'We have some tea and bread-and-butter in our rooms about eight o'clock, and then at midday we all meet for a *déjeuner à la fourchette*, or what you English call a solid meal. I'm just going to have *my* tea now, and we will order some for you as well. Here, Vaska!' (Basil).

'Your Brightness?' replied a deep voice, as a man appeared from behind the bushes with a tea-tray in one hand, while with the other he made a stiff military salute to his young master.

Harry looked with no small interest at the new-comer, whose tall, spare, upright form, measured step, and scarred, weather-beaten face proclaimed him to be an old soldier as plainly as if he had carried it written on his cap. Such, indeed, he was—a veteran of the Crimean war, who had brought away the scars of English sabres from the fatal field of Balaklava, and had been in Count Bulatoff's service ever since leaving the army.

'Vaska,' said the boy-count in Russian, 'bring some more tea for the English *barin*' (gentleman).

'I hear, Yury Feodorovitch,' replied the veteran; and back he came in a trice with another tea-tray, equally well covered.

But, unluckily for our hero, Vasili, eager to do his utmost for his young master's guest, and determined that, whether the latter's taste leaned to the Russian or to the English way of drinking tea, it should be gratified, placed a small jug of milk beside the brimming tumbler of tea and sliced lemon; and Harry, not thinking of what he was doing, poured in *the milk along with the lemon*—with what result may be imagined!

All Yury's good-breeding could not repress a laugh, and a momentary grin flickered over the iron face of Vasili himself; and the peace of the household was once more in danger.

But the untiring Vasili promptly repaired this mishap; and over the tea and bread-and-butter—both first-rate of their kind—the two lads gradually became more confidential. Yury laughed heartily at Harry's account of his father's exploit in the refreshment-room at Jmerinka; and Harry, on his part, finding the young count, as he had expected, utterly ignorant of the noble game of cricket, volunteered to teach it to him as soon as the necessary appliances could be got ready. The discovery that Yury could ride and shoot came just in time to check the rising contempt which his cricketless barbarism had begun to inspire in the Winchester athlete's mind; and when the Russian offered to show Harry his horse, our hero marched off with him as amicably as if they had been chums of ten years' standing.

Meanwhile Mr Archer and his host, who had got through *their* breakfast much more expeditiously than their respective sons, were holding a long conference in Bulatoff's study, in the course of which they examined enough maps and overhauled enough ancient coins and other antiques to stock a museum. At length the Englishman said suddenly:

'By-the-by, I had better go and see what that young man of mine is about; he is sure to get into some mischief or other if he is left to himself for half-an-hour.'

'Oh, I don't think you need trouble yourself about him,' rejoined the count, laughing; 'he can hardly get into any mischief *here*. Most likely he has met my Yury somewhere about the garden, and they have made friends; and I'm sure I shall be very glad if they do, for Yury is neither so strong nor so brisk as he ought to be, and perhaps your Monsieur Harry may put more life into him.'

Hardly were the words uttered, when there arose outside a clamour that might have awakened a country policeman on duty. Doors were banging, dogs barking, feet trampling to and fro, and a dozen voices at once kept calling out in tones of amazement and horror:

'They'll be killed! They'll both be killed!'

'What on earth is all this?' cried Archer, darting out like a rocket.

But this question was no sooner asked than answered; for one glance showed him what had happened, and he cried out angrily:

'Put more life *into* him, indeed! From what I see, he is much more likely to knock all the life *out* of him!'

In truth, the tableau that met his eyes and those of his host—who had hurried out after him—was certainly one which might well startle even *them*.

Right on the top of the house, nearly fifty feet from the ground, Yury, with a very pale face and a general appearance of being anything but comfortable, was clinging to a rickety gable with the clutch of a drowning man. On the ridge of the roof, which was barely wide enough to give him footing, Harry Archer, at the imminent risk of his neck, was springing up at a huge, overhanging bough, which seemed to elude his grasp as persistently as the fruit-tree eluded that of Tantalus. On the lawn below, the Tartar coachman and groom, the Russian cook and housemaids, the German lackey, and three or four hangers-on of the household were gazing upward, with startled eyes and muttered exclamations of horror, at their young master's peril; and, to crown all, the old soldier Vasili (who was the only one that appeared to retain any presence of mind), in attempting to drag out a long ladder that lay in the courtyard, had slipped and gone sprawling on his back, with the ladder atop of him.

As if all this were not enough, the wind, which was now fast rising to a gale, swept furiously across the exposed roof, making the position of the unsheltered boys on their dizzy perch more perilous every moment; and when Harry's cap, torn from his head by a violent gust, came whirling down into the garden, the short, quick gasp of horror that broke from the spectators foreboded the fall of its owner in the same way.

But Archer and Bulatoff, vexed and angry as they were, saw that this was no time for scolding, and that the first thing to be done was to get the boys out of their scrape.

'What on earth have you been at, Harry?' cried his father, who, in spite of his vexation, could hardly keep from laughing at this queer dilemma.

F

'Showing Yury how to climb,' hallooed the young athlete in reply. 'I thought it would be rather fun for him.'

Archer had his own opinion of this 'fun' as he eyed the rueful face of the Russian boy-martyr for whose benefit it had been contrived. But ere he could speak again Harry shouted to his comrade :

'Sit firm, Yury; I've got it at last!'

In fact, our hero had at length managed to clutch the swaying bough, along which he scrambled like a squirrel, and clambering down the tree, dropped lightly to the ground from a height of more than ten feet, and ran to help Vasili, who was still struggling with the unmanageable ladder. In a trice the ladder was reared against the side of the house, close to where Yury was clinging; and Harry ran up it as nimbly as a sailor, hardly touching it with his hands.

'Now, old fellow,' cried he cheerily, 'come along and show 'em how handily you can get down!'

And, in fact, the boy-count—whether it was that he had begun to get used to the situation, or that the native courage of his gallant race revolted against the idea of showing any sign of fear before so many witnesses—came down the ladder as boldly as his fearless comrade, and reached the ground in safety, amid a burst of cheers from the anxious spectators.

This being the first time that he had seen his father that day, Yury greeted him by ceremoniously kissing his hand, to the no small wonder and amusement of his friend Harry.

'Well, that's a queer notion, and no mistake!' muttered he. 'I wonder what daddy would say if I were to bid *him* good-morning that way!'

As they all re-entered the house Bulatoff whispered to Archer :

'Pray do not scold your son for this, for he has really done me a very great service without knowing it. This is the first time that I have ever seen Yury try anything so daring ; and now that he has once done it, he will have more confidence in himself ever after.'

Mr Archer did not scold Harry, but he spoke to him very kindly and seriously, warning him to remember that he must not expect this delicate Russian boy to be as strong and sure-footed as himself, and that, had he been the means of killing or crippling for life the only son of their kind host, he could never have forgiven himself ; and Harry, not a little startled by this new aspect of the case, promised earnestly to be more careful in future.

Later on in the morning Count Bulatoff (the general having gone off before daylight to his own residence, a few miles away) showed his guests over the house ; and Harry, whose head was full of the old mansions of Harrison Ainsworth and Sir Walter Scott, was charmed with the grim old chambers, secret stairs, hidden vaults, and unexpected trap-doors with which this Russian chateau seemed to abound. And when he found himself actually sitting down to lunch in a long, paved hall, with a huge, carved fireplace at one end, and its walls hung with Circassian helmets and mail-coats, and the antlered heads of mountain-deer, our hero's delight knew no bounds.

'I shall hope to show you something better than this to-morrow, Monsieur Henri,' said the count, smiling good-humouredly at the boy's enthusiasm, 'for I find that the Grand-Duke is expected at his palace yonder either to-night or to-morrow morning. In fact, those soldiers that you saw to-day were the escort of his baggage, which he has sent on ahead ; and as I shall have to go up to pay my respects to him, you and your father may as well come too. As a rule the palace is shown only in his absence, but I'm sure he will be glad to let *you* go over it, especially when he knows who you both are.'

Lunch over, the young Wintonian, by way of putting in practice his good resolutions of the morning, invited Yury to go for a walk with him through the town, prudently calculating that they could not well get into any danger *there*. But Yury, who had been a good deal shaken by his recent adventure, pleaded that he was tired, and wanted to sit still; so Harry was forced to set off alone, muttering as he did so:

'Poor little chap! Fancy a trifle like *that* tiring him! As if any fellow should *ever* want to sit still, unless he's fairly knocked up! However, I suppose he can't help himself—he's never had the luck to be at school!'

Such was indeed the case, for (as usual in Russia) Yury's education had hitherto been conducted by a tutor living in the house—which, to our hero's sturdy British prejudices, seemed only one degree better than being looked after by a nurse!

Left to himself, Harry turned his back on the town, and set off on a rattling tramp through the woods, up hill and down dale; across rude wooden bridges spanning tiny waterfalls; along the brink of dizzy precipices; over steep, crumbling slopes, where the loose stones pattered down like hail; till at length, in the depths of the gloomy pine-forest, he came suddenly upon a small open space, over which were straying half-a-dozen tiny black pigs, covered with thick bristly hair.

'Can they be *wild* pigs, I wonder?' cried Harry. 'What fun to meet a real, live wild-boar *here!*'

Never was any wish more suddenly and fatally granted. A fierce snort, a sharp crackle of broken twigs, and out from the thickets burst a monstrous wild-boar, with the foam flying from its huge, tusked mouth, and its small, round eye glowing like a live-coal!

Harry had no weapon save a spiked staff lent him by the count; but he at once brought it to the 'charge,' and stood firm, with a passing recollection of how Louis XI. of France had faced the boar's rush in *Quentin Durward*.

But the brave boy had no better luck than his royal prototype. On came the furious beast, at a speed truly wonderful for so heavy and clumsily-made a creature; and our hero's levelled point, in place of piercing the monster's chest, glanced off from its bristly shoulder, and our amateur hunter went sprawling on his back.

Luckily his fall saved him from the stroke of the terrible tusks, and the impetus of the boar's charge carried it some way past him; but it turned ere he could regain his feet, and all seemed over with poor Harry, when, just at the critical moment, there came a flash and a crack, and the whiz of a bullet, and the savage beast, as if struck by lightning, fell dead within a yard of the prostrate boy, just as a tall man, with a smoking gun in his hand, stepped forth from the thicket beside him.

CHAPTER IX.

NIKOLAIEVITCH THE FORESTER.

HE new-comer wore the picturesque dress of a Circassian mountaineer, which set off to great advantage his strong, active frame and bold, handsome, manly face. The firm lines of his mouth were partly hidden by a heavy moustache, but his shaven chin had a solid strength that told of an iron firmness of purpose which nothing could shake.

'Thank you very much,' said Harry in Russian; 'you've saved my life, whoever you are.'

'I am a forester of these woods,' said the other, 'and you may call me Nikolaievitch.'

'Well, I'm glad to hear it, for *I* took you for a robber!'

'A robber!' echoed the forester, with a laugh that lighted up his dark face very pleasantly. 'What made you think that?'

'Well, they say some of 'em ran off toward this side when General Naprashkin broke up Krovolil's gang the other day.'

At these last words the stranger started slightly, and seemed about to ask further questions; but ere he could do so our hero broke in:

'I say, Mr Nikolaievitch, I wish you'd tell me the nearest

way to Borjom, for I haven't the least idea where I've got to.'

'I am going that way myself,' replied the hunter, 'and I shall be glad to show you the road, as soon as I've done with this gentleman here.'

So saying, he turned to the slain boar, and drawing his short sword, hewed off the beast's head at one stroke, with an ease ominously suggestive of long practice—perhaps on other subjects than wild-boars.

'Do you mind carrying this head for me,' said he, 'if I take the carcass?'

'Can you really?' cried the boy, eyeing that huge mass, which was indeed a heavy load for even a strong man.

'I think so,' said Nikolaievitch coolly; and swinging up the vast bulk on to his shoulders, he set off down the hill as briskly as ever.

'Did you not say,' asked he of Harry, who tramped along beside him with the boar's head, 'that General Naprashkin had just broken up a band of robbers?'

The boy replied by telling briefly all that he had learned from the general himself.

'Good fellow, Naprashkin; he always does his work thoroughly!' said the forester, with a grim smile.

'I think he might do it a little more mercifully, though,' cried Harry. 'Knocking men over in fair fight may be all very well, but when it comes to starving them to death'——

'Would it be more merciful to let them escape to rob and murder scores of quiet folk who are living honestly?' broke in Nikolaievitch, with a frown that darkened his noble face like a thunder-cloud.

'Well, anyhow,' rejoined the boy, somewhat abashed, 'he need not talk of all that as if he enjoyed it.'

But his guide made no reply, and Harry, thinking that he had offended him, hastened to change the subject.

'What's that ruin up there, Mr Nikolaievitch? Is it an old castle?'

A sudden break in the wall of dark trees around them had just disclosed to him a stern gray tower, high on the crest of a bold ridge far away to the right, which, half-hidden as it was by weeds and bushes, had a grim massiveness of outline that at once suggested to the romance-loving Harry one of those ancient feudal fortresses in which he delighted.

'That's just what it is,' said his companion, smiling. 'There are plenty of them among these hills, but this particular one has a rather curious history. A good many hundred years ago that tower, and another that used to stand close to it, were held by two brothers, who were wont to vary the customary amusement of gentlemen in those days— namely, robbing and murdering all passing travellers—by getting up an occasional feud among themselves, and doing a little private family killing on their own account. These innocent sports at length developed into a quarrel so serious as to threaten the personal safety of these shining ornaments of society, and their friends unanimously agreed that the affair must not be allowed to go any further; so all the good old country gentlemen of the neighbourhood came in a body to give these two nice young men "a good talking to," and persuade them to shake hands and say no more about it.'

'And *did* they do it?' cried our hero, rather shocked at the idea of such a tame conclusion to what he had expected to be a very exciting story.

'I blush to say that they did,' said his guide, with a quiet smile; 'but, unluckily for the public peace, it was, of course, impossible for this reconciliation to go off properly without being celebrated with a tremendous revel, and when the wine began to flow freely the irrepressible brothers soon got to sharp words, and thence to sharp swords likewise. The kind old gentlemen who had reconciled them, forgetting their own rôle of peacemakers, drew *their* swords and laid about them most manfully. The men-at-arms backed their masters, and this peaceful and joyous entertainment ended in the two reconciled brothers killing each other on the spot, while their friends kept up the fun so vigorously that (as the admiring chronicler pithily tells us) " ere they parted sixty men lay dead on the floor." '

As the two became more confidential, Harry talked freely to his new friend, and told all about himself and his father, and their previous travels in Russia. At the mention of 'Livingstone Archer' the Russian's face lighted up as if the name were familiar to him; and he seemed not a little interested in their romantic meeting with Count Bulatoff and their strange introduction to the Czar.

Then the forester, who appeared to be a keen sportsman, began to tell, in his turn, a number of exciting hunter-stories, with which our hero was so well entertained that it was quite a surprise to him when they suddenly emerged from the wood, and saw the Borjom valley only a little way below; and he was more surprised still to espy, not twenty yards away, his father, Count Bulatoff, and Yury, all taking a stroll along the hillside together.

But all these surprises were nothing to the amazement of the adventurous Wintonian when he saw the count doff his hat with a low bow to the tall forester, and heard him say in a tone of deep respect:

'I am glad to have the chance of offering my homage to your Imperial Highness rather sooner than I had expected.

Yury, come and present your respects to the *Veleeki Knyaz*' (Grand-Duke).

'What!' cried Harry, staring blankly at the calm face of his guide; 'are *you* the Grand-Duke Mikhail Nikolaievitch?'

'At your service, Monsieur Archer,' answered 'Mr Nikolaievitch,' with a good-natured smile; 'and I hope you will pardon my having given you only half my name at our first introduction.'

CHAPTER X.

INSIDE THE PALACE.

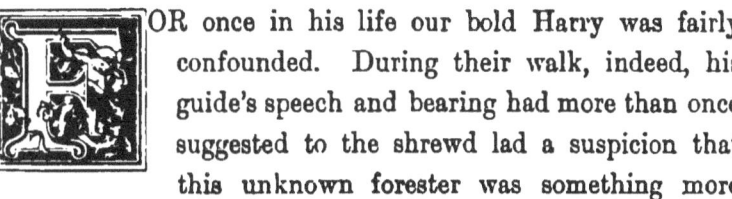OR once in his life our bold Harry was fairly confounded. During their walk, indeed, his guide's speech and bearing had more than once suggested to the shrewd lad a suspicion that this unknown forester was something more than what he seemed; but that he should prove to be the Viceroy of the Caucasus, and brother to the Czar himself, was a flight of romance beyond Harry's boldest imaginations, and his thoughts turned once more to *Quentin Durward*, and to the young Scot's memorable walk through the woods with the disguised king of France.

Nor were his friends less astounded to find him on terms of such close intimacy with the very Prince to whom they were about to present him as a perfect stranger; and there was a pause of general amazement, which was broken at length by Mr Archer.

'I had hoped for the honour of presenting my son to your Highness to-morrow; but I find that I am forestalled, for he seems to have presented himself.'

'I had the pleasure of his company during a part of my walk,' said Michael courteously; 'for, hoping to fall in with some game, I came home on foot through the woods with my gun after leaving the train, as I often do.'

'And a good job for me, too!' cried the irrepressible Harry; 'for, if it had not been for him, this brute here' (and he held up the boar's head) 'would have made short work of me.'

And then the Grand-Duke, in reply to Mr Archer's inquiring look, briefly related the adventure, and received the Englishman's hearty thanks for his timely aid.

But at that moment some of the Prince's servants (who had, no doubt, recognised their master as he descended the slope) came hurrying up from the palace, which lay about a hundred yards to the left.

'Children,' cried Michael to them, 'take this carcass down to my soldiers at the barrack yonder, and say that their general begs them to accept a share of what God has sent him; and let the head be dried and stuffed, and hung up in my hall.'

And then, as his men went off with the game, the Prince turned to Mr Archer and Harry, and said with his usual frank courtesy:

'Well, gentlemen, I hope that, though our acquaintance has begun in a somewhat unusual way, it is not to end here. To-morrow, when I have had time to get it into a little better order for you, I shall be glad to receive you at my house yonder. I dare say that my young comrade here would like to go over it.'

'Indeed I should!' cried Harry bluntly; and then, recollecting himself, he added with more tact, 'since your Highness is so kind as to offer it.'

'As for *you*, Feodor Alexandrovitch,' added the Viceroy, turning to Count Bulatoff, 'an old friend like yourself needs no invitation, and I hope you will bring your son along with you. At twelve o'clock to-morrow, then, gentlemen, I shall hope to have the pleasure of seeing you all at such a breakfast as a sportsman can offer you. *Au revoir.*'

'Why, he's every bit as good a fellow as the Czar himself!' said Harry warmly as the Grand-Duke turned away. 'And so *these* are the sort of men that those sneaks of Nihilists, or whatever they call 'em, are always wanting to murder! I only wish I could catch one of 'em trying it on. I'd punch his head if he were as big as a house!'

. . . .

As may be supposed, the four visitors were punctual to a moment in their arrival at the palace next day; and, quickly as they passed through the garden, our keen-eyed Harry did not fail to note the dainty little fountain that splashed and sparkled in the centre; the smooth, well-kept walks; and the array of splendid roses, whose size and rich colouring would have made any horticulturist's mouth water. In the anteroom—adorned with a number of beautiful photographs of various interesting spots in Central Asia, not a few of which were at once recognised by Archer as places that he had himself visited—they were met by the Grand-Duke in person, still in the Circassian costume of the previous day, which, indeed, he habitually wore, as a compliment to his wild mountain subjects.

'Good-morning, gentlemen! You are very welcome. Will you be pleased to step this way? Breakfast is just ready.'

The great dining-room, into which the hospitable Prince ushered his guests, was furnished in a style more frequently met with in the Middle Ages than now, but certainly appropriate enough in the house of such a born sportsman as Prince Mikhail Nikolaievitch. The chairs, the chandeliers, and the very candlesticks were made of *stags' horns* skilfully joined together; while other horns, and even entire skulls, hung thick on every wall, each marked with the name of the fortunate hunter by whom the game was brought down. High over all, a mighty head, with huge branching antlers that would make the heart of a Scottish deerstalker leap for joy, displayed an inscription telling that its owner was shot among the woods above the palace by the Grand-Duke himself, whose skill as a marksman was still further attested by the tusked head of an enormous wild-boar, even larger than Harry's recent assailant, on the opposite wall.

The English boy, who was passionately fond of every kind of sport, and had at his finger-ends almost every book that Captain Mayne Reid ever wrote, was so taken up with all these wonders that for once he almost forgot his breakfast.

'Do not neglect your food, Monsieur Henri,' said the Grand-Duke, smiling, as he clapped a huge slice of boar-ham on Harry's plate. 'I kept this bit of our wild-boar specially for you, for it is no more than justice that you should try your teeth on a brute that so nearly tried his on you.'

'Did you really kill that boar up yonder yourself?' asked our hero, who was still so absorbed in the marvels around him that when he mechanically began to eat he all but stuck his fork into his eye instead of his mouth.

'Indeed I did, and hard work I had of it. My first shot only wounded him, and I might have fared badly but for old Ruslan.'

'Ruslan?' echoed the boy. 'What! General Naprashkin's dog? Was *he* with you?'

'It was I who gave him to the general,' said Michael. 'You know him, I see.'

'I should think I did!' cried Harry; and then, to the no small confusion of his father and the count, he coolly related at length, for the Grand-Duke's benefit, the story of Ruslan's theft of the meat-pies.

During the whole meal our hero was specially struck with the perfect self-possession of Yury, who, boy as he was, seemed quite as well versed as his father in every detail of court etiquette, and replied so composedly, and in such well-chosen words, to the few remarks that the Prince addressed to him, as fairly to astound the less experienced Harry.

'One would think he had been chumming with kings and princes all his life,' mused the Wintonian; 'and perhaps he *has*, by-the-by, for his father seems to be hand-and-glove with every swell in Russia.'

'I hope you like this cream, Monsieur Henri,' said the Grand-Duke. 'I can recommend it, for it comes from my own dairy.'

'What! have you a dairy of your own?' cried the boy, to whom the idea of the Czar's own brother keeping a dairy (for so *he* understood it) seemed very funny indeed.

'Well, it's rather my wife's than mine,' said Michael; 'and I am sorry she is not here to show it to you herself, for I can assure you we are both very proud of it. It is being repaired just now; but in a day or two, when the work is done, I hope you and your father will come up and see it for yourselves. Now, gentlemen, if you cannot be persuaded to take anything more, I shall be happy to show you my house.'

And, in truth, the house was well worth showing. First came a snug and tastefully-furnished library, among the well-bound books of which Harry espied Charles Reade,

Henry Kingsley, and other pet authors of his, and also (to his great delight) a large illustrated copy of *Robinson Crusoe*.

'I suppose you recognise an old friend *there*, Monsieur Henri,' said the Grand-Duke, smiling, as he pointed to the famous volume.

'*Rather!*' cried the boy enthusiastically. 'Isn't it splendid?'

'I quite agree with you,' laughed Michael. 'My boys are just wild about it; and, to tell you the truth, it was the first English book that *I* ever read myself.'

But when they passed from the library into the Prince's private cabinet beyond, they seemed to make one step from Europe to Asia. The cabinet was furnished wholly in the Eastern style, the very paper-cutters on the table being shaped like Syrian daggers. The spacious divans, with their soft carpets and vast cushions, might have suited Mehemet Ali himself; and all the recesses were adorned with that curious fretwork which decorates the great mosques of Tashkand and the grave of Timur at Samarcand. In fact, the only European feature of the whole room was the charming little oil-paintings on the walls, most of which were the work of the Grand-Duchess herself, whose autograph, 'Olga,' was visible in the corner of each. But, indeed, the traces of *her* hand were visible in every chamber. Here a beautifully-painted transparency; there a trim little work-box; yonder a pretty piece of embroidery or a tasteful drawing, diffusing through every nook of the deserted palace that aroma of womanly grace and neatness which is the crowning charm of any home, whether palace or cottage.

In the centre of the drawing-room stood an enormous white swan hollowed into a water-bowl, and an excellent half-length photograph of the Grand-Duke himself when a young man, as he might have appeared on the memorable day when he and his brother Nikolai watched their father's soldiers rushing upon the bayonets of the 'Western heretics' on the historic ridge of Inkermann. Even more striking were the splendid likenesses of the Czar and Czarina in the adjoining bedroom, though it was painful to see how strongly the *doomed* look stamped on the fine face of Alexander II. in his last years came out even in his portrait.

'My eldest boy is a great Napoleonist, as you see,' said Michael, as he led the way to the upstairs rooms inhabited by his children; and, in fact, nearly all the books were lives or memoirs of the famous conqueror, whose portrait hung between the windows, harmonising well with the large ornamental shield on the opposite wall, formed of countless photographs of Russian officers in full uniform.

One hasty glance from the roof over the splendid panorama of forest and precipice, foaming torrent and sunny green upland, that lay below, terminated their sightseeing; and as the outer gate closed behind them Harry said emphatically:

'Well, if all kings and princes have such jolly places as this to live in, I shouldn't so much mind being a king myself!'

CHAPTER XI.

THE PERSIAN DAGGER.

UR hero did not forget the Prince's invitation to go over the Grand-Duchess's dairy, which lay not far from the palace itself, a little way down the road skirting the river; and, three days after their breakfast with the Grand-Duke, he and Yury Bulatoff set out to have a look at it.

The famous dairy was a neat little plank cottage at the foot of a wooded ridge, from the brow of which the stern gray ruins of an ancient Georgian castle looked sulkily down upon it, as if shocked at the unheard-of spectacle of so many cows being within reach and no one allowed to steal them. Here they were received by a ruddy, jolly-looking Russian dairy-woman, as neat and clean as the spotless pans and milk-bowls around her, who served out to them a liberal measure of *kefir*, or thick cream flavoured with small mushrooms, which Harry swallowed with marked approval.

Thence they went on to the cow-house itself, where a slim, active little Czech from Southern Bohemia exhibited to them the Princess's 'Swiss' cows (which really came from Novorossisk on the Black Sea, at a cost rather more than triple their original price), and showed them, marked on a slate at the door, the quantity of milk yielded daily by the different animals, which were kept beautifully clean, and looked very well altogether.

But this was only the first of many excursions which the two lads made together; for, utterly unlike as they were (and perhaps for that very reason), they soon struck up a close friendship, and ere long were all but inseparable. Yury, with the wonderful imitative power of a true Russian, picked up the rudiments of cricket in a way that earned Harry's warmest praise; and Harry, by talking Russian with his new chum every day and all day long, made such progress that he was soon able to talk fluently to any one whom he met.

In most of their expeditions the two friends had the escort of Ruslan the mastiff, which General Naprashkin, having to take a journey on which the company of his big dog would have been inconvenient, had left with the count till his return. The dog had specially attached itself to Harry, as if to atone for the theft of his pastry at their first meeting; and our hero, who had taken a fancy to the gallant beast from the very first, never lost a chance of 'trotting him out' along with them.

In addition to the protection of this redoubtable guardian, both lads were well armed, Yury carrying his own double-barrelled gun, and Harry a light rifle lent him by the count. Nor were such precautions needless, for the encircling woods were haunted not by wild-boars only, but also by wolves and bears; and though these were less dangerous at this season than in the early spring, after their long winter fast, yet a meeting with them in the lonely forest was not a thing for any unarmed man to desire.

One fine evening in the first week of June the two boys and their four-footed crony were out on one of their customary rambles over the hills, which they had extended a little farther than usual, in order to visit the ruins of an old native monastery which crowned the summit of one of the more distant ridges; and the adventurous lads enjoyed to their hearts' content the sight of the ivy-clad towers and broken but still massive walls, the graceful creepers that had trailed their long sprays and great bell-like flowers over masses of fallen masonry, and the crumbling gaps that had once been windows, which looked down upon the intruders with the blank, unseeing stare of the blind.

But a loud, fierce bark from Ruslan among the thickets outside suddenly startled them both; and hurrying to the spot, they found the mastiff standing in a menacing posture over the prostrate figure of a man.

But, in truth, it seemed a cruel mockery to give the name of 'man' to such a spectre, for never yet had the startled boys beheld so miserable a wreck of humanity. His wretched clothing, torn to rags by the briars through which he had forced his way, barely sufficed to cover his wasted frame, which was so frightfully emaciated that, wherever it was exposed to view, every bone stood out beneath the shrunken skin almost as plainly as in an actual skeleton. His matted hair, caked with dirt and with the blood that had issued from a fearful gash on the side of his head, hung in elf-locks around his hollow, skull-like face, the only sign of life in which was the gleam of hungry and wolfish eagerness in his sunken eyes.

'Down, Ruslan; down, sir!' cried Harry. 'He must be starving, poor fellow; and we have no food with us, worse luck!'

But Yury interpreted more truly the look of agonised entreaty in the hollow eyes of the helpless wretch, who was evidently quite unable to speak, and he ran to fill his

The fainting man sucked in the cool draught with a frightful eagerness.
PAGE 99.

water-flask at a tiny brook that went dancing and sparkling down the hillside not many yards away, and held it to the sufferer's lips.

The fainting man sucked in the cool draught with a frightful eagerness that told its own story; and then, visibly revived, he raised his head and struggled to speak, though feebly, and with a convulsive gasp for breath at almost every word.

'You are—the only living things—that have had pity—on me,' he panted; 'and this is all—I can give you—for thanks;' and, drawing from his tattered silken girdle a splendid Persian dagger with a jewelled hilt, he offered it to the young Russian.

'Those dogs of peasants showed me no mercy,' he went on more distinctly after a pause. 'When I prayed them to give me just one morsel of bread to keep me alive, they cast stones at me and wounded me in the head—mischief take them for it!'

'I think he must be one of Krovolil's gang,' said Yury to his friend in a whisper; but, low as it was, it did not escape the ear of the outcast, whose senses appeared to have been sharpened rather than dulled by the torture of famine and the approach of death.

'Krovolil—ha, ha!' said he, with a spectral laugh; 'they think he is dead. They will see presently!'

'And *isn't* he dead, then?' cried Harry, to whom these last words were like an electric shock.

But the castaway made no reply, his attention being suddenly diverted by a distant sound of hoarse voices calling to each other, and a crackle of broken twigs which came nearer and nearer every moment, as if a number of men were forcing their way through the thickets.

'Here come the soldiers,' said he faintly; 'but they're too late—I'm dying—ha, ha!' and, with a ghastly grin at the disappointment in store for his pursuers, the hunted bandit sank back and died.

So quickly had all this passed that the two boys were still standing beside the body in silent bewilderment, hardly realising even yet what had happened, when a dozen Cossack soldiers broke from the bushes around them, and uttered a savage growl of disappointment as their eyes fell on the lifeless form of the robber.

'The dog has balked us after all!' cried one fiercely.

'But here are two more of the gang, anyhow,' put in a second, pointing to the two lads, whose boyish aspect was not at once apparent in the deep shadow of the thickets, and whose disordered hair, muddy clothes, and blackened hands and faces certainly made them look sufficiently brigand-like.

'Yes, that's always something!' said a third, levelling his piece at Yury Bulatoff. 'Throw down your dagger this moment, you young rascal, and give yourself up, or I'll send a bullet through you!'

Ere Harry Archer, whose English blood was up at once at this rough address, had time to reply, Yury, to his friend's utter amazement, stepped boldly forward, and drawing up his slight form so proudly that he seemed to the startled gazers to grow larger on the spot, waved the armed men haughtily back.

'Dogs!' cried he sternly, 'do you dare to speak like that to *me*, the son of Count Bulatoff, and nephew of the governor himself? Ask pardon at once for your insolence, or you shall have such a taste of the *rozgi* (rods) as you will not soon forget!'

Harry listened to this tirade with his eyes starting out of his head; and he was more amazed still to see how these big, strong men—the least of whom could have crushed with one hand the half-grown boy that was threatening them—shrank and quailed before him as they suddenly realised their mistake. In fact, one or two of the soldiers, having been in attendance on Yury's uncle, the general, during his last visit to Borjom, knew the lad's voice the moment he spoke; and his words were suddenly confirmed by the appearance of the governor's well-known mastiff, which came bounding back just then from a run among the trees.

'*Vinovati!*' (We are to blame!), stammered all the Cossacks with one voice.

'Forgive us, your honour; how could we tell?' added a big sergeant who seemed to command the party.

'I forgive you; but take care not to be so hasty another time,' said Yury, as grandly as if he were Edward III. dismissing the six burghers of Calais. 'Four of you pick up that dead fellow yonder, and carry him down to Borjom; there's a reward for him, dead or alive, you know, if he belongs to that gang.'

His orders were obeyed without a word; and Harry, who had been watching in blank amazement this unlooked-for demonstration on the part of his 'quiet' chum, muttered to himself, as the party moved on down the hillside:

'Well, this is coming it strong, and no mistake! He puts on as much "side" as if he were commander-in-chief of all the armies in Russia! Well, they may say what they like about "military despotism," but it *is* a useful kind of thing now and then, after all.'

'Sergeant,' said Yury to the leader of the party, who was tramping along beside him, 'that robber yonder said something about Krovolil himself being still alive; but I suppose it was all nonsense.'

'I only wish it were, your honour,' faltered the veteran, whose bold brown face had suddenly grown pale as death; 'but it's as true as the lives of the blessed saints. The "Blood-shedder" *is* alive, and we have all of us seen him only three days ago!'

Looking up in surprise at this unexpected voucher for the dying man's wild words, Yury read a new and startling confirmation of them in the faces of the soldiers; for at the very mention of the dreaded name that seemed to act upon them like a baneful spell, these strong and daring men, who would have charged up to the muzzles of an enemy's cannon without a sign of wavering, were already looking as nervous as frightened children.

'Are you sure it *was* he whom you saw?' asked the young Russian, turning again to the sergeant. 'My uncle told me that he and his men had driven the fellow over a precipice, and *he* is not a man to leave such a thing in doubt.'

'There is no mistaking the "Blood-shedder," your honour; there are not two such men in all Russia,' said the old soldier gloomily; 'and as to precipices, there is not a precipice in the Caucasus deep enough to make an end of *him*. He is in league with the Evil One, and nothing can harm him till his time is up.'

More and more disturbed, Yury questioned the man closely, and Harry did the same; but cross-examine him as they might, they could not stir him one whit from what he had already said. Krovolil was still alive, and at large among the hills—of that he was quite certain; and his men declared positively that they had all seen and recognised the brigand-chief only a few days before, though unable to catch or even to wound him, do what they would.

This news set both lads thinking. It was but too likely to be true, for twelve men, who had every reason to think Krovolil dead, would hardly have been all possessed at the same time with a sudden conviction of his being still alive unless they had some very good cause for it; and, moreover, the tale, wild as it was, had been confirmed in advance by their own encounter with one of Krovolil's band.

The more our heroes thought over the matter the more serious did it appear; and on reaching the valley the first thing that they did was to go straight back to the house and tell all that they had just learned.

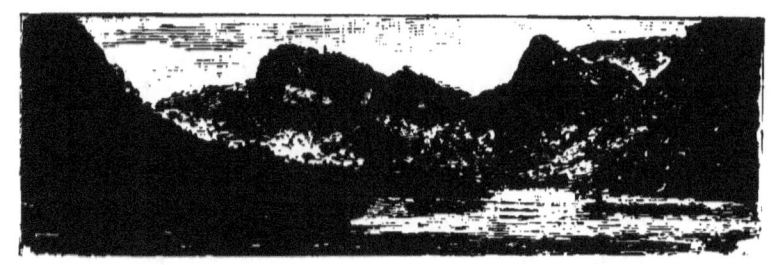

CHAPTER XII.

AN UNEXPECTED SUMMONS.

N hearing the story, and seeing the Persian dagger given to Yury by the dying bandit, Archer and the count looked very grave; and the latter declared at once that until the destruction or capture of the robber-chief and his whole band was placed beyond a doubt, the boys must never again go so far from home without an armed escort.

But, as if two such adventures were quite enough at a time, the life of our young heroes for some time after this was singularly uneventful. June passed into July, and July into August, without any occurrence worthy of note; and Mr Archer, in spite of the hospitable entreaties of his kind host to stay as long as he liked, began to think that he had inflicted a long enough visit upon the count, and to meditate moving elsewhere.

It was during this interval that Archer at length found out the meaning of something that had been puzzling him not a little for some time past—namely, the extreme interest, almost amounting to awe, with which he himself seemed to be regarded by the servants of the count's household and the lower-class Russians of the little town.

That men who could not read, and who had very possibly

never seen an Englishman before, should be familiar with his travels, seemed out of the question. Yet they had plainly heard *something* about him which made them regard him with special admiration, not unmixed with fear, as was clear enough from the way in which, whenever he appeared, they stared and pointed at him, and whispered to each other, even turning their heads to gaze after him when he had passed.

The count, to whom he applied for a solution of this mystery, was quite as much at a loss to explain it as himself; but chance at length gave them the clue, and they discovered, to their unspeakable amusement, that some vague rumour of the Englishman's renown as an explorer, coupled with his name of *Livingstone* Archer, had impressed these simple fellows with a conviction that he was no other than the great Dr David Livingstone himself, whose fame had reached even them, and of whose exploits they had just then been hearing a good deal. And certainly, if they believed about him one-half of the marvels which Archer heard related one morning by Vasili, the ex-soldier, to a crony from the town, they had good cause to regard him with such awe-stricken admiration.

'I tell you, brother, if this Dr Davidovitch Livenshtonn had not been a great magician, he could never have done what he did; for how could any mere man go all across Africa, beyond thrice-nine lands, where the heat turns all the people black, and the fish in the rivers come to the surface *boiled?* In some of those places, you know, nothing can live but the lions; so the wizard-doctor turned himself into a lion, you see, and went wherever he liked. I know it for a fact, for I've heard my master say, once and again, that this Englishman was "one of the biggest *lions* of the season." *
But it wasn't all honey for him in that business either, for he

* The word has the same double meaning in Russian as in English.

met another lion, and had a fight with it; and though he killed it, he got his own right arm—paw, I mean—broken in the scuffle, and that's why he is always using his left instead.'

Archer, who had trained himself to be 'ambidexter,' called to mind how often he had written notes or flung stones with his left hand in Vasili's presence, and chuckled inwardly at the queer misconception to which it had given rise.

But during that uneventful summer the energetic traveller was by no means idle. He made constant excursions through the surrounding country (sometimes with his son and sometimes alone), visited more than a dozen ruined castles and monasteries, and pushed his researches as far as Kutaïs, where he spent a whole night by himself in the ruins of the ancient stronghold of 'Prince David the Restorer'—the Georgian national hero of the tenth century—seemingly without any fear of falling in with the redoubtable 'Bloodshedder,' who had been last heard of near that very spot.

But when at Borjom in the intervals of these expeditions, Archer took little or no part in the public amusements of the place; and, somewhat to the chagrin of his host, who had promised himself no small pleasure in presenting to the local circle so famous a brother-traveller, he very seldom appeared at the club which was the regular evening resort of the Borjom fashionables, and when he *did* appear there, kept himself as much as possible in the background.

'I am always glad to meet such men as *you*, Feodor Alexandrovitch,' said he, in reply to the count's remonstrances, 'and the more of *them* the better; but as for what is called "publicity," I would much rather be without it. Indeed, I never could understand how any man of sense can find pleasure in a notoriety which, after all, he only shares with the last new thief and the last new murderer!'

In fact, the only way to get this British hermit into the fashionable circle was to promise him a sight of some quaint national sport or antique custom ; and so it came to pass that his only appearance at the club during the last two weeks of July was due to a 'children's fête,' at which—so the count told him—the little people were to perform some curious native dances of considerable antiquity.

This idea pleased Harry as well as his father ; and on the appointed evening the two explorers and their sons appeared on the scene of action in good time for the anticipated spectacle.

And a very picturesque spectacle it was. The club-house stood just at the entrance of the great park, and in front of it, in a blaze of lamplight, lay a wide circular space of smooth green turf, forming the central point of a broad, straight walk between two lines of tall, dark trees, from the boughs of which hung scores of coloured lanterns, giving quite an Eastern character to the whole scene. Gaudy flags of every form and colour, suspended from cords of twisted silk, made a kind of canopy overhead ; and beneath these gay hangings eddied a ceaseless flood of merrymakers in every variety of local costume, from the smart olive-green jacket and glittering gold or silver lace of the Russian officer to the small, flat, muffin-shaped cap of the Georgian lady, with its long, white veil flowing half-way down the back.

All at once the regimental band, in their trim little gilded 'stand' on the other side of the lawn, struck up the lively popular air of *Kogda ya buil Arkadskim Printzem* ('When I was an Arcadian Prince'), and marching in time to the music, the procession of children came filing up the walk, two and two, to the front of the club-house.

Harry Archer uttered an emphatic 'Bravo !' as the

Lilliputian host went by; and, in truth, the procession made a very charming picture. The boys, many of whom were not more than seven or eight years old, were dressed so as to represent all the various races of the district, some wearing the uniform of the Russian line and shouldering toy-muskets; others displaying the embroidered jacket and black velvet knickerbockers of the Georgian warrior; others still flaunting in the laced coat and high cap of the Black Sea Cossack; and not a few copying exactly, with the aid of pasteboard and tinsel, the pointed helmet, chain-mail hood, and scarlet tunic of the terrible Circassian horsemen who rode at Shamyl's back through the gorges of Daghestan. The little girls, in like manner, were arrayed as Russian, Mingrelian, Georgian, or Armenian women, even their hair being dressed in each case appropriately to their costume.

The procession of children marched twice round the bandstand, and then came to a sudden halt, forming a circle around the lawn, and continuing to clap their hands loudly, in measured time—a part of the performance that seemed very much to the taste of Master Harry, who pressed eagerly forward to the very edge of the clapping ring, and made as much noise by his own unaided efforts as any other half-dozen.

'Now you will see something worth looking at,' said Count Bulatoff to Mr Archer. 'I know what they are going to do now; it's the famous "Lesghian" dance, of which Dumas says so much in his book on the Caucasus.'

'I have heard of it, though I never saw it before,' said his friend. 'It seems to be somewhat after the style of the Spanish "Manola;" and a very pretty sight it must be when performed by children.'

And a very pretty sight it *was*, sure enough. As he spoke

there stepped forward with perfect self-possession into the centre of that living ring (which was by this time thickened with a double row of grown-up lookers-on) a boy of eight and a girl of seven, the tiny cavalier being dressed as a Russian Life-Guardsman, and his little lady as a Georgian princess.

The two little people bowed to the audience with a grave dignity that drew forth a good deal of applause, and some slight laughter as well; and then the band changed from the Russian march that it had just been playing to the wild music of the mountain-dance, and the performance began.

As Archer had said, it was a good deal like the famous 'Manola' of Spain, being, in fact, not so much an actual dance as a pantomime in dumb show. The knight advanced towards his lady, and seemed by his gestures to be desirous of accosting her and taking her under his protection; but she, as if scorning such aid, moved haughtily away as he approached, and in this way they made the round of the circle three or four times, the one pressing on and the other retiring. Then the scene changed. The heroine suddenly assumed a look of terror, as if menaced all at once by some unlooked-for peril, and moved toward her cavalier with outstretched hands, as if imploring his help and protection. But it was now the knight's turn to be offended (as, indeed, he well might be) at the way in which he had been treated; and he receded in turn, followed by the distressed damsel, amid the now unrestrained laughter of the ever-growing throng of spectators. Finally, both knight and dame appeared to 'give it up as a bad job,' and drew apart to opposite sides of the ring; but, with a somewhat far-fetched politeness, they seemed resolved not to turn their backs upon one another even then, and, still facing each other, actually danced *backward* for some time—no easy feat on that smooth, dry, slippery turf, though these nimble little folk performed it with perfect ease. Then they once more approached each other ceremoniously, and a low bow on either side closed the exhibition.

Renewed applause from all the lookers-on (among whom Harry was conspicuously vehement) rewarded the small performers; and then several more children executed various other native dances with equal dexterity. But at length—no one could tell how—a call arose amid the throng for one particular mountain-dance, the name of which Archer could not catch; but it must have been a very hard one, for even these active little dancers hung back from attempting it, some saying that they had never learned the step, while others declared that they could not possibly make their feet move quick enough.

'Is there no one here who can do it?' asked a portly, richly-dressed lady seated on the steps of the house, who was no other than the wife of the local military commandant. 'I should so like to see it once more.'

'I will gladly do my best to satisfy you, madam, but I cannot promise to be perfect,' said a clear voice from the crowd; and into the ring stepped a slim, graceful, young fellow in a Russian cavalry uniform, whose pale, handsome face was (but for his small, black, pointed moustache) as smooth and delicate as that of a young girl, though the tiger-like suppleness of all his movements showed that he lacked neither agility nor strength.

'That's Prince Shervashidze, a descendant of the old Georgian nobles,' whispered the count to Archer. 'We have plenty of them in our army now, and in other employments too; for the last time I was in Tiflis I saw—terrible as it may sound—several of the oldest names in Georgia over *shops!*'

A forward heave of the crowd hid from Archer the opening steps of the dance (which was evidently a general favourite), and what he *did* see was a quick, stamping movement, not unlike a mazurka, increasing in rapidity every moment, till the beating of the dancer's feet on the ground sounded like the roll of a drum, and reminded the Englishman of the famous 'Sailor's Hornpipe' that he had so often witnessed at sea.

'Well done, Geoŕgii Davidovitch!' said Bulatoff to the panting performer, as the dance ended amid universal applause. 'I have seen that dance often, but I never saw any one so nimble at it as you.'

'I had need be nimble at it,' replied the young man, with a strange smile, 'for the last time I danced it I did so to save my own life!'

This startling announcement attracted general attention, as, in truth, it well might, and an eager crowd gathered round the two men to hear the Prince's reply to Bulatoff's query how such a thing could have come to pass.

'Well,' said the young noble, laughing, 'it is really not much of a story after all, though it seemed a good deal to me at the time. I dare say you have all heard of Krovolil the brigand, for he seems to be pretty well known in these parts just now.'

The sudden thrill that pulsed through the crowd at that terrible name was a sufficient answer to his question.

'Well, a few months ago, just before that train-robbery that made so much stir, I was picked up by Mr "Bloodshedder" and his gang while I was out shooting on the hills above Kutaïs, with no one with me but a trooper who acted as my servant. The rogues killed the poor fellow on the spot, and dragged me away with them—whether for ransom or for torture I never found out; and when they got me to their camp one of Krovolil's fellows (who seemed to know me, though I had no recollection of *him*) began to make fun of me, saying that if I could run as well as I could dance, they would never have caught me at all.

'"Are you such a great dancer, then?" said Krovolil to me. "Can you dance the 'Rattle'?"

'It happened to be my favourite dance, and I said so.

'"Good!" said the chief; "it is *my* favourite dance too, and my comrade Loris, here, is by way of being the best hand at it in the Caucasus; so, if you can keep it up longer than *he* can I'll let you go free; but if not (and he smiled a horrid smile that made me feel cold all over), so much the worse for *you!*"

'This did not sound very hopeful, but it was evidently my only chance; so one of the robbers struck up the tune on his *skribka* (fiddle), and to work Master Loris and I went.

'I don't know how long we were at it, but to *me* it seemed like a year. Do what I would, the fellow went on and on as if he would never tire, while I felt my limbs aching and my strength failing, and the perspiration pouring down my face, as the merry music trilled and frolicked along like some demon mocking my agony; and all the while I could see the eyes of the robbers around me lighting up with a cruel, hungry eagerness, like wolves when they are close upon their prey; for it seems that one of Master Krovolil's favourite amusements was to torture his prisoners to death, and I suppose they were looking forward to some such sport with *me* as soon as my strength gave way. And, sure enough, it *would* have given way in a very few minutes more; but just as all seemed over with me, Master Loris tripped on a stone and gave his ankle a wrench that settled the business.

' " Well done ! " cried Krovolil, who seemed to have been enjoying it very much—which was more than I did. " I did not think there had been a man alive who could keep it up against Loris as long as that. Well, you have shown good sport, and you can go free; but take care that I don't catch you again ! " '

'What was this man Loris like ?' asked Yury Bulatoff, who had been listening most attentively.

The young Prince gave a brief but minute description of this dancing robber.

'Well,' said Yury gravely, 'allowing for the effect of hunger and weariness, that's just the description, point for point, of that brigand that we met on the hill, who gave me the Persian dagger.'

For a few days to come this startling episode gave the two boys plenty to think and talk about; but as its novelty wore off, the depression that had begun to creep over them returned with tenfold force.

And well might it be so. They had by this time exhausted every walk in the immediate neighbourhood, and, as we have seen, they were forbidden to go farther away on account of the brigands. General Naprashkin was still absent, and the Grand-Duke Michael had been called away to some other part of his extensive province ; and though his Highness, before leaving, had given our heroes a full and hearty permission to visit the palace and its grounds in his absence as often as they liked, yet even this began to pall upon them after a time.

In truth, Borjom is seldom very gay in summer at the best of times. Like Piatigorsk, and other Caucasian 'spas,' it is essentially a winter resort; and very few of those who come from the north in the colder months to take the baths or drink the mineral waters (a happy compound of the flavour of bad eggs and old shoes) are wont to remain over the spring.

And now came a harder trial still; for with the opening of August set in one of those spells of wet weather that are so common in these mountains, making the beautiful landscape as dull as a story 'written with a purpose,' and as hideous as a plate of the fashions. The hills pulled down their caps of mist over their brows, and the gray, sullen sky was striped with slanting lines of rain, and the weary drip, drip, drip of the big drops from the eaves went on hour after hour in its dismal monotone, and the drenched woods and muddy paths loomed drearily through brooding clouds.

All this, however, failed to keep the restless boys indoors; for Yury, living almost wholly in the open air, and trained to daily feats of strength and agility by his new comrade, had improved so much in health and vigour as to be by this time almost as indifferent to bad weather as Harry himself. But, with all their energy, they found it anything but easy work; and Master Harry now learned, to his cost, why all the Borjom pedestrians—ladies included—were wont to carry about with them spiked walking-sticks very much like an abridged edition of a Swiss 'alpenstock.' The higher mountain paths, up which, even in dry weather, they had had to drag themselves by clinging to bough after bough, were now, beneath this unceasing pour, just like a skating-rink set up on end; and the two lads had cause to think themselves lucky if they did not go sprawling on their faces in a puddle every five minutes or so, or vary the performance by sliding down twenty or thirty feet on their backs into a clump of briars.

Moreover, it happened but too often that a treacherous 'break' of seeming fine weather misled all but the most

experienced into thinking the rains at an end, tempting out the ladies in their most attractive summer costumes, and then suddenly driving them home again drenched and dripping—
'To weep for slaughtered satins, and for martyred muslins mourn.'

In the meantime, however, Harry had made several friends among the residents, in whom he was greatly interested, and not without reason. One afternoon, in a brief interval of sunshine, he had a long talk with an old Russian general, who in his youth had seen Circassian Shamyl himself face to face in battle, and had cut his way through a whole band of the great chief's mail-clad horsemen. On the same evening another officer showed to him, among other trophies of a campaign in Daghestan, two long Persian guns with ivory stocks and damascened barrels, the work of a famous armourer who lived more than two hundred years ago. At a dinner-party a few days later his neighbour at table was the widow of the first Governor of Baku, who seemed to have been an eye-witness of every exciting event in the Eastern Caucasus for twenty years past, and had actually been a prisoner for several weeks in the hands of the fierce Circassian mountaineers; and he lunched on the following morning with a man who had entertained Stanley when the great explorer was on his way to Persia years before, and who still had a vivid recollection of the 'gay American,' as he called him.

'Well,' said Yury, with a grin, as he and his English chum came splashing and sliding home one evening, wet to the skin as usual, 'if that worthy fellow, Krovolil, is out in all this weather, we have not much to fear from *him*, for he will certainly be laid up with rheumatism!'

'Or else,' chuckled Harry, 'he 'll catch such a cough that we can hear him long before he can get at us, same as a rattlesnake. Well, I wouldn't mind if he *did* come, for it's really time for us to have another adventure of some sort.'

So, too, thought Archer and the count; and, in fact, all four were in equal need of a change, which, just then, they seemed very unlikely to get. But, as third-rate authors always say when they want to be impressive, 'the hour was coming, and it came.'

Early on the morning of the 15th August, Mr Archer, who had slept a little longer than usual, was aroused by the bursting in of the count, waving an open letter.

'News for you, my friend!' he shouted. 'The Emperor has another job for me to do in Central Asia, and he says (let me see—ay, here it is) that, if you like to go with me, he will gladly give you every facility, as some slight amends for that unfortunate mistake at Moscow.'

'Hurrah!' cried Archer, springing up as briskly as a boy. 'When shall we start?'

'Whenever you're ready; to-morrow, if you like!' replied the Russian, with equal eagerness. 'On with your clothes, while I get a map and show you our route over the Tartar deserts!'

The map was brought, and for the next ten minutes both men were fully employed in tracing the line of their adventurous journey, which passed through more than one region where any traveller would carry his life in his hand.

'Hollo!' cried Archer suddenly; 'I was forgetting something. What on earth am I to do with Harry? He could never get back to England by himself.'

'Well, why should he? You can just leave him here till we come back.'

'Oh, that really won't do. Why, to quarter him upon you for months and months, you know'——

'Come, my dear fellow, don't talk nonsense. If there *is* any obligation in the matter, it is all on my side; for that boy of yours has done my Yury more good than twenty tutors could have done, or doctors either. Why, you must have seen for yourself how wonderfully improved he is in every way since your son came. Don't say a word more about it; the thing's settled.'

It was; and on the following day the two bold travellers, having taken an affectionate leave of their respective sons, and promised to send word of their progress so long as they were within reach of posts at all, set joyfully forth on their long-wished-for journey—to meet their fate.

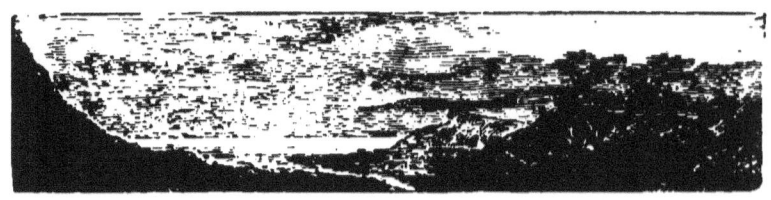

CHAPTER XIII.

THE MIDNIGHT STORM.

WO days after the departure of their fathers, the two lads also left Borjom; for the count, hearing that General Naprashkin was not to be back for some time yet, had found time to telegraph, just before starting, to his widowed sister at Tiflis, Countess Sobolyeff (the aunt with whom Yury had been staying before the arrival of the Archers), asking her to receive Yury and his friend for a short visit, till the general's return. Her assenting telegram reached Borjom the morning after the travellers left it; and on the following day our young heroes set off for Tiflis in high glee, under the escort of Prince Shervashidze, who was on his way to rejoin his regiment at the Caucasian capital.

This time their drive down to Mikhailovo was done in broad daylight, and so different did it all appear that Harry could hardly believe it to be the same road. Now, for the first time, he saw at its best (for by good luck the day was beautifully fine) one of the most picturesque routes in the whole Caucasus—the endless windings of the steep mountain road between the great ridges that piled themselves up on either side, terrace above terrace, into the very sky, wooded from base to summit; the dazzling southern sunshine and warm, rich blue skies; the glittering foam of the river seen in glimpses through the clustering leaves, which displayed every varying tint of green, with a dash of orange, scarlet, or pale gold thrown in here and there by the approach of autumn. Ever and anon a broad, deep, whitish-gray scar amid the overhanging masses of foliage showed where some landslip had torn away the leafy covering, and left the bare limestone cliff towering gauntly hundreds of feet overhead, in all its grim and ghastly desolation. And when to all this was added the spectacle of the wild Georgian peasants tramping past in their picturesque native dress; the quaint, old-fashioned mountain carts with wheels made of one round piece of wood, without spokes or tire; the vast black bodies and curled horns of the buffaloes wallowing in deep, still pools; and the ruined castles and half-destroyed bridges of a period that history has well-nigh forgotten, it was no wonder that Harry's admiration became so emphatic as to satisfy even the young Georgian prince beside him.

They had not long to wait at Mikhailovo—for, by some miracle, the train was not more than ten minutes late—and off they went again, rather pleased at the idea of being among the first travellers who had gone by rail to Tiflis, the line having been completed only a few days before.

But as they got into the train, Harry noticed for the first time that a very important appendage of his friend's usual dress appeared to be missing.

'I say, Yury,' cried he, 'what's become of your Persian dagger—the one that that robber gave you, you know? Have you put it in your luggage?'

'No; I gave it to my father to take with him,' said Yury, little thinking how all-important that gift was one day to be. 'I'm not likely to want to stab any one in the streets of Tiflis, whereas *he* may find it useful where he is going.'

Harry was delighted with the famous Suram Pass—one of the finest bits of scenery on the whole line—with its green hollows and plunging torrents, its frowning cliffs and deserted hamlets, its creaking wagons drawn by broad-horned oxen, and its tiny black goats perched on narrow rock-ledges a hundred feet overhead, like chimney-ornaments on some monster mantelpiece. But he was still better pleased with the steaming cabbage-soup and savoury *bitki*, or cakes of chopped meat, set before him in the neat little station at the farther end of the pass, where the train halted half-an-hour for dinner.

'This is something like!' said he, with his mouth full.

'But you will not always fare so well on this line, Monsieur Archer,' laughed Prince Shervashidze. 'At Rion, the last time I came this way, they gave me something which *they* called cabbage-soup, but which seemed to *me* very much like lukewarm water into which a very stale cabbage had tumbled by accident.'

By the time they set off again the sun was already beginning to sink behind the purple hills that framed the vast shadowy plain which was now opening before them; and all the rest of the journey was a flitting magic-lantern vision of dark mountains and glimmering rivers, and black wastes of moorland, and stations flashing out for a moment in sudden lamplight from the surrounding gloom. At length Harry awoke from a confused dream—in which he was the Wandering Jew, ·going round the world on a self-acting bicycle worked by the steam of cabbage-soup—to find the train just coming to a stand-still with a long, creaking groan; and then there was a shouting and bustling all around, and in a few minutes more he and his companions found themselves jolting and bumping through the flaring streets of a great town, and he began to realise that he was fairly in the capital of the Caucasus at last.

It was after midnight ere our heroes got to the house, at the door of which the young Prince took leave of them; and Countess Sobolyeff, who kept earlier hours than most Russian ladies in the Caucasus, had already gone to bed, having left orders with her *klyootchnitza* ('key-woman' or housekeeper) to let the boys have all that they required. But the next morning she was up betimes to attend to her guests, and Harry was agreeably surprised to see, instead of the cold, stately, distant woman of rank whom he expected, a brisk, bright, cheery little old lady with a round, fresh, kindly face, and 'not a bit of stiffness or nonsense about her,' as our hero remarked approvingly to Yury, who quite agreed with him.

Harry made friends with her at once, and the three were just in the midst of their plans for that day and the next, when a servant brought in a letter addressed to Harry Archer, which had been left at the door, he said, by a Russian soldier.

'It's my father's handwriting!' cried the boy, pouncing upon it. 'Isn't it fine to hear from them so soon!'

'Your father has given you good measure, Monsieur Archer,' said the countess, smiling; 'I did not think you English wrote each other such long letters.'

'You are quite right, *tyotushka*' (auntie), cried Yury, with a grin. 'An Englishman's letter generally goes like this: "Dear Sir, nothing doing at present. Excuse haste, and believe me yours, So-and-So."'

'Well,' retorted Harry, slightly nettled, 'that's as good, anyhow, as your Russian way of beginning, "Most merciful

Sir," and ending, "Your obedient, humble servant," to some fellow whom you'd be glad to kick all round the town!'

'If there is nothing private in your letter, Monsieur Archer,' dexterously interposed the lady, as Harry unfolded the two sheets of close pencil-writing, 'I shall be glad to hear how my brother and his friend are getting on. I think I know English enough to understand you pretty well.'

And the boy began to read aloud as follows:

POST-HOUSE OF BYELI-GORI, MOUNT KAZBEK,
August $\frac{1}{13}$, 1871.

'I always think it looks so queer,' commented Harry, 'to have *two* dates on one letter. It's because your reckoning is twelve days behind ours, isn't it, Yury?'

'Well, why not?' laughed the young Russian. 'If *you* lived in Russia, you know, you would have *two* sets of birthday presents instead of one.'

'So I would, by-the-by!' cried the Wintonian; 'and I remember that my father had some joke about a sick man in London, who, hearing that in Russia the 13th of the month was reckoned as the 1*st* with *them*, went there that he might have twelve days more to live! But I must not keep on talking when I ought to be reading.'

And he went on with the letter thus:

MY DEAR HARRY,—We have reached the highest point of our journey (for the present at least), and here we are up above the clouds, on the great 'dividing ridge' of the Caucasus, crammed into a little wooden box just big enough to hold ourselves and the old postmaster, and trying to keep warm by swallowing scalding tea and thinking of the hot places to which we are going. But, though we have had some excitement on the way (as you shall hear presently), we are all right so far; and my friend the count wishes me to tell his sister and Yury (to whom I also desire to be kindly remembered) that he never felt better or brisker in his life. It will be all downhill with us now, too, when once we can get horses ; but just at present there are none to be had.

We got to Tiflis from Borjom the same night ; but as we had to buy some things for the journey, and to see about one or two other matters, it was after eleven next morning when we set off again, in a ramshackle vehicle not unlike the top of a bathing-machine knocked into the bottom of a butcher's cart, in which we lay full-length like two babies in a cradle (for the Russian post-chaises have no seats, you know), jammed in between two walls of baggage to keep us from flying out head-foremost.

But, once fairly off, we began to enjoy it in earnest. Wasn't it Dr Johnson who defined supreme happiness as the sensation of being whirled along in a post-chaise? Well, the old gentleman was not far wrong, after all ; for, flying at full speed along these splendid military roads, with the fresh mountain breeze stirring one's blood like the breath of life, after the hot, stifling closeness of the dusty plains—a bright blue sky above, and such a panorama as the Central Caucasus all around—one has really nothing left to desire.

And the farther we went the more savagely magnificent the scenery became. Smooth green slopes at first, crested with waving trees, and dotted with black, wild-looking goats ; then bolder and bleaker ridges, rising ever higher, and steeper, and darker, with here and there the roofless and windowless shell of some ruined castle hanging on the very brink of a grim, black precipice ; and then, toward nightfall, a wide green plain overhung by purple mountains, through the passes of which the setting sun came streaming in a flood of golden glory.

It was just about sunset when we stopped to change horses for the fourth time ; and not long after we started again I began to notice the first signs of a coming storm. Far away to the north-east a ghostly dimness hovered low down in the sky, against which the great snow-peaks of the highest range stood out white and ghastly ; and the last gleam of sunset looked red and angry, and the breeze had died away, and all was deadly still—the kind of stillness that always means mischief.

I could see plain enough, by the way our new driver kept looking back over his shoulder, what *he* thought of it ; but he showed no sign of hanging back, for he was one of those neck-or-nothing Tartars who, if you give them twopence extra, will plunge into a flooded river or up to the muzzle of a loaded cannon.

But none of us needed to be told what a risk we were running; for we had now got fairly in among the mountains, and were getting higher and higher every moment; and if the horses took fright on that narrow road (as they were certain to do at the breaking-loose of such a thunder-storm as was coming upon us now), the chances were that we, and they, and everything else would all go tumbling over the precipice together!

By this time the sun was down and the full moon up; but it looked very wan and sickly, for the gathering blackness behind the hills had now risen high above them, and was fast blotting out the moon altogether.

'Well, Feodor,' said I to Bulatoff, 'I have run a good many races in my life, but I think this is the first time I ever raced a thunder-storm!'

'It will be a pretty close race, by the look of things,' said he, as cool as a cucumber; 'but we *may* manage it yet. What do *you* say, my lad?' he added, turning to the driver.

'*Avoss*' (Maybe), answered the man; and then, tightening his belt with a business-like air and pulling up the collar of his thick sheepskin frock, he gave the reins a furious shake, and encouraged his horses with a succession of screeches worthy of a scalded cat. But the poor beasts needed no urging, for *they* knew what was coming quite as well as we did, and tore along as if there were a pack of wolves at their heels.

Meanwhile the rising storm-clouds had swallowed up the moon, and the whole sky above us was like a roof of black marble. So deep was the darkness, in fact, that, even with our lamps lit, we could hardly see the precipice along the very edge of which we were rushing; but by the way we were whirled from side to side of the narrow road, we could tell that we must be mighty near the brink every now and then.

After that no one spoke another word, but we all sat waiting for what was to come.

By ill-luck this particular stage was a very long one (to say nothing of its being all uphill), and the horses, having been out once that day already, were not so fresh as they might have been; so that, as you see, the chances were sorely against us. I was just loosening my dirk-knife in its sheath, to be ready to cut the traces—our only chance of life if we were upset *there*—when I felt the count grip my arm in the darkness, and, looking up, saw far away in front of us, in the midst of the utter blackness, a single spot of fire, which I knew at once to be the light of the next post-house!

But just then—as if to warn us not to rejoice too soon—before I had even time to speak, there came pat, pat, pat, two or three heavy drops of rain from the great black void above us—the first drops of the coming storm!

The horses seemed to feel it too, and to know what it meant, for away they dashed as if they had but just begun. On we flew, tossed and banged hither and thither, rocking and reeling from side to side in the darkness like a ship in a heavy sea; and then all at once our driver set up a yell that awoke all the echoes far and near, and the wooden palisades of a courtyard seemed to start up around us in a sudden glare of lantern-light, and there was a clamour of hoarse voices beside us as the Tartar ran our team in under a low shed, while we jumped out and darted into the post-house like acrobats.

We were not a moment too soon. Hardly had the door shut behind us, when there came a blinding glare over the whole sky, as bright and fierce and sudden as if a furnace-door had opened and closed again instantly. The queer little cross-beamed room, and the knives and glasses on the rough deal table, and the gilt-edged portrait of the postmaster's patron saint in the far corner, and the white, scared faces of his two children were all terribly distinct, for just as long as a man might draw breath. Then, quick as thought, all was black as pitch once more; but through the blackness came a thunder-clap like the crash of a hundred pieces of brass cannon all fired at once, echoing and re-echoing among the unseen mountains outside as if it would never end. And then there was a rush and a roar, and the whole house shook as the whirlwind struck it like a battering-ram, while a volley of rain came rattling and hammering on the roof and against the windows, as if it would dash them all to pieces.

But the old postmaster (who was well used, no doubt, to such little disturbances) set to work quite coolly to get us some tea, while the hut trembled to its foundation, and the timbers cracked and groaned, and the thunder crashed and banged overhead, and heavy bullets of rain came rattling against wall and roof, and flash after flash showed us the tall trees outside bending and swaying like bulrushes in the furious blast. Every now and then, when the uproar lulled for a moment, we could hear the snap of broken boughs and the boom of falling rocks; and then the thunder would break out again louder than ever, while the postmaster's two little girls hid their poor wee frightened faces in my lap, and asked piteously 'when that nasty noise would be over.'

But, little by little, the uproar began to die away; the clouds broke; the moon shone forth again; the thunder melted into a low growling and muttering in the distance; and the stolid postmaster announced, as coolly as if such a storm were the regular accompaniment of a change of horses:

'*Vashé blagorodié, loshadi gotovi*' (Your honour, the horses are ready).

And off we went again through the drenched woods, the drip, drip, drip of which sounded like the ticking of a hundred clocks at once, while the swollen torrents roared hoarsely far below. Up, up, up we went, higher and ever higher, till all trace of vegetation disappeared, and our path began to wind amid heaped-up masses of black, broken rock and boundless fields of eternal snow, which looked doubly weird and spectral beneath the cold splendour of the moonlight.

At last, in spite of the joint-cracking bumps and jolts of our car, and the piercing cold that seemed to bite us to the very bone as we ascended, we both fell fast asleep, and went journeying for hours over the shadowy roads of dreamland, waking at length to find ourselves on the very summit of the pass just as day began to dawn, very cold, very damp, very sore, very hungry, and very cross.

But I must break off now, for here comes the postmaster to say that our horses are ready. God bless you, my dear boy!—Your affectionate Father, L. ARCHER.

Here ended the letter; but in folding it up Harry caught sight of a postscript over the leaf, which, like many other postscripts, contained the most important fact in the whole despatch:

P.S.—A Russian officer who has just come up from Vladikavkaz, on the other side of the mountains (and who will kindly take charge of this letter to Tiflis), tells us that this mysterious brigand of ours, Krovolil the Blood-shedder, has really been captured at last, and packed off in double irons to go with the next chain-gang to Siberia.

CHAPTER XIV.

ON THE BRINK OF THE ABYSS.

'WISH Monsieur Harry were here to see this; it is just what *he* would enjoy.'
'Well, I must try and give him some idea of it the next time I write; but, upon my honour, I don't know any words large enough to describe such a view to any one who has not seen it.'

And well might Mr Archer say so. From the summit of the great central ridge on which he and his comrade stood— down which the Russian officer who bore their letter to Tiflis was just disappearing—they looked down upon Asia on one side and Europe on the other. Far down the steep incline the endless curves of the road by which they had ascended melted into the sea of mist below. All around, the mountainside was gapped and rent with yawning chasms, left by the fall of the huge shapeless boulders that lay strewn on every side, like a battlefield of giants. At the very feet of the gazing travellers gaped a fathomless gulf, from the dim depths of which came booming up the hollow roar of an unseen waterfall. Beyond it vast black precipices thrust themselves up against the clear morning sky, like rising thunderclouds. And, high over all, with its great white pyramid shining like tried silver in the growing splendour of the sunrise, towered the glorious Kazbek, lifting itself heavenward in silent, eternal prayer.

'As we have to travel through such places,' said Archer, 'it is just as well for us that our good friend Krovolil has been captured.'

'Captured, but not killed,' rejoined the count meaningly as he scrambled into the queer little car that had just drawn up beside them.

'Well,' cried Archer, getting in after him, 'he is hardly likely to escape, surely? After having so much trouble to catch him, they would scarcely give him the chance.'

'Such prisoners are not easy to keep,' replied the Russian, with sombre emphasis, as they rattled off down the farther slope.

And then, after a moment's pause, as if hesitating whether to utter the thought that was in his mind or not, he said in a low voice:

'You would not call me *superstitious*, would you?'

'No man less so,' said the other, looking surprised—as he well might.

'Nor should I call myself so; but I will own that not merely am I certain that Krovolil *will* escape, but I feel equally sure (though I could not tell you why) that we shall sooner or later fall in with him ourselves!'

'Since when have you had that feeling?' asked the Englishman, looking fixedly at him.

'Ever since that lady in the train spoke of him as having been among those robbers who broke into her house at midnight and killed her servant. Laugh at me if you like, but it is so.'

'I can't very well laugh at you,' said Archer gravely; 'for, if I *must* confess it, I have the same feeling myself, and have had it (so far as I can remember) ever since the very same time!'

Their car being a light one, and the way all downhill from this point, they disposed of the two next stages at a much brisker rate than those which had preceded them; and the count was just beginning to joke his thoughtful comrade on being 'deep in meditation as to what he should order for dinner at Vladikavkaz '—suggesting at the same time that an Englishman's first duty on reaching any new place abroad was 'to look about for something fit to eat,' and his second duty to abuse it as 'nasty foreign trash, not fit for a dog'—when there came a startling interruption which made them both serious enough.

The horses given them at the last posthouse were young and skittish beasts, evidently quite new to their work, as was also their driver, a slim native lad, who seemed hardly more than a boy, and would plainly be wholly unequal to the holding in of so fiery a team if anything went wrong. Archer was just making some remark of this kind to his friend— more, however, with the air of a man making a casual observation than as if in any way anxious or uneasy about the matter —when, just as they entered upon a steep downward path, or rather ledge (zigzagging between a perpendicular cliff on the right hand and a terrific precipice on the left), the clatter of a falling stone gave the excitable creatures the shadow of an excuse which they wanted for 'bolting,' and with a crash and a rattle they were off, along the very brink of the abyss!

The driver, with a muttered exclamation of dismay, put forth all his strength to pull them in, but he might as well have tried to rein up an express-train; and his vain efforts to check their speed only enraged the furious beasts, which at length, with one frantic plunge, tore the reins from his nerveless hands, and left him perfectly helpless!

There are times when men appear to live a whole lifetime in a few seconds, and this was one of them. Whole years of deadly peril and maddening excitement seemed crowded into those few moments in which the frail car, tossed and banged about from side to side of the narrow path, staggered on the brink of the precipice, with the flying pebbles crashing around it, and the hammering hoofs striking fire from the splintered rock. Escape seemed hopeless; for, whether they were dashed against the cliff on one side or hurled into the gulf on the other, their destruction was equally certain.

Both Archer and the count had sprung up to try and seize the reins, but they were instantly flung down again by a furious bound of the car; and ere they could gain their feet once more, the end came. The near horse, entangled in the trailing reins, fell suddenly, dragging down the other along with it; and the car, after wavering for one terrible moment between the precipice and the cliff, turned over against the latter, hurling out Bulatoff and the driver with terrific force, while Archer, who clung desperately to the inside of the car, was the only one that escaped unhurt.*

The rest were not so fortunate. The unlucky driver was lying stunned and senseless beneath the car. Count Bulatoff, though saved by the packages that fell out along with him from being crushed against the rock, was bleeding freely from a fearful gash on the forehead; and the horse that had caused the overturn, maddened by the pain of a broken leg, was lashing out wildly in every direction.

Two slashes of Archer's long hunting-knife freed the poor beast from the entangling harness; but scarcely was this done when a furious plunge sent it headlong over the precipice.

* The author once had a similar adventure.—D. K.

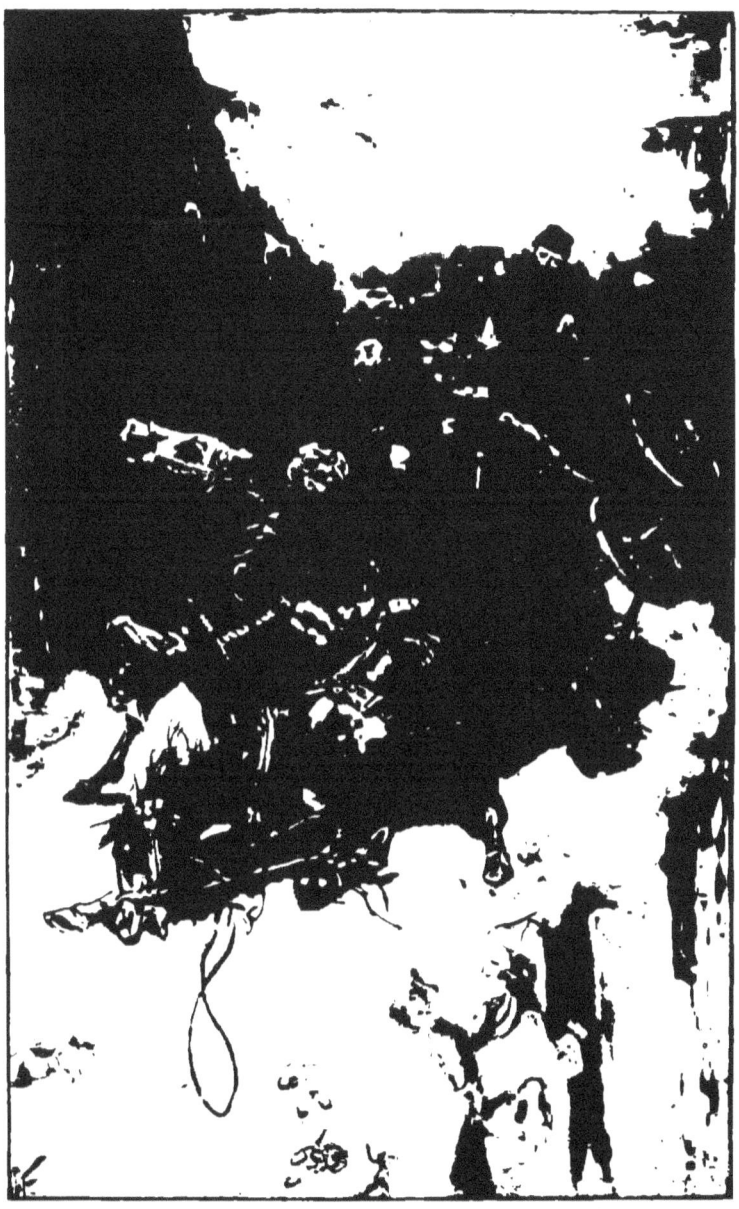

Wavering for one terrible moment between the precipice and the cliff.
PAGE 130.

'I'm afraid this poor lad has broken his arm,' said the Englishman, dragging out the still insensible driver from under the car. 'The best plan will be for me to mount this horse that is left, and ride back to the posthouse for help; for, as we stand now, we can do nothing to help *him*, and are only blocking the road for every one else.'

'Better let *me* go,' cried the count, who had just finished binding up his wounded head. 'I know their ways better than you, and every moment is precious.'

'But won't that broken head make you feel sick on horseback?' asked his friend doubtfully.

'I haven't *time* to be sick just now,' said the brave Russian simply; and away he went on the remaining horse, which, spent with its own violence and cowed by its comrade's fate, was now as quiet as a lamb.

The interval that followed, though really less than an hour, seemed endless to the impatient Englishman, left alone as he was with this suffering lad, who began to writhe and groan piteously as consciousness returned to him. But at length the count was seen coming back with men and horses; the hurt man was borne away, the car set up again, and a fresh team harnessed to it; and away went the two travellers toward Vladikavkaz, as if nothing had happened.

'See the good of having an autograph letter from the Czar!' chuckled Bulatoff. 'Just at first the fellows were inclined to be as lazy as a Cossack on a holiday; but when I showed them that letter I can promise you it made 'em nimble enough. If I had only had an ordinary *podorojnaya* * I might have been there yet.'

But Archer hardly noticed what he said; for by this time

---

* Literally a 'by-the-way'—a kind of travelling-pass, without which one cannot obtain posthorses.

they had got fairly down into the depths of the great ravine, and the Englishman, who had never been through it before, was wholly absorbed in surveying the savage grandeur of a defile that may bear comparison with the Via-Mala itself—the far-famed Dariel Pass. Mile after mile they struggled through the gloomy depths of a tremendous chasm, walled in by sheer precipices many hundred feet in height, which, leaning toward each other as they towered upward, narrowed the sky itself to a tiny blue ribbon far overhead; while the swollen torrent beside them, roaring and lashing itself into foam against the huge, black, fallen boulders that obstructed its course, overflowed at every turn the narrow, zigzag strip of gravel and big stones which, contributed by landslips from above and floods from below, was imaginatively called a road. But, little by little, the great rock-walls became lower and less steep; the deep, black gorge opened out into a sunny valley; the path grew clearer and more level; till at length, toward afternoon, they came out upon the vast green plain on the southern border of which clustered the painted church-towers, and straight, wide, dusty streets, and quaint, many-coloured houses of the neat little town of Vladikavkaz ('Lord of the Caucasus').

But even here there was no rest for these untiring 'globetrotters,' who had barely time enough left to reach the Caspian port of Petrovsk ere the weekly steamer should sail thence for Astrakhan. A hasty dinner, a good wash with their own soap and towels (both articles being extras in these parts), and they were off again, heading over the boundless level toward the distant hills that hung like hovering clouds upon the north-eastern sky.

And then, for hours upon hours, the vast, green, silent steppe, with here and there a grass-thatched Cossack hut, or a queer little post-house with its striped black-and-white doorposts—at first all ablaze with hot, cloudless sunshine, then gradually blurred into indistinctness by the creeping shadows of night, and then awakened by the rising moon to a ghostly resurrection. And all night long they were scurrying through a wild and dream-like confusion of broken roads and pebbly streams; horses yoked and unyoked; dark, bearded, brigand-like visages starting out in sudden gleams of lantern-light; big Cossacks shouting and brawling over their liquor; and lonely wastes of dark prairie, voiceless and lifeless as the grave.

Then the sun rose again, and the long, burning, monotonous day went slowly on—the same loneliness, the same dust, the same heat, the same unending level—varied only by a hasty gorge of half-raw meat at Khasaf-Iourt, a straggling timber-village of the true Caucasian type, along the one street of which the ridges of mud left by the recent rains had suddenly hardened, causing a jolting to which all that our heroes had yet endured was a mere joke.

Here again there was a slight difficulty as to the getting of fresh horses; but, as before, the Czar's autograph letter worked wonders, and the fat, greasy, half-drunken postmaster—at first disposed to reply insolently to the demands of two strangers whose outward appearance (after two nights in an open post-cart, and such a 'spill' as they had just had) was certainly none of the most respectable—was ready to kneel down and kiss the mud off their boots when he found out who they really were.

Night came round once more—the third night that our travellers had spent on the road without resting; but to these veterans it was nothing to sleep as soundly through the worst jolting of a Russian postcart as they had often slept in a storm-tossed boat or in the saddle of a moving horse.

'We *must* catch that boat, come what may,' said Archer; 'and, bar accidents, I think we shall do it yet.'

Soon after dark they plunged once more into the mountains; and all night long they were struggling up and down steep, crumbling ridges, over crunching gravel-beds, through splashing fords, along black, tomb-like gorges, till at length, just as morning dawned, a glittering streak along the eastern horizon announced the presence of the Caspian Sea.

Half-an-hour later they were in Petrovsk at last, and aboard the trim little coasting-steamer, which had already got her steam up for departure.

'Well,' cried Count Bulatoff cheerily to his friend as they stepped on board, 'our adventures are over for the present, for we can hardly get up any kind of excitement between this and Astrakhan!'

The count was an old traveller, and one of the shrewdest men in Russia; but, as will shortly be seen, he was no prophet.

CHAPTER XV.

MR ARCHER SEES A FACE.

HE boat that carried our heroes was the *Rusalka* (Water-nymph), newest and best of the light steamers plying weekly between Astrakhan, at the extreme north of the Caspian Sea, and Ashur-Adé, at the extreme south of it. Like many Russian steamers, she had her first-class deck forward and her third-class aft; and at this season both were usually crowded to excess. But, by rare good luck, most of her passengers on this particular voyage had landed at the intermediate ports, and our two pilgrims had the small raised platform that served as a promenade-deck almost to themselves.

'The last time I was here was in the autumn of 1869,' said the count, as they stood looking back at the straggling houses and tiny stone pier of the miniature seaport, and the queer little toy fort (very much like an overgrown inkstand) perched on a low rising-ground just behind it; 'and *then* I was bound for Mikhailovsk Bay.'

'Oho!' cried Archer, 'did *you* go with that expedition that was sent out two years ago to establish a fort and naval station at Krasnovodsk, on the eastern side of the Caspian?'

'Yes, I was one of the privileged,' said the Russian,

smiling; 'and, in fact, it was from there that I began my journey to the Tien-Shan Mountains, from which I had just returned when I met you in Moscow last April; but, after all, I did not set off in time to get the start of *you*—eh, Lyoff?'

(It may be observed that the count, being now on intimate terms with his English rival, had substituted for the latter's name of 'Livingstone'—which he could never manage to pronounce—the Russian name 'Lyoff;' to which Archer could hardly object, as it not only had the complimentary meaning of 'lion,' but was also the Christian name of the great Count Tolstoi himself, one of the Englishman's chosen heroes.)

'Well,' said Archer, 'I suppose I shall have a chance of seeing before long what they have made of that Krasnovodsk business, for we shall be down there next week, shall we not?'

'I hope so. We must go up to Astrakhan first, to meet the boat that is to carry us down—more's the pity, for working up the mouth of the Volga is always a tiresome job —but, once off from there, we shall run right down the east coast to Krasnovodsk.'

Then followed a short silence, which Archer was the first to break:

'Those fellows seem to be no end of a time getting breakfast ready; they have been chinking away with their cups and saucers for this last half-hour and more, and yet I don't see any signs of a meal. There they go again—do you hear?'

The count started slightly at the sound, as a man might do on suddenly hearing a well-known voice in some strange place, and then he broke into a loud laugh.

'Cups and saucers, do you say?' cried he. 'My dear

fellow, *those* cups belong to a breakfast that you would hardly like to share. Come with me and I'll show you what they are like.'

Archer followed him wonderingly to the after-deck, the chinking growing louder as they advanced; and near the stern of the vessel they found, seated on the deck, a group of four stalwart and very handsome young men, in white tunics and high Cossack caps, who were laughing loudly over an old-fashioned Russian game of cards which they were playing against four gray-coated, weather-beaten soldiers, who seemed to be getting rather the worst of the game.

So far Mr Archer had seen nothing to explain the mysterious chinking, which was just then heard once more, louder than ever. But a slight sign made by his friend directed his attention to the feet of the white-jacketed players, and he saw, with a slight thrill of emotion which all his self-command could not wholly restrain, huge rings of steel clutching both ankles, and linked together by a heavy chain!

The mystery was fully explained at last. The sound that he had heard was the clinking of *fetters;* these four handsome, merry young fellows were convicts on their way to Siberia; and the four friendly soldiers, who were laughing and jesting with them so frankly, were their appointed jailers!

Archer was still eyeing with some interest (as well he might) these respectable fellow-passengers, when the signal was given which announced the long-expected breakfast; and the two explorers, whose long mountain drive had considerably sharpened their naturally good appetite, lost no time in setting to work upon it. But all through the meal the Englishman seemed thoughtful and silent; and no sooner was it over than he left Bulatoff to write some letters which were to be posted at Astrakhan, and went aft for a second peep at the chain-gang.

At the first glance he saw that two new personages had been added to the group, the one being a man who was lying at full length close under the bulwarks, apparently fast asleep. His face was hidden by the arm on which it rested; but his fettered feet showed that he too was a convict.

The other new-comer was the Russian corporal in command of the party, a scarred veteran with a few tell-tale streaks of gray in his thick yellow moustache. Something in this man's face struck Archer as familiar, and looking closer at him, the Englishman recognised an old acquaintance.

'Hollo, Corporal Nikeetin! Do you remember that spring morning three years ago, when you and I, and six more, stood at bay behind a breastwork of flour-sacks, against fifty Turkomans?'

The old soldier looked up with a start, and his hard brown face brightened into a joyful grin as he answered, with a stiff military salute:

'Hey, father! is it *you?* I have good cause to remember that job' (pointing to one of the deepest scars that seamed his iron visage); 'but it was *that* that made me a corporal, so I need not complain. "He who remembers bygones, let him have his eye knocked out!" But whence has God sent you to us?'

'I have been staying at Borjom, brother, with your great traveller, Count Bulatoff; and he and I are going off to the East together to do a little business for Father Alexander Nikolaievitch' (the Czar).

'Count Bulatoff! That's he whom they call "the Wandering Jew," because he is always on the march somewhere. I have heard enough of him, and I am very glad to meet him at last.'

'And *I* am very glad to meet *you*, my lad, though I could wish you a better duty than shepherding those rogues yonder.'

'You're right, father; it's foul work for any man! But what can one do? Orders are orders, you know.'

'Very true; but surely these fellows of yours are very young to be ripe for Siberia already. What have they done?'

'What *haven't* they done?' growled Nikeetin. 'I'll just tell you a few of their tricks, and see how you like 'em.'

And he poured forth a bead-roll of crimes so black and frightful as to make even Archer's strong nerves tingle with horror.

'What! have those mere lads done all that? Nice fellows they must be, upon my word!'

'Ay, it's sad to think such boys should have sold themselves to the Evil One already. I shall be glad to get 'em safe to Astrakhan; and I shall be glad, too,' he added, with a sombre emphasis that awed Archer without his knowing why, 'if we ever get there ourselves!'

'What do you mean?' asked the Englishman, somewhat startled. 'This is a good, stout boat, and there is no sign of bad weather.'

'Maybe,' said the old soldier, with a gloomy shake of his gray head; 'but we have *one* man aboard here who is enough of himself to sink the best ship in the Russian navy!'

Archer, in spite of himself, began to feel vaguely uneasy; and he looked keenly all around him, expecting to see some

J

hideous face start up from the deck with the brand of a hundred crimes on its ruffianly features; but he could see none.

'Where *is* this dreadful man, then?' asked he, forcing a laugh. 'I don't see anything of him.'

At that moment the sleeper beside the bulwarks awoke, and rose slowly from his lair.

As he did so he revealed a face which, to the Englishman's startled eyes, seemed to have come fresh from the wonder-working hand of Guido or Raphael. In truth, no archangel ever painted by those great masters, in all the splendour of his eternal youth, could have surpassed the beauty and brightness of those fresh, smooth, child-like features, framed in soft, golden hair, and lighted up with a joyous smile that sparkled like the dancing ripples of the summer sea. Yet, beautiful as it was, that face would have disquieted any close observer with a weird, haunting sense of something *wanting* in it, though it was not easy to say what.

'There,' said the corporal in a hoarse whisper, 'that's the man!'

'*That* the man?' echoed Archer, looking in bewilderment from the speaker's sombre face to the young Apollo at whom he pointed. 'You must be joking, brother; that lad has the face of an angel!'

'Ah, father!' said the veteran gloomily, 'there are angels of *darkness* as well as angels of light. Do you know who he is? *Krovolil the Brigand!*'

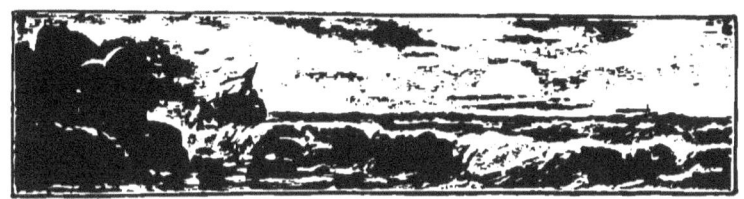

CHAPTER XVI.

IN DARK WATERS.

FOR once in his life even the cool and hardy Englishman was fairly struck dumb with amazement; and, in truth, the sudden discovery that this handsome, smooth-faced, innocent-looking lad was really the monster of crime and cruelty who was the terror of the whole Caucasus, and whose very name had long been the symbol of all that was vile and murderous and devilish, was enough to startle any man alive.

'It *can't* be!' cried Archer vehemently. 'Do you mean to tell me that that young lad yonder, who looks like a pretty girl in boy's clothes, is the savagest cut-throat in the Caucasus, whom even General Naprashkin and all his men could not kill?'

'Well, if you won't believe me,' replied the corporal, with the same ominous gravity, 'look and see for yourself how even his fellow-rascals yonder shrink away from him.'

In fact, the mere rising of this man from his place had sufficed to break up the group of players as if a bombshell had fallen right in the midst of it. The soldiers started to their feet and put their hands hastily to their short swords; and even the very convicts drew back with a nervous start (one of them actually letting fall his cards) and crossed themselves instinctively, as if at the approach of an actual demon.

Glancing from the startled men to the object of their terror, the quick-eyed Englishman noticed that the latter's hands were chained as well as his feet, and called to mind at once that the Russian officer who had told him of Krovolil's capture had spoken of the bandit-chief being 'packed off in *double* irons.'

Convinced at length in his own despite, Archer looked keenly at the smooth, handsome face of the terrible 'Bloodshedder' in quest of some token of what he really was. But there was absolutely none. The countenance of Archer's own son could not have looked more bright and fresh and innocent than that of this man of countless murders, to whom the dying agonies of tortured captives were a favourite sport and pleasure.

'So much for physiognomy!' said the traveller to himself. 'Catch me ever judging a man by his looks again!'

But Archer's keen glance did not fail to note that at sight of the terror which Krovolil seemed to inspire in those around him, the bandit's eyes lighted up with a sudden gleam of childish amusement and self-satisfaction, which told its own story to the shrewd Englishman.

'Vanity and conceit,' he muttered, 'are at the bottom of more crimes than people think; and there are plenty of men (or rather beasts) who would much rather be known by the worst villainies than not be known at all. Well, who would ever have believed this? I must go and tell Bulatoff at once.'

Cool as he was, the count was visibly startled by the news of this unexpected fellow-passenger, and said, with an air of unusual excitement:

'Did we not both say that we should fall in with this fellow sooner or later? And so we have, sure enough, earlier than we expected. It is, perhaps, just as well for us that our other presentiment—about his breaking loose again, I mean —has not been realised too.'

'Not *yet*,' said the other meaningly; and then *he* in his turn sat down to write a letter, while his friend went hastily aft.

The corporal, guessing at once who he must be, saluted him respectfully by name; and at the mention of 'Count Bulatoff' the soldiers, and even the convicts, eyed him with an air of interest, and even Krovolil himself looked up quickly.

The count exchanged a few words with Nikeetin; greeted the soldiers with 'Be fortunate, my children;' and then, to the manifest terror of all who saw it, walked deliberately up to the spot where the 'Blood-shedder' was standing, and seated himself close to him on the very edge of the bulwarks, in such a position that one touch would, apparently, have sufficed to plunge him headlong into the sea.

'Suppose I were to give you a push with my shoulder and send you overboard?' said the robber-chief, with an insolent grin. 'It would make no difference to *me*, you know, for I'm going to Siberia for life as it is!'

'Are you quite sure that you *could* do it?' asked the count, as coolly as ever.

'Well, perhaps not,' said the brigand, eyeing the sinewy strength of the speaker's tall, wiry frame with the knowing air of one who was a judge of such matters; 'but if General Naprashkin were sitting in your place, I'd *try*, bound as I am.'

'Well, I dare say you are not over-fond of the general,'

replied Bulatoff quietly, 'for I have heard that he and his men hunted you till they drove you over a precipice, and thought they had killed you!'

'They were not so clever as they thought, though, after all,' chuckled Krovolil. 'They saw me disappear over the precipice, but they *didn't* see me clutch the creepers that clung to the face of the rock, and swing myself down safely by *them*. I fooled 'em finely that time—ha, ha!' and a laugh as clear and musical as a silver bell expressed the ruffian's enjoyment of his own superior cleverness.

Just at that moment Archer, having finished his writing, was seen coming aft again to see what his friend was about.

'His Excellency the Count is a bold man,' said Corporal Nikeetin to the Englishman, with a side-glance at the spot where Bulatoff sat perched on the bulwarks, close to Krovolil. 'To be made a colonel I would not do what he is doing now.'

'But hark you, brother,' cried Archer, 'why on earth *are* you all so much afraid of this fellow Krovolil? He is only a common criminal after all, like any other convict.'

'Like any other convict?' echoed the soldier. 'Why, father, what are you saying? If he *were* just an ordinary convict, we would not fear him if he had killed as many men as Yeruslan Lazarevitch, who slew a whole army of pagans in one day; but don't you know he's in league with Satan?'

Archer's face probably expressed some doubt on this point, for the veteran went on at once, in a tone of grave rebuke:

'You may laugh, father, but you can't get rid of *facts* just by laughing at them. Judge for yourself. If this fellow were not helped by the Evil One, how else could he come alive again after being killed half-a-dozen times over?

How else could he slip through the fingers of the best soldiers in the Caucasus again and again? How else could he be as merry and gay as a peasant at a fair when he's on his way to Siberia in chains? Take my word for it, you will see, before this voyage is over, what happens when a man forsakes God and gives himself up to evil!'

The ominous words had hardly been spoken, when they were suddenly and startlingly confirmed.

A large gray cat, the pet of the ship's company, came sauntering past at that instant, purring loudly as one or two of the soldiers, who seemed to have the Russian fondness for animals in full measure, stooped to caress it. But when it came near Krovolil it stopped short and shrank hastily away, arching its back as if in presence of an enemy.

The rough soldiers exchanged looks of silent horror; but the robber himself seemed amused rather than offended by the beast's evident fear of him, and, as if wishing to tease it, he was just extending his fettered hands to bar its retreat, when, scared either by the rattling of the chains or by some other cause, the cat sprang at him with a kind of frightened fury, and gave him a deep and severe scratch on the back of the hand.

Words cannot paint the instant and horrible change that distorted the young man's bright and beautiful face as he dashed the poor creature to the deck with one crushing blow of his heavy irons, and then pounded it with his chained feet into a shapeless mass, on which he kept stamping furiously long after all life had been crushed out of it.

For some minutes no one moved or spoke; for, even to these stolid and hardy soldiers, the presence of an actual demon could hardly have been more appalling than the hideous transformation that they had just witnessed. At length a sailor came forward as cautiously as if venturing into the den of a hungry tiger, and, keeping at a safe distance from the dreaded 'Blood-shedder,' drew away the mangled carcass with a long boat-hook, and dropped it overboard.

Turning away in disgust, Archer caught old Nikeetin's eye fixed upon him with a look that said more than any words.

'What do you say *now*, father?' asked the old man in a hollow whisper. 'Would any.man but one possessed by a demon go on like that? I tell you, this man has *no soul;* and the Evil One, finding the house empty, has gone into it.'*

Few men were less open than Livingstone Archer to terrors of any kind, natural or superstitious; but after what he had just seen, the veteran's gloomy words, and the ominous look that pointed them, impressed him more than he would have cared to own.

'Such things *never* happen nowadays, of course,' said he half-aloud, as if he really needed such an assurance to give him confidence; 'but if ever a man could be possessed by an evil spirit, this fellow would be the one!'

And then rose up in his mind, all at once, a haunting memory of the weird scene in Lord Lytton's *A Strange Story*, where Margrave, the 'soulless man,' kills, in a similar paroxysm of beast-like ferocity, the squirrel that had bitten him; and the very words of the tale suddenly stood before him as if written in letters of fire: 'The human animal *without soul* may, like the tiger or the serpent, tear and

* It must be remembered that I only describe this man as I myself saw him, and as he impressed me and others who came in contact with him at the time. I can well believe that, to any one who has *not* seen it, such a dreadful perversion of nature must appear impossible; but, could one imagine a man actually without a soul, he would certainly be just such a one as the frightful creature of whom I have here tried to give some faint idea.—D. K.

destroy, and then sport harmless and rejoicing in the sunlight, because, like the tiger and the serpent, it is incapable of remorse.' And what text was that which spoke (as the old soldier had just spoken) of an evil spirit finding his home in a human heart, 'empty, swept, and garnished,' and entering in to dwell there?

For an instant the brave man stood in silent and gloomy thought; but the next moment he threw back his head as if shaking off some heavy oppression, and then—either angry with himself for having yielded even passingly to so extravagant a fancy, or moved by that combative spirit which always impels an Englishman to rush upon danger instead of awaiting its coming—he walked right over to the spot where Krovolil was standing, and seated himself beside him, in the very place that Count Bulatoff had just vacated.

As he did so, a quick, convulsive movement of the convict drew Archer's attention to him, and the Englishman saw that the bandit's cruelty had brought its own punishment, for his bleeding hand had attracted swarms of the terrible 'stinging-flies' which abounded on board the boat (as they did everywhere in that climate at that season), and which were goading the wretch to madness by their persistent attacks on the torn flesh, his chains making him powerless to repel them.

At that sight Archer's British instinct of helping, as a matter of course, any one who was in trouble overpowered for the moment even his horror of the monster before him. He at once produced a strip of rag from a pouch at his side (for, as has been seen, a journey by post in Russia is seldom achieved without a good many cuts and bruises), and wiping the blood from the torn hand, bound it up as dexterously as any surgeon.

'Thank you; that's a great deal better,' said the brigand, who had received this kindness with marked surprise. 'It *did* hurt a good deal, though, and those plaguy flies made it ten times worse. I see *you* are not afraid of me, anyhow, like those fellows yonder.'

'Not I,' rejoined Archer bluntly; 'I am an Englishman!'

'An Englishman?' echoed Krovolil, looking up quickly. 'Think of that, now! I've never seen one before!'

And this fell destroyer actually eyed the traveller from head to foot with the simple, eager curiosity of a child getting its first sight of some wonderful wild beast.

'Why do you stare at me so?' asked Archer, laughing in spite of himself. 'Did you think that Englishmen were differently shaped from every one else?'

'Well, I have heard a good many queer tales of them,' said the bandit, joining in the laugh with a simple, child-like merriment that made his frantic fury only a few minutes before seem as if it had never been.

'As, for instance'—— suggested the English explorer.

'Well, I've been told that those English can shut their voices up in a box,' said the robber, who had probably heard some garbled report of the newly-invented phonograph and telephone, 'and then send them to the other side of the world, and make 'em repeat, out there, all that *they* have been saying at home; and I've heard, too, that they have a trick of whispering into a hole, and making some one a thousand *versts* off hear every word they say. I only wish I could have learned *that* trick when I was up in the hills; it would have been very handy for letting my men know when there was a rich traveller coming.'

And again the 'Blood-shedder' laughed more heartily than before.

Archer was completely bewildered. This hearty frankness, this simple, boyish glee, seemed so glaringly out of place in a wretch to whom, if public report spoke truly, the worst cut-throat in Rome or Naples was a saint, that he began to doubt, for the first time, whether this man could really be what he was represented.

'Having once made out that he was possessed by a demon, these fellows would credit him with every crime on the face of the earth, and very likely put down to *him* alone the misdeeds of all the robbers in the Caucasus. I should not wonder if, after all, he turns out to be not so black as he is painted.'

But Count Bulatoff was by no means of the same opinion.

'I can believe *now*,' cried he, as his friend appeared, 'all that they say of that fellow Krovolil, and more.'

'Well,' said Archer, '*I* was just beginning to believe the contrary. Here as elsewhere, I fancy, a tale loses nothing by telling; and it really does seem impossible that any man who really *is* such a monster should show no sign of it whatever, either in looks, voice, or talk.'

'But how about that cat?' asked the count meaningly.

'Pooh! Any violent and untaught man might do such a thing in a fit of passion, whereas this fellow's worst cruelties are said to have been done in cold blood.'

'Ah! I see you don't know the Russians yet, Lyoff. There was a peasant in one of the villages on my own estate —a very kind-hearted fellow in his way, too—who, being disturbed one night by the crying of his baby, got up and strangled it, and went to bed again ; and when he was tried for the crime, he seemed quite surprised that any one should make a fuss about such a trifle, and only said—as if that were quite excuse enough—that the child would not let him sleep.'

'Well, at all events, I suppose you don't believe their stories of this man being a supernatural creature?' cried Archer, with a rather forced laugh.

'I don't say anything about that,' replied the Russian in an almost snappish tone that contrasted very startlingly with his wonted good-humoured composure; 'but I *do* say that I shall be very glad to get to Astrakhan!'

'And, to tell you the truth,' said his comrade, 'so shall I!'

That night, contrary to his expectation, Archer fell asleep as soon as he went to bed; but it was only to pass through an endless series of nightmares, each worse than the last. All at once there came a mighty shock and a tremendous crash, and he awoke to find himself sprawling on the floor, while at the same moment he heard Bulatoff shout through the darkness:

'Up for your life, Archer; *the ship's sinking!*'

It was a startling announcement to arouse any man from a sound sleep; but Archer had been shipwrecked before, and did not lose his head for an instant. Luckily he had lain down fully dressed, expecting to tranship before daylight into the flat-bottomed barge that was to carry them up the shallow mouth of the Volga, where the steamer itself could not pass; and in a trice he and his friend were on deck, side by side.

It was a wild scene that met their eyes. A sudden gleam of moonlight, breaking through the hurrying clouds, faintly showed the rocking, reeling deck, and the half-seen figures that flitted over it, ghost-like, to and fro, and the dim waste of dark waters all around. The steamer, with her port quarter completely stove in, was slowly settling down by the stern. Nothing was to be seen of the ill-fated sailing-vessel that had caused the collision, which (as was afterwards learned) had sunk at once; but far away to the north glowed amid the darkness one solitary eye of fire.

'That's Lighthouse No. 4; so we can't be far from the river-mouth,' said the count, with unruffled composure. 'It's all shallow water here, and if these sailors of ours can only lower the boats without some clumsy accident—ah! did I not say so? Look there!'

In fact, some awkwardness in lowering the only available boat (for the other was found to be leaky) brought her against the ship's side with a force that stove in two of her planks and made her utterly useless.

'Let us fetch up our boxes and knot 'em together for a raft,' cried Archer, darting below.

It was done in a twinkling; and as the last knot was tied the Russian asked as coolly as if he were at a picnic:

'Can you see what time it is?'

'Just half-past three,' said the Englishman, with equal composure.

'Then our barge and steam-tug cannot be far off,' cried the count, 'and they will be on the look-out for us. If they make haste they *may* be in time yet, for I fancy the steamer will take at least five minutes more to go down. Hark! I think I hear them coming now!'

He was right; but the rescue came barely in time, for the ship actually sank ere it could reach her; and well was it for our two heroes that they had their tiny raft to bear them up amid the whirl.

But when the chained convicts, who had escaped by clinging to planks and spars, were mustered on the deck of the barge, Krovolil was missing. No one had seen him, nor was a trace of him to be found; and the old corporal shook his head and said solemnly :

'The Evil One has taken his own. I said all along he was enough to sink any ship, and it's mighty lucky he did not sink *us* as well!'

CHAPTER XVII.

RIDING THE WHIRLWIND.

HILE their fathers were thus meeting with adventure after adventure, the life of Harry Archer and his Russian chum was, for the time being, as uneventful as ever; and the bold English boy might well have been as discontented as that enthusiastic youth who complained that he had been 'two whole months in India, and had not been bitten by a single snake yet!'

But, curiously enough, Harry, though by nature the more inclined of the two to rebel against inaction and lack of excitement, was just then the less dissatisfied of the twain. For this, however, there was a good reason; for the town which his companion already had by heart was quite new to *him*, and he was never weary of scrambling among the mighty precipices that shut it in on every side, admiring its rocky ridges and picturesque ruins, finding out fresh walks among its encircling hills, or getting up impromptu conversations, under every possible difficulty of language, with the various races that crowded its ever-busy streets.

In truth, there are few towns of the East better worth seeing than Tiflis, which, like Constantinople or Alexandria, is one of those places which every one can imagine, but which no one can describe. The monotonous sameness of Eastern cities, or the monotonous variety of Western ones, is easily sketched; but the mingling of the two at their point of intersection defies all the powers of language. How *are* you to believe in modern times among men who gravely show you the crag to which Prometheus was bound, and the rock to which Jason moored the *Argo* in his cruise after the 'Golden Fleece,' or display pedigrees tracing their lineal descent from Solomon?

So thought our young Wykehamist, as a five minutes' walk through the town carried him back a thousand years from the nineteenth century to the ninth—from the 'Russian quarter,' with its lamp-lit streets and brand-new brick houses (the staring red and white of which makes them look as if built of raw beef-steaks), to the 'Persian town,' along the narrow, crooked lanes of which, reeking with filth of every kind, passed the veiled ladies and bare-limbed water-carriers of the days of Haroun Al-Raschid.

'Well,' muttered Harry, eyeing with a broad grin the huge top-heavy caps of black sheepskin around him, ' I 'm sure one of *these* fellows might well have "a bee in his bonnet," as they say in Scotland, for the bonnet itself looks just like a tarred bee-hive!'

But this strange contrast of Past and Present rose to its highest pitch when, one quiet Saturday evening, our hero stood on the brow of the rocky ridge once crowned with the ancestral fortress of those ancient Georgian kings to whose last descendant Harry had been introduced on the previous day, in the person of a thin, dark, elderly gentleman in a black frock-coat, living on a pension allowed him by the Russian government.

Close beside the crumbling, ivy-wreathed ruins of the

ancient seat of Georgian royalty, groups of gaily-dressed promenaders were seated round the marble-topped tables of a trim little public garden, over their ice-cream or lemonade. At our hero's feet, in the centre of the wide green valley where native mountain-princes had held their court when the very name of Russia was still unknown, lay outspread in the glory of the sunset the serried roofs, and broad, straight, white streets, and glittering church-towers, and bridges black with creeping swarms of human ants, of busy, modern Tiflis. The old Mussulman caravansary in the great market-place, now turned into a concert-hall, stood facing a showy, white-fronted Russian hotel. A tall factory chimney rolled its smoke over the bank along which the hosts of Prince David the Restorer came marching home in triumph from the scene of his greatest victory; and a telegraph-wire ran across the grassy slopes down which the mail-clad horsemen of Georgia rode forth to battle a thousand years ago. And, over all this strange medley of ancient and modern, towered, far away on the northern horizon, the eternal snows of the Caucasus, watching the advance of Russia as they had watched the retreat of Xenophon's 'Ten Thousand' or the destroying march of Alexander of Macedon.

When Harry got home from his stroll he found the whole house in a stir. A carriage was drawn up in front of the door; several servants were bustling around it, and lifting out the packages which it contained; and in the doorway stood the countess herself, holding by both hands a sturdy figure that our hero recognised at a glance.

'What! Dmitri Ivânovitch? Are you back already? How's Ruslan? Are you come to take us home?'

'Ruslan is quite well, and will be very glad to see you,' said General Naprashkin, smiling at this volley of questions

K

as he shook hands heartily with his boy-comrade. 'I hear you've had news of your father already. I'm glad he and Fyodka have got on all right so far. As for taking you home, that won't be till the week after next, for I'm only in town for a day or two just now, on special business; but I may have something else for you to do in a few days' time, which I think you will like quite as well, if not better.'

This hint was more fully explained by the general at the supper-table an hour later. He had been summoned to Tiflis, he said, to confer with the Grand-Duke Michael (who had just arrived there from another quarter) about the progress and apparent prospects of various public works that had lately been set on foot in his district; and, that done, he was under orders to accompany the Viceroy on the following Tuesday or Wednesday, along with several other officers, to the opening of a new branch-line of railway among the hills, at which the Grand-Duke was to preside.

'And I have no doubt, Monsieur Henri,' he wound up, 'that, if you care to witness the ceremony, I can get leave to take you along with me, especially as the Grand-Duke himself is a friend of yours; and I should have been very glad to take Yury too, if he had not, unluckily, been on the sick-list.'

Poor Yury made a most rueful face at this news, as he well might, for, in fact, he *was* on the sick-list then, just at the wrong time. In his new-born zeal for athletics, he had forgotten that he had neither the long practice nor the splendid constitution of his English chum, and had imitated Harry's love of hard exercise and exposure to all weathers 'not wisely, but too well,' with the natural result of giving himself a very bad cold, by which he was for the present confined to the house.

But, delicate and petted as he was, Yury Bulatoff was far

too good a fellow to be sulky and envious because his friend
was going to have a treat which *he* could not share; and
though he evidently felt very deeply this severe disappointment, he did his best to bear it manfully; for one of the most
prominent doctrines in the code of schoolboy ethics impressed
upon him by Harry was, that no boy of spirit should ever
stoop to the weakness of making a 'fuss' about any calamity.
In truth, he had less reason to repine than he imagined; for,
little as he suspected it, this very fit of untimely illness, which
he was so bitterly regretting, probably saved his life.

When the appointed day came, General Naprashkin and
Harry Archer (who, as the general had foretold, at once
received permission to join the Viceroy's party) were the first
to appear at the station, where a special train was drawn up
in readiness. But they had barely time to make a hasty
inspection of it ere a deafening shout from the crowd around
the entrance, taken up and repeated again and again, told
that the Grand-Duke himself was at hand.

Sure enough, a few minutes later, the stately form and
handsome face of the Emperor's brother were seen advancing
slowly between the two living hedges of heated faces and
jostling shoulders that lined his way; and behind him came
ten or twelve men, some in uniform and some in plain
clothes, whose reception by the crowd showed that *they* were
celebrities likewise.

The Grand-Duke recognised Harry at the first glance, and
greeted him with a heartiness that delighted our hero, who
subsequently confided to General Naprashkin that Michael was
'not a bit like any of these stuck-up kings'—a comment that
not a little amused the worthy general, who naturally wondered
how many kings the boy had been intimate with in his life.

A special carriage had been provided for Michael himself, that he might be private if he wished; but this was not at all to the taste of the genial Viceroy, who insisted upon inviting all his guests into his own carriage. Harry was introduced to them all in succession as the son of 'the great English traveller, Monsieur Livingstone Archer'—a name that created a marked sensation in the circle; and our hero, with equal surprise and pleasure, found himself talking familiarly to half-a-dozen men whose names were then famous not only throughout Russia, but through all Europe.

The sleek, smooth-faced, innocent-looking man in spectacles, who greeted him so pleasantly in faultless French, was the great diplomatist, Count Born-Liaroff, who had just brought about the conclusion of a treaty that completely outwitted one of the craftiest and most ferocious despots of Central Tartary, secured to Russia certain advantages which she had for years sought in vain, and established his own reputation as surpassing all other Russians in the great art in which the Russians themselves surpass all the children of men—that of saying one thing and meaning another. Beside him stood a tall, dark, spare, bright-eyed man in a black velvet coat, who proved to be the famous Russian painter of battle-pieces, Gorian Choptheredzoff, whose admirable pictures of 'The Slaughter of the Janissaries,' 'Attila crucifying Roman Captives,' 'A Wounded Soldier devoured by Hyenas,' 'The Massacre of St Bartholomew,' 'Emmerich of Pavia torn Limb from Limb by Wild Horses,' and other paintings equally lively and well executed, were just then on exhibition in London.

Next after him came a fine-looking man in cavalry uniform, with a deep scar on his left cheek. This was Colonel Waudrin Jewski (the greatest living Russian traveller after

Count Bulatoff himself), who, finding no other means of making his way into a hitherto unreached district, had gained entrance to it by getting some one to sell him as a slave to a Tartar chief, and then, having seen all he wanted, had made his escape by the simple method of knocking his purchaser on the head and dressing himself up in his clothes. Then followed a round, ruddy, jolly, ever-laughing little fellow, whom our hero could hardly believe to be really the far-famed chemist and toxicologist, Dr Poison-soupoff, who had discovered more new poisons, and killed more animals with them, than any other man living, and who was now trying hard to interest the Czar in a 'humane project' for putting an end at one blow to the next Russo-Turkish war that might break out, by filling the air all round the Turkish army with the strongest essence of arsenic and prussic acid !

But Harry was more especially interested in a big, gray-haired, sad-eyed man who stood silent in a corner. The boy at first supposed him to be Count Tolstoi, but presently learned that he was the great Russian author, Ivan Gloomin, whose terribly true descriptions of the 'society life' of Russia had been translated into every language of Western Europe.

The Grand-Duke's 'special' flew along at a speed unknown to the creeping trains of Southern Russia; and though they had a good many miles to go, it was but little after midday when they reached their destination, a pretty little Georgian town in the heart of the western mountains, the inhabitants of which had turned out to a man to witness the ceremonial, and to welcome the universally popular Viceroy. The whole hillside was one flutter of gay flags and green boughs formed into arches ; and on the brow of the ridge stood, rising like an island above the black mass of the hurrahing crowd, the tiny train (consisting merely of an engine and tender and one carriage) which was to make its trial-trip, in the Grand-Duke's presence, over the new line that he had come to open.

A curious line it was, such as one seldom sees except in regions like the Higher Alps or the Himalayas. From the queer little station that stood perched like a nest on the very summit of the ridge, just above the town, the railway plunged down the farther slope—along a gradient as steep as the famous South African 'zigzag' through Natal to Pietermaritzburg, or the mountain-railroad that climbs up to Constantine from the Algerian port of Philippeville— down to a quiet little secluded valley, along which it ran to join, some miles farther on, a short offshoot of the main line from the coast to Tiflis. In descending or ascending this steep incline, the train was to be moved by the unwinding and winding-up again of a wire cable (as with the Brooklyn Bridge trains at New York), reserving its steam to propel it over the flats below.

The local *golora* (mayor) had coughed and stammered out his official address; the Viceroy had replied to it in a few kindly and well-chosen words; the customary 'bread and salt' had been presented in the form of a light native cake and a glass of mountain-wine; and then came the question, who should go with the train on its first trip?

The Grand-Duke had wished to do so himself; but he was strongly dissuaded by those about him, and more especially by the general, who urged that on this steep descent there was always a possibility of accident, and that a life so important must not be lightly risked. Michael unwillingly assented, and stepping back, invited such of his guests as wished it to take their seats.

The artist and the author got in at once; the chemical doctor instantly followed; but the general hung back, saying:

'With your Imperial Highness's gracious permission, I would rather take my place in the tender itself, from which I can better watch the working of the train than from this carriage.'

'By all means, general; we could have no better judge of such a matter,' said Michael, with a courteous bow.

'May I go with you, please, Dmitri Ivânovitch?' asked Harry eagerly.

'Certainly,' replied the general, whose bold spirit fully sympathised with the boy's love of perilous adventures; 'but mind you sit still, and, above all, take care not to lean over the edge.'

And the two scrambled to their places.

The next moment came a rush of steam and a sharp clank of metal; and then, in place of the lusty cheer with which the lookers-on were about to hail the starting of their first train, there broke forth from the whole multitude a wild cry of amazement and horror, which made the very air ring.

For this strange excitement, however, there was only too good reason.

It being uncertain whether the Grand-Duke and his guests *would* care to go with the train, the coupling of the wire cable to their carriage, and of their carriage to the tender, had been deferred to the last moment. It was afterwards conjectured (for, as will be seen, no one has ever had a chance of arriving at any certainty on the subject) that the engine-driver, who was a stolid, dull-witted fellow, had taken the leaping of Harry and the general into the tender as a signal to set off, and started the engine, without any idea that it was *not* attached to the restraining cable.

Most unluckily, both Naprashkin and his boy-comrade happened to be looking forward at the moment, and thus failed to notice that they were not coupled to the passenger-carriage. But the cry of terror that broke from the crowd made them turn quickly round, and the fearful truth flashed upon them at once.

Quick as thought the general sprang to his feet, and thrusting aside the two strong men like children, darted forward and turned off the steam. But it was too late. They had already traversed the tiny strip of level ground along the summit of the ridge, and had reached the brink of the perilous descent beyond, over which engine and tender shot like a boat over the edge of a waterfall, vanishing, as if the earth had swallowed them, from the eyes of the terrified beholders!

'Thank God that Yury is not here!' muttered the General. 'Now, Harry, we must just do what we can to save ourselves. Be ready to jump when I give you the word!'

'All right, general,' said the young Wintonian promptly.

Harry's face was a trifle paler than usual, and his lips were firmly set; but his eye was as bright and his voice as cheery as ever. Up or down, in play or in peril, there was no 'white feather' about Harry Archer.

Just then was heard, close beside the doomed travellers, a heavy thud, and then a stifled cry. The poor stoker, scared out of his senses by this sudden and horrible peril, had flung himself wildly out, without even looking whither he was going; and, whirled forward like a stone from a sling by the impetus of the train, he came head-foremost against a pine-trunk with the force of a battering-ram, and that faint cry was the last that he ever uttered.

The fate of his comrade seemed to complete the prostration

of the luckless engine-driver. It was in vain that Naprashkin spoke to him, shook him, and strove to make him understand what they were about to attempt, and persuade him to join them. As if paralysed by sheer terror, he sank down all of a heap in one corner, and moved no more.

But, in truth, the danger that now stared them in the face might well have tried the strongest nerves. Down they flew, down, down, down; while trees, rocks, and thickets went racing past them like hurrying clouds, and the very air seemed to shriek in their ears as they rushed along. That the engine should keep on the rails at all was little short of a miracle; but the experienced Russian knew too well that it could not do so long, and that its first swerve would hurl them out headlong, to be crushed into a shapeless, mangled mass, or, worse still, to be left lying among the cruel stones, torn, bleeding, shattered, but still alive, to die by inches in lingering agony.

But the cool and practised soldier was just the man for such a crisis, and amid all the maddening excitement of that death-race he had never lost his head for a moment, and had even found time to single out the very spot where their leap for life and death was to be made.

About midway between the crest of the ridge and its foot the hillside was cleft by a deep, narrow chasm, over the bridge spanning which the train must pass. On the nearer brink of this chasm, close to the bridge itself, the workmen had left a huge mound of loose earth, which the general, with that keen eye that nothing escaped, saw at once to be the only spot in the whole descent where they could take their leap with any hope of escaping alive.

The sight of Naprashkin's coolness did more than anything else to steady our hero, just as it had often steadied the general's young soldiers on their first battlefield; and as the terrible moment drew near, the veteran saw with stern satisfaction that his young comrade was fully prepared for it. He made a last effort to arouse the helpless engine-driver from his torpor, and to give him a chance for life; but it was all in vain, and he was forced to leave the poor wretch to his doom.

There was indeed no time to lose. They were fast nearing the steepest part of the descent; and all around the little station that lay almost under their feet in the valley below, the frightened country-folk, who had by this time caught the alarm, were flying back from the path of the coming destruction, with cries of terror that came plainly to the ears of the forlorn pair, and seemed to give them a foretaste of the bitterness of death.

'Jump!' roared Naprashkin all at once; and as the word was spoken our hero found himself shooting through the air like a rocket.

A sudden shock, an instant of sick, numbing dizziness, and then Harry opened his eyes once more, and shaking off the earth that covered him (for the tremendous force with which he alighted had buried him in the loose soil right up to the very chin), stared about him in bewilderment, hardly knowing yet whether he were alive or dead. He did so just in time to see the engine leap from the rails as it came dashing into the level space below, fly across it like an arrow, and burst right *through* the little wooden station building, which vanished with a deafening crash into a cloud of dust that hid everything from view for a moment.

It is needless to say that the ill-fated engine-driver was killed on the spot; but fortunately his life and that of his mate were the only sacrifices, for every one else had already fled from the fatal place.

But when Harry and the general turned their attention from the gloomy spectacle below to their own position, both stood motionless with amazement; and well they might. They were, indeed, lying on a vast mound of loose earth, the softness of which had saved them from any injury beyond a few bruises; but it was on the *farther* side of the chasm, and they now saw, to their utter astonishment, that the tremendous impetus communicated to their leap by the rush of the train had carried them not only over the first mound, but right across the gully itself, bridge and all, landing them in the midst of a second mound beyond it!

The two looked at each other, but said nothing; and, in truth, there was nothing to say.

When the leap was measured next day, the total length of their flight through the air, reckoned from a large white stone that had been just abreast of them as they made their spring, was *thirty-seven feet*, which, as Harry truly said, ' broke the record for a broad jump out and out!'

It was some days ere the general and our hero wholly shook off the effects of this adventure; but thenceforth the comradeship of danger drew them closer together than before, and the growing affection felt by the stern old soldier for the bold lad who had shared so fearlessly the deadliest of his many perils, was destined to produce, at no distant date, very strange and momentous results.

CHAPTER XVIII.

MOBBED BY MOHAMMEDANS.

'WELL, Lyoff, here we are in Meshid at last!'
'Here we are, Feodor, sure enough; and the next thing to do, I suppose, is to deliver the letter of introduction which Mr Barak-Ali, or whatever his name was, gave us in the train on our way to Odessa!'

The speakers were Mr Archer and Count Bulatoff, more than a thousand miles farther on their way since we saw them last, but still far, very far from the goal of their journey, and unconsciously on the eve of a series of fresh sufferings and dangers to which those that they had already encountered were as nothing.

But in the three weeks that had passed since their midnight shipwreck in the Caspian Sea (for it was now near the middle of September) the wanderers had seen many a strange sight and had many a strange adventure. They had beheld the massive white towers of the great cathedral of Astrakhan rising amid a forest of masts above the quiet, overpowering filthiness of the thick, greasy waters of the Volga. They had sighted, after a dreary coasting voyage of two days, the smooth landlocked basin of Mikhailoff Bay, and glided into it between the queer little timber town of Krasnovodsk,

straggling along a curving ridge on the north, and Fort
Mikhailovsk, perched on a bare, sandy promontory to the
south, from which, only a few years later, Russia's famous
'Trans-Caspian Railway' was to start on its long journey
over desert and mountain to the gates of Samarcand. Thence
our travellers had started south-eastward across the terrible
Khiva Desert (called by the natives 'Kara-Koom,' or Black
Sand), and had crossed at Moolah-Kari, fourteen miles from
their starting-point, the dry, stony gully through which the
mighty Oxus poured its waters into the Caspian ages ago,
ere a Mongol conqueror turned it away to the north, to fill
that huge, shallow foot-bath facetiously called 'the *Sea* of
Aral.'

More fortunate than the ill-fated Russian column which,
two years later, tried vainly to cross the same desert from the
Caspian in its fatal march upon Khiva (losing three-fourths
of its camels on the way), our travellers got safely to Kizil-
Arvat, and found a strong band of desert Turkomans encamped
in the crumbling ruins of the ancient Persian fortress, which,
then encircled by a vast and voiceless solitude, was so soon
to be stared out of countenance by a brand-new Russian railway station.

Fortunately for the two daring men (for robbery is one of
the fine arts with the Turkoman, who will steal a sewing-
machine or a Latin dictionary for the mere pleasure of taking
what is not his own), Count Bulatoff recognised in the leader
of this party, to his no small satisfaction, an old chief with
whom he had made friends in one of his former expeditions.
This 'father of the desert' was delighted to meet his Russian
friend once more, and regaled them both with a *sheet* of bread
six feet long by half-an-inch thick (which, as Archer said, the
baker must have shaped out by lying down and rolling on it),

several enormous bunches of dried grapes, the least of which would have been enough even for an English schoolboy, and a full measure of that curious gingerbeer-like liquid which is now so widely known by the name of *koumiss* (fermented mares' milk).

The meal over, the chief invited them to be his guests for the night; and the spectacle of the grim old ruin lighted up by the red glow of sunset, as it streamed through the countless clefts of the crumbling masonry upon the wild faces and picturesquely barbaric dress of the Turkomans, flitting ceaselessly to and fro amid the mouldering walls, formed a tableau worthy of Verestchagin himself.

Nor did the old warrior's kindness end here. When his guests took leave of him, he sent along with them one of the trustiest of his own followers, under whose escort they passed in safety the great robber-stronghold of Geok-Tepé, with its huge, clumsy walls of dried mud, through which were to pour in irresistible might, not many years later, the shouting soldiers of a then unknown Russian officer of the name of Skobeleff. Pressing on toward the north-eastern border of Persia, the two adventurers and their guide skirted the bleak ridges of the Kooran-Dagh, and crossing the range by a steep and difficult pass not far from Mahomedabad, came down at last —with beards worthy of a Turkish Pasha, and faces almost as brown as the swarthy Asiatics around them—into the wide sweep of bare upland in the midst of which, three thousand feet above the sea, stands the big, dirty, bustling town of Meshid or Mash-had, once the capital of Eastern Persia.

Their first proceeding was to install themselves in a huge, dreary, barrack-like building called by courtesy an 'inn,' though it offered them little beyond the mere shelter of its bare walls; for the cells that ran cloister-like along all four sides of its vast, bare, muddy courtyard were wholly innocent of furniture, and the old *khanjee* (innkeeper) would have laughed to scorn the unheard-of idea of *his* supplying the food and bedding that every guest was expected to bring along with him.

In this choice retreat Mr Archer sat down by himself— the count and his Turkoman having gone into the town to make some inquiries—to hold a review of their stores and camp-equipage, and see what damage had been done by their passage of the mountains.

But his worst fears fell short of the ghastly reality. The smoked sausages were 'all awash' with the contents of a broken phial of castor-oil, the fragments of which were fraternising with those of a box of army-biscuits. The flask of cold tea was standing on its head with the cork out, and mingling its last drop with that of a smashed ink-bottle in the middle of a map of Central Asia. The soda-powders were fast merging their identity in that of the too completely *pounded* sugar; and in the thickest of the tea (which pervaded everything like an impalpable essence) lay what appeared to be a bruised stick of chocolate.

'Come,' cried Archer, 'here's a chance of a new experiment in cookery; let us see how chocolate and tea will taste together. Here goes!' and the strangely-mingled ingredients went at once into his camp-kettle, which was almost the only thing left unshattered in the whole paraphernalia.

The water was not long in boiling, and Archer, having filled his wooden cup with the mixture, and sugared it to his liking, proceeded to drink.

The English globe-trotter had made trial of every kind of startling flavour in his time, from the ant-paste and bat-soup of South America to the 'Mogul tea' of Tartary, with salt for sugar and melted mutton-fat for milk; but never in all his life had he met with so nauseous and abominable a taste as that which startled him now. His first thought was that he was poisoned; but as he had done all the cooking with his own hands, it was hard to see how this could be. Then he thought that perhaps the cup itself might not be clean; so he flung away the remainder of the dose, and having thoroughly rinsed the cup, he refilled it from the kettle and tried again.

If the first 'brew' had been loathsome, the second was so infinitely worse that Archer threw *it* away at the first mouthful. But this time a curious *froth* at the bottom of the cup attracted his attention, and suggested a frightful suspicion, which was changed to certainty when he emptied out bodily the contents of the camp-kettle; for it then became only too evident that the supposed chocolate which he had just been mixing with his tea was neither more nor less than a piece of brown *soap!*

Just at that critical moment the stately form of the Turkoman guide appeared in the doorway.

One glance at the empty kettle, the half-melted soap, and the Englishman's convulsed features told the whole story to the keen-witted 'son of the desert;' and instantly this grave and dignified Asiatic (who looked as if he had never laughed in his life) threw himself flat on his back upon the floor, kicked up his heels in the air, and screamed and howled like a madman till his breath failed; after which he started up, and stood solemn and stately as ever, just as if it were some other man who had been making all this noise and *he* were quite ashamed of him!

Behind the Turkoman came Bulatoff, who was as prompt as he to take in the whole import of the situation; and all his fear of vexing Archer could not keep him from echoing, with all the power of his lungs, the laughter in which the Englishman good-humouredly joined.

But the news brought by the count soon made both men serious enough.

'That fellow Barak-Ali might well say that this brother of his, Ahmed Mirza, is well known in Meshid; for every ragamuffin in the bazaar seems to know his house as well as I know mine.'

'Is he a prince, then, or what? He ought to be, by his name.'*

'No, he's a sort of saint—the chief "holy man" of the place, in fact; and *they* often assume royal titles, you know. But, anyhow, prince or saint, he has the whole town at his beck and call, and can do just what he likes; so he might be a very useful ally to us, only that by ill-luck he is not at home now.'

'And when *will* he be at home, then?'

'Well, the people here say that he is to preside at some grand ceremony which is to take place here to-morrow, and that our best plan is to wait for him at the gate of the great mosque just about midday. But mind this, that we must be very careful how we deal with him; for if we happen to displease him in any way, he has only to say one word and we shall both be torn in pieces by the mob in less than half-a-minute.'

'Well, then, we must just hope that we *won't* happen to displease him,' said Archer as coolly as ever; 'but, whether or no, we will go and make his acquaintance to-morrow.'

---

* The word 'Mirza' placed *after* a Persian name has the meaning of 'prince;' when put before it, it means simply one who can read and write.

Punctually at noon on the following day, accordingly, the two friends and their Turkoman guide posted themselves, to await the coming of Ahmed Mirza, just *outside* the gate of the great mosque; for they knew well that it would be certain death to enter it under the eyes of the savage Mussulman zealots who were now flocking into it from every side.

But the less privileged Europeans were fain to content themselves with obtaining a passing glimpse, through the stately gateway, of the vast paved court within—one of the finest in all Persia. It was nearly five hundred feet square, and the towers and buildings that encircled it were all one blaze of many-coloured mosaics, flashed into countless rainbows by the dazzling sunlight that streamed over them; and far within—one great glow of shining splendour—stood the famous 'silver shrine' given to this holy place by Nadir Shah, one hundred and thirty years before, from the plunder of India.

'Not so many years ago,' said Archer to his comrade, 'my friend Eastwick, during his official residence in Persia, had a hairbreadth escape of his life in this very mosque; for, though the man who ushered him into it was one of the most powerful and venerated of their own priesthood, the mere sight of an "unbeliever" in the sacred place was quite enough for the orthodox rabble of the town, and if his friends had not smuggled him out by a back-way, there would not have been much left of him.'

'And it strikes me,' whispered the count, facing about as an ominous murmur in the crowd behind him caught his quick ear, 'that we shall stand a good chance of being served in the same way ourselves if this worthy Ahmed Mirza does not come soon; for, by the black looks of some of our Moslem friends here, I judge that they don't at all approve of our presence.'

Archer faced quickly round in his turn, and saw, not without some secret anxiety, that his friend was quite right.

Both men had been perfectly quiet, and had neither done nor said anything that could possibly be construed into a cause of offence; but the mere presence of two 'Western unbelievers' was quite sufficient to arouse the innate ruffianism of a Mohammedan mob, which is fully a match in brutal and ignorant ferocity for the lowest savage of Central Africa. Dark looks were cast at the two strangers by the foremost of the throng, while many of those behind were seen tightening their girdles and whispering excitedly to each other (always a bad sign in a Moslem crowd), and already a mutter of threatening words had begun to buzz through the mass of lowering faces, growing louder and louder every moment.

'What do these Feringhee (European) infidels here? This is no place for such as *them!*'

'Whose dogs are they, that they should presume to venture so near the holy shrine?'

'And to dare to plant themselves in the path of our sainted Ahmed Mirza, too—as if *they* were worthy to kiss the dust off his sacred feet?'

'Shall we suffer this, brothers? Shall we let the holy place be profaned by the presence of unbelieving dogs?'

Bulatoff's Turkoman follower had heard and understood, and drawing up shoulder to shoulder with the count, he loosened his short sword in its sheath with a business-like alacrity that made the nearest blackguards draw hastily back.

But though this menace cowed the rioters for a moment, it enraged them all the more; and the two travellers began to perceive, with inward dismay, that in bringing this wild ally along with them they had really done more harm than good.

Both had calculated, with some show of reason, that the presence of one who was unmistakably an Asiatic and a 'true believer' would be a kind of protection to them amid the fanatical mob that this ceremony was sure to draw together. But they had failed to take into consideration the rooted scorn of the free desert warrior for the inhabitants of cities, and the bitter hatred with which that scorn is always repaid.* Their warlike guide was evidently 'spoiling for a fight,' and, on the other side, the growing fury of the mob needed only the slightest additional impulse to make it break loose; and at that very moment the impulse came.

Through the thickest of the crowd came forcing his way roughly a half-naked, wild-looking native pilgrim, covered with dust and dirt, and clutching a heavy club. By ill-luck he emerged from the throng just at the spot where our two travellers were standing, and the moment he caught sight of them he shouted, or rather screamed:

'Who hath brought these Christian dogs hither? Let their faces be defiled with dirt, as they deserve!' and snatching up a lump of half-dried mud, he flung it full in the Englishman's face.

Till then Archer had controlled his temper admirably, though his British blood boiled at the coarse insolence of the vile creatures around him; but at this crowning insult prudence and self-command went to the winds together.

---

* Among the savage highlanders of the Persian border the word *shehcree* (man from the town) is habitually used as a term of the grossest abuse.

Springing forward like a roused lion, he wrenched the club from his assailant's hand, and with one smashing blow laid him senseless on the earth, with his jaw broken and his face covered with blood.

For an instant the yelling rascals around were startled into silence, and there was a visible backward heave all along the front rank of the crowd; but those behind, as they saw the pilgrim fall, broke forth in a burst of wolfish cries that made the air ring.

'Who dares to harm a holy pilgrim?'

'Down with the dog of an unbeliever!'

'Kill the infidels! Cut them in pieces! No mercy!'

Stones, potsherds, and lumps of hard clay began to fly like hail; knives and daggers flashed out on all sides; and, with one rush, the mass was upon the three forlorn men like a wave.

Three blows did Archer deal into the press, and each blow felled a man; while his Turkoman comrade, drawing his sword, sliced off at one stroke the ear of the nearest brawler, and sent a second reeling back, with his cheek cut open like an orange. Meanwhile the count had whipped out his revolver, and knowing the superstitious fear of these ignorant Asiatics for 'the-short-gun-that-goes-on-talking,' he sent a bullet through the turban of his foremost assailant, taking care, however, to avoid his head. Then, as the rabble of greasy scoundrels recoiled from the dreaded weapon, he shouted in a voice of thunder, through a momentary lull of the uproar:

'What means this? Who dares to molest *us*, the friends of the saintly Ahmed Mirza?'

The last words fell like a thunderbolt upon the savages around him, who exchanged blank looks of doubt and dismay;

and the foremost rioter, lowering his uplifted club, faltered out:

'Say'st thou, O Christian, that ye are friends of Ahmed Mirza, the holy one?'

'It is a true word, though an evil mouth hath spoken it,' said the Russian sternly. 'To visit *him* are we come hither, and to bring him a letter from his brother, even from Barak Ali, who dwelleth afar off in the land of the Oorooss (Russian). Behold the letter! And if there be any man among ye who can read, let him come forward and see whose name is written thereon.'

There was a momentary pause, and then a grave-looking, elderly man, in the dress of a native trader, stepped forth from the throng and looked keenly at the letter that Bulatoff held out toward him.

'Children,' said he in a faltering tone, 'methinks this unbeliever speaks truly; for the name on this letter is indeed that of our saintly Ahmed Mirza—may it be ever fragrant as sweet incense!'

'And in very deed, brothers,' put in a bare-limbed porter beside him, 'the taller of these two Kafirs (infidels) is the very man who asked me yester-night, in the bazaar, where Ahmed Mirza's house was to be found.'

'Tush!' cried a brawny butcher fiercely; 'will ye let these infidels laugh at your beards with lies? How could any Christian dog ever be a friend of the holy Ahmed Mirza?'

A low growl ran through the mob, and the attack seemed about to be renewed, when all at once a strange voice said from behind:

'Who hath spoken my name? If any man have need of Ahmed Mirza, Ahmed Mirza is here.'

The voice that spoke was as quiet and gentle as a summer breeze; but the loudest thunder-clap could not have had a more appalling effect on this rabble of grimy scoundrels. Intent on their fell work, they had never noticed the parting of the crowd behind them; and as in the East the coming of a great man is always greeted with a reverent silence, instead of the lusty cheers of Western races, none of them were aware of Ahmed Mirza's approach till he was actually in the midst of them.

There he stood—one solitary, quiet old man, in a flowing robe (hardly whiter than the long, silky beard that streamed over it) and a green turban, the badge of his descent from the Prophet Mohammed himself.

In height he was but little, if at all, above most of those around him; but, standing erect amid the savages who crouched and cringed before him, he seemed to tower over the whole throng like a giant. And as he stood there alone, looking calmly round upon the wild faces and brandished weapons that hemmed him in, he might well have been taken for some great enchanter of Eastern legend, turning to stone with one potent word the contending hosts of a battlefield.

Amid the universal hush of dismay, Count Bulatoff, to the visible terror of his assailants, stepped up to Ahmed Mirza with a friendly salute, and handed him Barak Ali's letter. The other opened and read it, and then faced round upon the shrinking brawlers with a look before which the fiercest of them cowered like beaten curs.

'What is this that ye have done?' said he in a voice which, low as it was, seemed to sweep through the silent and trembling multitude like the rush of a mighty wind. 'Do ye dare to lift your hands against the strangers who have come hither in peace, under *my* protection? Will ye that I let fall my curse upon you, and'——

What was to happen *then* the terrified rioters did not wait to hear, for ere he could utter a word more they were all wallowing in the dust at his feet.

'Spare us, O saintly one! Lay not thy curse upon us, or we are lost! Forgive our misdeed, O noble strangers, and plead for us with the holy one, that he curse us not!'

And, in their agony of superstitious terror, the ignorant savages clasped entreatingly the feet of the very men whom they had just been trying to murder!

'It is enough—I forgive you,' said Ahmed; 'but beware that ye offend not again. And mark this, these Christians are *my friends*, and he who shall dare to harm them in any wise, whether by word or deed, it were better for him that he had never been born!'

The scared faces of the listeners showed how fully they believed his words. Not a few slunk away home without entering the mosque, as if fearing that their saint might change his mind and curse them after all; and those who remained made way for the two 'unbelieving dogs' as reverently as for Ahmed Mirza himself.

'On my head be it, O friends of my brother,' went on Ahmed, turning to the travellers, 'that none can grieve more than I that ye should have been so treated by true believers in the city where I dwell; but be assured that whatever service I can do you to make amends shall be given as freely as Allah giveth His rain from heaven.'

The old Moslem was as good as his word. During the rest of their stay in Meshid they were, as Archer said with a grin, 'the kings of the whole place;' and when they set off again—having sent back to his tribe, with their warmest thanks and a goodly array of presents, the friendly Turkoman who had followed them so far—they were attended by a skilful guide from Chinese Tartary, placed at their disposal by Ahmed Mirza, and pledged on the Koran to pilot them safely through the wild 'No Man's Land' which lies between China, Afghanistan, and Asiatic Russia.

CHAPTER XIX.

MEETING A HIGHLAND CHIEF.

HARRY ARCHER'S ride on the runaway engine was his last adventure for several days to come; for the fall had wrenched his ankle so violently as to cripple him outright for the time being. This mishap was all the more provoking, since it delayed their departure for General Naprashkin's house in the Western Caucasus, whither Harry, having by this time seen all that there was to see in Tiflis, was now eager to return. But there was no help for it, and our impetuous hero was fain to bear the delay with what patience he possessed—that is to say, with none at all.

Nor was this the only disappointment in store for him; for on the very first day when he was able to walk abroad the general came to breakfast with an open letter in his hand, and said, with a compassionate glance at the boy's eager face:

'I fear you will get tired of waiting for me to start, my friend Harry; but it seems that our journey to Byelaya-Gora (the general's residence) will have to be put off once more. The fact is that I have just got a letter from the Viceroy saying that the Servian Patriarch* and a friend

---

* This ecclesiastical dignity has no exact equivalent in our Church, being something between a bishop and an archbishop. The now historical visit of the Servian Patriarch to Russia really took place in 1867, when I met him at St Petersburg.—D. K.

of his are just about to visit Tiflis, and that, as there is no one else to entertain them and show them round the place in his absence, he wishes *me* to do it.'

'As if there was no other time for these bothering fellows to come here,' muttered our hero discontentedly, 'that they must come just at this particular time and spoil our trip!'

But the Russian visit of the Patriarch and his 'friend' (of whom the English boy was destined to see and hear a good deal more yet) was fated to have other and more important results than the spoiling of Harry's trip; for it was the first link in a chain of events that were to startle all Europe, and to culminate, only a few years later, in the Servian outbreak against Turkey, the 'Bulgarian atrocities,' and the great Russo-Turkish war of 1877. But all this was still in the future, and little did the bold lad dream, as he growled at this fresh postponement of his expected journey, that that very postponement was soon to connect *him* with events which would hereafter fill many pages in the history of the world.

Harry Archer's first impulse when anything whatever went wrong with him was to indulge in a burst of violent exercise, or, as he said, to 'work it off;' and so, finding his damaged foot equal to a walk, he started out as soon as the meal was over, and was right in the midst of the 'Persian quarter' ere he took the trouble to think where he was going.

All at once a clamour of hoarse voices drew his attention to a crowd a little farther up the street, in the midst of which (as our young athlete was quick to perceive) two men were wrestling.

One of the two was a tall, lanky fellow in a soiled white

jacket, evidently a Cossack soldier, though somewhat more shambling and 'weedy' than is usual with those born athletes. The other (who plainly had with him the sympathies of the crowd) was fully half a head shorter, but square, thick-set, and brawny as Friar Tuck himself; and Harry's father would have recognised him at a glance as one of the formidable Bashkirs of Central Asia, whom France knew to her cost in the great invasion of 1814.

Just as Harry came up they closed for the second time, and at first it seemed as if the Cossack would have the best of it; but he had put forth his full strength too soon, and speedily began to give way before his adversary's superior weight and muscle. Feeling his danger, the Russian made a desperate effort, and succeeded in tripping his opponent; but the Mussulman cleverly recovered himself, and, with a mighty heave, hoisted White-jacket right off his feet and brought him to the ground with a dull crash, falling heavily upon him, amid the clamorous applause of the Moslem spectators.

'So let it be with all infidels!' cried the Bashkir (evidently a Mohammedan of the old school), stroking his thick black beard complacently, with a scornful glance after his late antagonist, who limped away abashed. 'When there is fair-play, assuredly no Christian dog can stand against a true believer!'

'Are you quite sure of that?' asked a voice from behind, which, though perfectly calm, had in its deep, mellow tones a stern impressiveness that made every one start.

Harry faced round like the rest, and his eyes remained fixed on the new-comer with a look of wondering admiration which was certainly not without cause; for never before (though the last few months had introduced him to a perfect gallery of striking figures) had he looked upon such a man as this.

The stranger, though a giant in strength and stature, was so splendidly proportioned that only by noticing how far he overtopped the tallest men around him could one estimate truly his magnificent height. His face was a model of manly beauty, though a keen observer might have read something menacing and terrible in the firm setting of the lips beneath the heavy black moustache, and the quick, piercing glance of the large, bright eye.

His dress was as striking as himself—a long white coat, left open to display a crimson vest richly embroidered with gold; a gaudy sash of various gay colours; sky-blue knickerbockers; snow-white stockings; strong shoes, or rather sandals, laced with gold thread; and a black *biretta* (round flat cap) with a crimson top.

In cool blood the swaggering Bashkir might not have fancied an encounter with this brawny giant; but now, emboldened by his victory and put on his mettle by the presence of so many lookers-on, he turned sharply upon him and said insolently :

'Hast thou a mind to try thy strength against mine that thou speakest thus?'

'I have,' replied the unknown curtly. 'Come on!'

And, without another word, they closed in a desperate grapple.

The Bashkir had science as well as muscle, and twice brought into play a wrestling-trick which, with such strength to back it, would have laid low any ordinary man; but the stranger, too, was no novice in the sport, and, though shaken, still kept his feet. The Moslem was just making a third effort, into which he threw his whole strength, when all at once (no one could tell how, so quickly was it done) his feet flew from under him, and he shot away like a rocket, not only across the street, but right through the window (luckily open) of a butcher's shop, where he made a 'cannon' off the butcher and his son, and all three came to the ground in a crumpled heap, overwhelmed with an avalanche of raw mutton!

There was an instant rush of the dismayed crowd toward the prostrate man, for it seemed hardly possible that any one should sustain such a fall without harm to life or limb. It took some time to ascertain that the Bashkir, though stunned and badly bruised, was not dangerously hurt; and when they at length turned to look for the unknown victor, he was gone.

Harry set off home at once, eager to tell this adventure; but on the way he met his friend Prince Shervashidze, who was just back from a term of duty in the hills. The Prince's quarters being close by, he invited our hero in; and both had so much to tell and to hear that it was well on in the afternoon ere the boy reached home.

Entering the drawing-room in his usual headlong fashion, he found General Naprashkin engaged with two visitors. The one was an elderly man of dignified aspect (in a large, brown, monk-like robe, over which his long silky hair flowed down almost to the jewelled crucifix on his breast), whom Harry afterwards found to be the Servian Patriarch himself; but in the other he recognised at a glance the hero of the wrestling-bout, and was not a little surprised to hear him announced by the general as 'Danilo Petrovitch, a relation of the reigning Prince of Montenegro.'

'Well,' cried Harry, with his usual outspoken frankness, 'if the Prince himself is anything like his relation, he ought to be well able to keep his people in order!'

And then he proceeded to explain this blunt comment by a full-length account of the Montenegrin's recent exploit, to which both Naprashkin and the Patriarch listened with marked approval.

Our hero had read and heard so much of the warlike highlanders of Montenegro that he was overjoyed to fall in with one of them at last, and to meet with a genuine 'Highland chief' so far from the scene of Sir Walter Scott's imperishable portraits. The English schoolboy and the Montenegrin warrior struck up a friendship on the spot; and during the next few days Danilo, pleased to find a stranger so much interested in *his* native land, told his young comrade so many stirring tales of the strange national customs of this miniature Scotland, its giant warriors and grim precipices and pathless mountains, its hunting-parties and winter marches through the snow, its ceaseless battles with the savage Albanians and Bosniaks, and its long and gallant resistance to the swarming hosts of the Turk, that Harry secretly made up his mind to persuade his father (as soon as the latter came back from the East) to go and see Montenegro at once, and take *him* along with him.

But this question was fated to be settled for our hero sooner than he expected, and in a widely different way.

One afternoon, when the general came back from showing the Patriarch and his Montenegrin friend over the town Museum (where both were much interested in the oyster-shaped human skulls that had just been dug up in making the new railway), he found a big, official-looking letter awaiting him, which he read with an air of very unwonted excitement.

'Here's a chance for you, Master Harry!' cried he. 'The Emperor wishes to send a special envoy to Montenegro, and he has been good enough to pick *me* out as the man. I am to go back with Prince Danilo when *he* goes; and if you like to join us, I'll take you.'

'And I need hardly add, Monsieur Henri,' said Danilo Petrovitch heartily, 'that if you care to visit my country, you may be sure of a real Montenegrin welcome!'

'Oh, Dmitri Ivânovitch! will you *really* take me?' cried the boy, hardly able to credit such overwhelming good fortune.

'Well, as a rule, I don't care to be cumbered with boys on an expedition,' said the blunt old soldier; 'but I saw that *you* were one of the right sort on that day when the train ran away with us at Nikolsk, and if you like to go with us, go you shall.'

Harry's face grew radiant; but it clouded again as he asked:

'And what about Yury?'

'Oh, Yury shall go too,' said the general. 'I've always thought he would be all the better of a little " roughing," as you call it; and this is just a good chance for him to get it. Besides, I really don't know with whom I could leave him if he *didn't* go, for I shall be away some time. So, as soon as Prince Danilo and his holiness here are ready to start, we'll all be off together.'

And off they went, sure enough, the very next week.

CHAPTER XX.

THE PHANTOM CITY.

ORNING on the Upper Sir-Daria—one of those splendid October mornings that seem to revive midsummer in the end of autumn. In the glory of the brightening sunrise the wide, smooth sweep of the great river shines like silver between its low, grassy banks. To the north-west, far as eye can reach, the gray, dreary, unending level of the 'Hungry Steppe' stretches away into the dim distance. On the opposite side, the shadowy mass of the great mountain-rampart that walls off China from Russian Turkestan hovers like a cloud along the eastern sky; and in the foreground of the picture, above a dark, glossy belt of rich semi-tropical vegetation, stand up like sentinels two tall, white, slender towers, marking the spot where, amid its countless gardens, lies, 'like a sleeping child cradled in roses' (as a Persian poet has truly said), the charming little town of Khojend—the farthest point reached by Alexander the Great in his conquering march through Bactria two thousand years ago.

Early as it is, the usually silent and lonely river-bank is now humming like a hive with all the life and bustle of a passing caravan on its way from the south to Tashkand, the capital of Russian Turkestan. Around the huge, clumsy,

M

iron-bound raft which, towed by a rope made fast from bank to bank,* does duty as a ferry-boat, flat caps and white turbans, red shirts and loose mantles, high boots and broad-toed sandals, are coming and going like bees. In the background the big, roomy tents of gray felt and the charred circles of extinct camp-fires mark the scene of last night's bivouac; and beyond them the camels are feeding side by side with the wiry little Tartar horses, or lying crouched, with their long pipe-like necks outstretched upon the warm, dry earth, in lazy enjoyment.

But it is now time to start, and for a brief space the habitual indolence of the Asiatic gives place to a spasm of unwonted activity. To work go one and all to prepare for their journey, in the old traditional fashion that has not changed one whit since Abraham mustered *his* caravan to go down into Egypt forty centuries ago. Ropes are knotted and noosed; bales, boxes, and casks dragged hither and thither; the Tartars catch and saddle their hardy little horses, gaunt, sinewy, and untiring as the wolves of their native wilds; and three or four lean, brown, piratical-looking fellows, who have been paddling in the river, hurry on what few clothes they have, and hasten to join the throng.

And now, at the signal-cry of 'Tchok!' the camels double up their long shambling legs like a foot-rule, and lie flat on the ground, while their masters place a square wooden frame on the hump, and then proceed to cord to it bundle after bundle and chest after chest, till a short, angry grunt from the independent animal warns them to beware of that 'last straw' which proverbially 'breaks the camel's back.'

But who are these two stalwart figures in white forage-caps,

---

* When I reached Khojend two years later a bridge was being built across the river at this spot.—D. K.

knee-high boots, and ragged linen jackets, with faces which, sunburned as they are, are too light for any Asiatic? Surely we have seen them somewhere before, and their Tartar attendant too, though all three are sorely changed since they took leave of Ahmed Mirza at Meshid, only a few short weeks ago, on their way to cross the Desert of Merv, pass the Oxus at Tchardjui, and work north-eastward through Bokhara toward the Tian-Shan (Celestial) Mountains of the Chinese border.

'Well, Lyoff, here's the first half of our work done, anyhow.'

'Yes, you've surveyed the route of your proposed desert-railway from the Caspian Sea to the Oxus, sure enough, though I suspect you will find it harder to make than to plan. But if, as you say, you mean to search through the Tian-Shan Mountains till you find a place to establish a direct caravan-route right through them into Western China, it strikes me that the hardest part of your work is still to come.'

'Very likely; but it *may* turn out easier than it looks, after all. By far the most difficult part of the work was done when we got the Chinese Government to agree to it; and, moreover, I've always had an idea that such a route *did* exist there once upon a time, somewhere or other, and that, if we were only to look carefully enough, we might find some traces of it still.'

'With all respect to your greater experience, my dear Feodor, I don't think *that* very probable. You and I have both been a good deal about in those parts, and we have never found any traces of it yet. Moreover, if the hunt is to be a long one, so much the worse for *us;* for we are in the third week of October already, and *you* know what travelling through those mountains in winter means better than I can tell you.'

'True enough; and I must say I wish his Majesty had hit upon this idea a little earlier in the year, or that, having hit upon it, he had chosen a different season for carrying it out. However, it is no use to say anything about that now; orders are orders, and must be obeyed. But what does this fellow want?'

'This fellow' was a gaunt, long-armed, monkey-like creature, whose round, yellow face, half-buried in a huge, shapeless, goatskin cap, looked very much like a half-boiled pudding escaping from its bag. For some minutes past he had been observing, with a close though stealthy attention, not only themselves, but their Tartar henchman likewise; and just at that moment he came slouching forward and addressed them.

'Have my lords any need of a guide?' asked he in tolerable Russian, but with a strange snuffling accent. 'If my lords are minded to go up into the eastern mountains which border Kitai (China), their servant knoweth those mountains well, and would gladly guide the noble Khans thither.'

Archer, annoyed at this interruption, was just about to tell the intruder, in no sugared terms, that they had a guide already; but a warning gesture from the count, so slight that no eye less keen than his own would have noticed it at all, checked the words on his lips.

'We thank thee, friend,' said Bulatoff to the Mongol, 'and had we need of a guide, assuredly we would not slight thine offer; but now that we have joined this caravan we need none.'

'Go my lords to Tashkand, then?' asked the other, with a momentary look of disappointment at which the wily Russian inwardly chuckled. 'I had thought that they might be bound for the hills.'

'Do men travel through the hills, then, when *winter* is nigh?' rejoined the count, with a slight smile at the absurdity of the idea.

And then he began to ask various questions about the time that it would take them to reach Tashkand, the risk of bad weather on the journey, and, above all, the chances of finding the way unsafe from thence to Semipalatinsk; for, the Russian conquest of Central Asia having been completed barely three years before, the whole country was still in a very unsettled state.

Archer listened with some surprise, for he knew well that his friend had as much idea of going to Semipalatinsk (a border-town of Siberia, far out of their present route) as he had of going to the moon. But the shrewd Englishman easily guessed that his wary comrade, mistrusting this man's honesty, wished to mislead him as to their intended journey; and this suspicion was confirmed when they found themselves alone again a few minutes later.

'That fellow's one of the Khan of Ala-Tau's men,' said the count, 'and they are all robbers to their finger-tips. I should not wonder if that fellow is spying upon us yet, and we must contrive to give him the slip some time to-day, before he can bring down his comrades on us.'

Accordingly, as soon as the caravan halted for its midday rest, the two men and their Tartar, under cover of some low brushwood, glided off to a little distance, and then, finding themselves to all appearance unobserved, struck away northeastward over the plain toward the distant mountains.

'There must be some ill-luck,' laughed the count, 'in this Persian dagger which that brigand gave to my boy Yury.

Having belonged to a robber, I suppose it attracts to me all kinds of rogues, as moths are drawn to a candle.'

And Bulatoff was to have still better cause to say so ere that day was over.

The vast plain that stretched before them, right up to the foot of the great mountain-wall, though not· wholly without traces of cultivation, was almost as voiceless and lonely as the formidable 'Hungry Steppe' itself; for in this wild border-land, where the might of Russia had not yet had time to make itself felt, there was not sufficient security for life and property to tempt either agriculture or commerce. But it was not long ere they came upon a startling proof that this strange region, however dreary and deserted it might be now, had once been far different.

The sun was already touching the horizon, and the wide, bare plain looked vaster and drearier than ever beneath the creeping dimness of night, when suddenly a deeper and darker shadow started up right in front of them—misty and impalpable at first, but growing more solid with every moment.

As they approached, it shaped itself into a huge oblong wall, as high and massive as the rampart of Samarcand itself; but over the whole place brooded a dreary silence, an air of utter lifelessness and decay, which contrasted weirdly with its grand proportions. As the last gleam of sunset flashed it into sudden light, they could see that the mighty walls were gaping with unnumbered clefts, that the gateway itself was well-nigh blocked with heaps of ruins, and that throughout the whole of the vast interior there was no living thing.

'Just what we want!' cried the count. 'In the open plain we should be at the mercy of any thieves who might pass; but behind these walls we can hold our own against an army. Let us camp here for the night.'

This idea was evidently not at all to the taste of the Tartar guide, who, having a firm belief in the grim, native legends that peopled such ruins with demons and evil things of every kind, had no fancy to venture among them at nightfall, and in the company of two 'unbelievers.' But when the count dexterously reminded him that no evil thing could possibly harm any friend of the holy Ahmed Mirza, he plucked up heart again, and followed the pair into the ruins as boldly as ever.

Just within the great gateway was a small chamber, or rather recess, which had probably served as the guardroom or porter's lodge of this ghostly fortress. Here the three established themselves and their horses for the night, and their first care was to make a blazing fire of dry brushwood, having learned to their cost that at that season there is often a difference of *thirty degrees* between the temperature of the day and that of the night. This done, they blocked up the narrow entrance with several armfuls of briars, and then made a hearty supper by the fire; after which—Archer having offered to take the first watch—the other two lay down to sleep.

The Englishman's watch passed without any alarm, and his Tartar henchman's was equally uneventful. Midnight was long past and the dawn already at hand, when Count Bulatoff, standing sentry in his turn, heard a slight noise outside, which might be the creeping tread of a wild beast, but sounded to *him* more like the stealthy step of a man.

Noiselessly as a shadow the wary Russian drew out his revolver, and lying down on the earth so as to get the doorway between him and the sky, waited to see what would happen. Presently there came a slight rustling and crackling among the briars that blocked the entrance, and the faint light of the dying fire showed to Bulatoff, framed in the opening, the dim outline of a man's figure, surmounted with a big, shapeless cap!

Crack went the pistol, and the phantom vanished with a sharp cry, which told the count that he had not fired in vain.

Snatching a brand from the fire, the Russian darted in pursuit, closely followed by his two comrades, who, aroused by the shot, needed no one to tell them what was going on. They hunted in vain, however, for their mysterious visitor; but just outside the doorway of their retreat they found a rough *goatskin cap*.

'Just as I thought,' said the count. 'That Ala-Tau rogue did not believe what I told him about our being bound for Tashkand, and he must have seen us slip away from the caravan, and have dogged us here. Well, I'm sorry he has slipped through our fingers; but, at all events (pointing to several dark stains on the grayish-yellow sand), he has had a pretty good hint not to meddle with *us* again.'

CHAPTER XXI.

ESCORTED BY THIEVES.

AFTER such an awakening none of the pilgrims felt inclined to sleep again; and before daylight they were on their way once more, in the hope of slipping off ere their prowling foes were ready to pounce upon them. But in this they were reckoning without their host; for hardly had they gone a mile, when the first beam of sunrise showed them a strong body of horsemen trotting leisurely toward them across the plain, with long guns slung across their backs and glittering lances in their hands!

Archer at once unslung his rifle with a business-like air; for he saw that one and all wore goatskin caps like that of their late visitor, and guessed instantly that these were the comrades to whom the spy had meant to betray them.

'These are the men of Ala-Tau—true servants of Shaitaun (Satan), every man of them!' muttered the guide, making ready *his* gun with equal promptness. 'We must fight for our lives, noble Agas (gentlemen), for these unsainted thieves know not the word *amaun!*' (peace).

'Keep still for your lives!' said the count in a low, emphatic tone. 'Let your weapons alone, and just leave it all to me!'

And then, knotting a white scarf to the end of his sheathed dagger, he held it aloft like a flag, and riding forward alone toward the advancing horsemen (who were now seen to be fully thirty strong), called out to them in their own language, in a tone of friendly greeting:

'Peace be with you, my friends!'

At such a salutation, offered by one unprotected traveller to a gang of robbers who were just about to fall upon him, the cut-throats halted in sheer amazement, and looked blankly at each other without making any reply.

'Ye are the warriors of the great Khan of Ala-Tau—is it not so?' went on the Russian as confidently as ever. 'Then he hath doubtless sent you to escort us to his sublime presence; for we bring him gifts from the Czar of Ooroosistan (Russia), who has heard the fame of his renown, and would make a league of friendship with him. Truly a lucky star shone upon us when we came hither to meet you; for your company will be as a strong wall to us in this unsainted wilderness, where robbers are as plentiful as summer flies. Lo! it was but yesternight that we were attacked, but Allah was with us.'

Not without an effort did Bulatoff keep up this bold and commanding tone, for just as he mentioned the attack of the past night his keen eye detected in the ranks of the Mongols the very man by whom that attack had been made, with his right arm bound up and in a sling from the effect of the count's shot! But the crafty Russian looked profoundly unconscious, and pretended not to have noticed him at all.

'We know nought of all this, O stranger!' said the leader of the party, with a hesitating and confused air. 'When we left the presence of the Khan nothing had been heard of your coming.'

'Ha! Then the messenger whom I sent to announce it hath been delayed!' cried the count, with an admirably-feigned air of surprise and vexation. 'But it matters little, now that we have fortunately met *you*. Turn your horses, then, brothers, and bring us quickly before the face of the great Khan, since he is expecting us.'

All this while Archer and the guide, not understanding the language in which this talk was held, were awaiting impatiently the explanation which Bulatoff was in no hurry to give; for, in truth, the wily count was well pleased that his friend *should* know nothing of what was going on, rightly judging that the idea of being mixed up with such a tissue of barefaced falsehoods would have been simply intolerable to the fearless and straightforward Englishman, and that, in his indignation, he might easily have betrayed them all.

But Bulatoff's trick, sly and underhand as it was, was completely successful; for the savages of Central Asia, though the sharpest of the sharp within the bounds of their own narrow experience, are helpless as children in the face of anything that they do not understand. To these ignorant ruffians the count's story seemed perfectly plausible. Ignorant as they were, they knew that Russia had conquered all Turkestan up to the very skirts of their mountains; and they had sense enough to realise that the power which had crunched like a nut the whole strength of Kokan and Bokhara would make very short work of them and their Khan. Moreover, they were well aware that the Russian Government was then sending embassies to many of the still independent native princes of Tartary; and what more natural than that such an embassy should be sent to their Khan, and that the messenger despatched to announce its coming should have arrived just after their departure? If this were so, their prince must indeed be expecting these men, and it was, of course, out of the question to offer them any violence, or even to delay their journey. And, moreover, if there were anything wrong with the story which Bulatoff had told, that was the Khan's business, not theirs; all that *they* had to do was to conduct the strangers to his presence.

Actuated by such feelings, the robbers gave a friendly welcome to the very men whom they had just been about to spear; and their captain offered his hand to the count, uttering in his turn, 'Peace be with you!' as gravely as if he had never had a thought of harming him. This done, the band closed around the travellers like a guard of honour, and away they all went together.

'I've told these fellows,' explained the count in English to the wondering Archer, 'that we are going to visit their Khan—as indeed we are, for to pass through his country without paying our compliments to him would be the shortest way to get all our throats cut—and *they* are to escort us till we reach him!'

Archer, having no suspicion of the real state of the case, chuckled not a little at the grim humour of thus turning the very men who had come forth to rob them into a guard against robbers. As for the stoical Tartar guide, he took his place among his new comrades without a sign of emotion.

But the Russian, as if bent upon being on the safe side, ranged boldly up alongside of the wounded marauder, and looking with well-feigned pity at the bandaged arm that his own bullet had disabled, said in a friendly tone :

'Thou hast been wounded, I see, comrade; let me offer thee consolation.'

The 'consolation' took the form of a twist of tobacco from Bulatoff's own pouch; and the cut-throat, after three or four whiffs of such a delicacy as he had seldom enjoyed, said with an air of marked approval :

'May Allah reward thee! This is indeed fit for a king! But why did my lord tell me that he was bound for Tashkand ?'

'How knew I that thou wert not a robber thyself, seeking to betray me to the swords of thy fellows?' replied the count, with perfect gravity. 'Assuredly there were many such in yon caravan. Hath not the wise man said, "He who telleth his business to strangers is a fool!"'

And the other savages, who had evidently heard the whole story already, applauded this diplomatic reply with a hearty laugh.

All that day they rode eastward, and ere night fell they had got fairly in among the hills, and the keen wind that came sweeping down from the higher mountains made our three pilgrims glad of the thick native cloaks, or rather blankets, with which they had provided themselves in Bokhara. Ere dawn they were off again, and during the whole of the next day and part of the ensuing night they kept getting deeper and deeper into the heart of the wild mountains, which shut them in on every side with an endless maze of bare, bleak uplands, dark peaks, frowning precipices, gloomy forests, roaring torrents, and black, tomb-like ravines, such as can hardly be found elsewhere in all Asia.

At length, a little after sunrise on the third morning of this strange ride, the Mongol leader pointed to a grayish-white spot far up the side of a dark, rocky ridge in front of them, and said impressively :

'Lo! the city of the great Khan!'

Brave as Bulatoff was, his heart beat quicker at the words,

which told him that he was about to enter the presence of a savage to whom mercy was unknown, and that one short hour more would decide the fate of himself and his comrades. All now depended on his being able to support to the end the character that he had so boldly assumed; for he knew well that, if once unmasked, they had nothing to expect but the cruellest death that Asiatic ferocity could devise.

Half-an-hour later the 'city' of the great Khan burst upon them in all the splendour of its twenty tiny mud-hovels, and its crowds of three or four people, perched on a precipitous ledge of rock. Midway along this shelf, like the citadel of this primitive metropolis, stood a rude wall of dried clay, enclosing an irregular terrace, in the centre of which rose a big, clumsy round tower of the same material, flanked by two smaller ones.

Beneath a kind of porch before the central tower, guarded by several dirty-looking spearmen, whose foul rags no decent scarecrow would have worn, sat a figure which Bulatoff rightly guessed to be the worthy Khan himself, whose round, fat face, small, dull eye, and broad, thick, slightly up-turned nose made him look so extremely like a monstrous pig squatting on its hams that Archer and the count, in spite of the deadly peril in which they stood, had hard work to keep from laughing outright.

But it was no time for laughter now; and when the Mongol captain had announced the visitors, and had received the Khan's gracious leave to 'permit them to kiss his feet,' the count stepped forward in turn, and, with a dignified bow, delivered the message with which he pretended to be charged—namely, that the Czar of Ooroosistan had heard the fame of the great Khan of Ala-Tau, and, wishing to make a league of friendship with him, had sent to him two of his warriors, with such gifts as one king might offer to another.

The royal Tom-Thumb of Ala-Tau (who, like most 'little great men,' thought himself very great indeed) was vastly pleased at this flattering compliment, and, with a condescending air which again put Bulatoff's gravity to a severe test, replied that he accepted the friendship of his brother-Khan in the West, and was ready to receive his presents.

The Russian, prepared for this, at once produced, as the gifts sent by the Czar, a small silver chain, an ivory-handled dirk-knife, a bright-coloured sash of flowered silk, a pocket-mirror in a smart scarlet case, and a beautifully embroidered pouch filled with the tobacco so highly approved by his friend the robber.

The first sniff of it filled this royal hog with delight; but he was still more enraptured with the mirror (the first, probably, that he had ever seen), and surveyed his own ugly visage in it with a self-satisfied smirk that tried once more the gravity of the two Europeans.

The count drew a long breath of relief, thinking that the peril was now past, and that they were saved. But he was fated to learn, to his cost, that a good deal of low cunning may exist in the mind of a fool; for just then the Khan asked pointedly, with a sharp, suspicious look in his small, gray, piggish eyes :

'Hath not the Khan of the Russians sent me a *letter* along with these gifts? I have heard that he hath done so to the other princes of our land ; and surely he would never pass over ME !'

For one moment the Russian's bold heart seemed to stand still, for now it did indeed appear as if all were over with him. The supposed gifts he could supply (as we have seen) from his own stock; but the *letter*—how was that to be represented?

For an instant he actually thought, in his desperation, of presenting the autograph letter given him by the Czar, which might easily be palmed upon savages who could not read; but after being thumbed by countless postmasters and petty officials, it was now so torn and soiled that even such a blockhead as this Khan could not be deceived by it. What was to be done?

All at once a brilliant idea struck him, and bowing to the Khan, he said quietly:

'Thou sayest truly, O Khan; such an affront could never be offered to *thee;* but it is ever our custom to give the presents first. Permit me now to lay the letter before thee.'

While at Meshid the count had received a letter from a cousin at St Petersburg describing the first public appearance of a young violinist in whom Bulatoff was interested, and enclosing the programme of a concert at the Alexander Opera-house, in which the young man's name figured. This letter he had preserved as the last communication that he was likely to have from the civilised world for some time; and now, while feigning to rummage in his pouch for the precious document, he took out of its cover the Czar's autograph commission, dexterously slipped into its place the *concert programme* (printed on fine gilt-edged paper, and adorned with the Russian Double-Eagle), and hastily closing it up, presented to the expectant Khan the big official envelope, which, with its huge red seal, looked very grand and imposing to the eyes of this ignorant barbarian.

The Khan opened it, took out the programme, and

eyeing it for a moment very much as a monkey might do in the same case, bade the guards call his *mirza* (secretary).

Once more the Russian's blood ran cold, for if this precious secretary were able to read Russian the trick would be discovered at once, and they would all be lost. But the thin, supple, crafty-looking Persian renegade who came at the summons inspected the so-called *letter* with perfect gravity, and did not seem to find anything wrong.

In fact, the worthy secretary, though unable to read Russian, had more than once had occasion, in his own country, to spell out the Czar's name on some official document; and so, when he saw the big 'ALEKSANDR' figuring beneath the well-known Double-Eagle, he could hardly be expected to guess that it denoted, not the Emperor Alexander, but the Alexander Opera-house.

'The letter is a true one, O King of the Mountains,' said he, with a low bow to the Khan, 'for it beareth the name of the Russian Czar.'

'It is well,' said the Khan majestically; 'let my ears be filled with his words.'

And the count, taking the concert programme reverently in his hands, read from it, with perfect gravity, an imaginary letter of florid compliments and good wishes, to which the worthy Khan listened with a fat self-complacency wonderful to behold. Having finished this impromptu, Bulatoff kissed the programme with the deepest respect, and handed it back to the secretary!

The victory was won at last. The supposed envoys were received with all honour, and the precious programme was respectfully placed in the Khan's private treasury, where the Russian soldiers found it when they captured the place a year later.

CHAPTER XXII.

THE BLACK MOUNTAINEERS.

EANWHILE Harry and his chum were having some equally picturesque if less perilous experiences, as may be seen by the following letter:

TSEITINJE, MONTENEGRO, *Nov.* 5, 1871.

DEAR DAD,—I don't know if you'll ever get this, for I fancy there are not many posts where you've gone to; but in case you do, I want to tell you that the general, like an old brick as he is, has taken me with him to Montenegro, just as he said he would; and here we all are at last, in the queerest little capital in all Europe, and in the midst of a country queerer still. It's just like *Jack and the Bean-stalk* over again—you climb up three thousand feet to the very top of the mountains, and there you find a new country right up in the air, with lakes and houses and villages and rivers, all complete!

I've made great friends with Prince Danilo, who seems to be a right good fellow, only perhaps just a *little* too fond of killing Turks; but I suppose every Mohammedan is fair game here, for when I said this morning that among these bare mountains they must sometimes be short of supplies, Danilo answered quite coolly, 'Lest we should be straitened, *God gave us the Turk!*' I asked him the other day how many Turks he had killed himself, and he said he'd reckoned up to thirty-five and then he lost count!

But first of all I must tell you how we got here. We all came by Black Sea steamer from Poti to Constantinople, along the coast of Anatolia; and a very pretty sight it was in the bright October sunshine—smooth green hills and snug little valleys turn about, with now and then a glimpse of great white snow-mountains beyond, the biggest of which, as the general told me, was Mount Ararat itself. And certainly *he* ought to know, for he lay within sight of it for weeks and weeks in '55, with the army that was besieging Kars.

At Trebizond (the place where Xenophon's 'Ten thousand' first sighted the sea, you know, and sang out 'Thalassa! Thalassa!') two English fellows came on board, who had got there from Persia slap through Kurdistan and Armenia—a pretty awkward job, if all tales are true. And what do you think? The minute they heard my name they asked if I was any relation of 'the great Mr Livingstone Archer' (fancy that!); and when I told 'em, they made as big a fuss over me as if I'd been the Prince of Wales. It *must* be fine for you to have people all over the world knowing your name and feeling to you like old friends, though you've never seen 'em in your life!

When we got to Constantinople we had to tranship into an English steamer, which didn't sail for three or four days; so I had time to see all the sights, and the general and I went up to the palace, and had a talk with the Sultan himself—not such a bad-looking fellow for a Turk, if he hadn't been so awfully fat. The old chap was very civil, and gave me his portrait, and such a big box of 'Turkish Delight' that, though we served out a lot to all the passengers every night after dinner, we didn't get through it till we were almost in sight of Athens.

We did not touch there, though, but went on round Cape Matapan, which they say is the southernmost point of Europe; and a queer place it was, just like a great stone fist stuck out into the sea, with the waves lashing and tearing all around it—not at all a nice place to be wrecked, I should say. Then we worked up the west coast of Greece, touching at one or two of the islands (stunning grapes they have there, and no mistake!), till at last we got to Corfu. And just fancy, it's the very same place that used to be called Corcyra, about which old Thucydides is always talking. I had to draw a map of it once at Winchester; but I never thought *then* that I should really go and see it some day myself.

At Corfu we transhipped again, into one of the Austrian-Lloyd steamers that go right up the Adriatic, touching at a lot of small ports on the way. But before she sailed we had a drive round the town, and saw the church of St Spiridion and the citadel that old

Schulemberg defended against the Turks ; and some Greek fellows showed us a rock at the mouth of the harbour, and told us it was Ulysses' ship turned to stone ! I wonder if they expected us to *believe* all that bosh !

It was after dark when we left Corfu, so we did not see much that night; but when the sun rose next morning, there were the Albanian mountains all along the starboard side, ridge above ridge and range beyond range, as if they would never end.

Just then a sort of bundle unrolled itself almost at my feet, and up rose, out of a big sheepskin cloak, a grand old Turk with a long gray beard, whose face would have been quite handsome but for a terrible scar right across it, which almost cut his nose in two. He had the queerest dress I ever saw—a short skirt just like a kilt, only white ; a red Turkish cap, an embroidered vest with gilt buttons, gray knickerbockers, scarlet shoes turned up at the toes, and a girdle of crimson silk, with enough pistols and daggers in it to set up a museum. Then I remembered what I'd read about the 'white-kilted Albanians,' and made sure that this must be one of them—and so he was.

The old fellow spread a small square carpet on the deck, and kneeling on it, began to say his prayers ; and he had just finished them, when I saw Danilo Petrovitch hovering about in the distance, as if he were looking for *me*. But the moment he caught sight of the Albanian he seemed to forget all about me, and forward he ran, and threw his arms round the old boy's neck ; and the two hugged each other just like two bears. And then Danilo drew up his sleeve and showed an awful scar on his left arm ; and the old Turk nodded and grinned, as much as to say, '*I* know all about that !'

'I see this old gentleman is a great friend of yours, Danilo Petrovitch,' said I, coming up.

'No ; he's a great *enemy* of mine,' said Danilo, laughing. 'He and his tribe live just on the other side of our border, and I've fought more battles with him than I can count. It was he who gave me this scar on my arm, and *I* gave *him* that slash across his face.'

And would you believe it ?—these two great strong fellows, who had been doing their best for years past to chop one another to bits, were so fond of each other that they could hardly bear to be separated. It was all I could do to get Danilo down to breakfast ; and the minute it was done up he flew on deck again, and forward he went to have another talk with his old Turk. And when the

Albanian got off at Durazzo (which was his nearest point for home, it seems) there was another hug between them that made my ribs ache to look at.

'Farewell, father,' said the Monteneg. quite sadly; 'we shall meet again in battle ere long, and try the edge of each other's swords once more!'

'May God grant it, my son!' answered the old chief, as affectionately as if he were giving him his blessing.

And so they parted; and I rushed away down to the cabin and laughed till I couldn't see.

Towards afternoon the next day I went down to see after Yury (who had been as sick as a dog ever since we left Corfu, poor fellow! the sea having been rather tumbly), and when I came up again we were close to the shore; and Danilo, pointing to a queer, grayish-yellow streak that went zigzagging up the face of a great black ridge in front of us, told me that that was the road up into Montenegro, and that it had *seventy-three* turns.

The sun was beginning to sink as we turned a sharp corner and came sliding into a queer little inlet with as many twists as a corkscrew, and so shut in by steep ridges that it looked as if the sea had strayed in there at hide-and-seek, and never found its way out again. Here and there we saw a tiny village pasted like a stamp on the foot of the precipice, as if it could not find ground to stand on; and so we went dodging and tacking about, now to port and now to starboard, and then going right ahead, and presently coming back again like a kitten running after its own tail; till, just as I was beginning to think that we must have lost our way, and would have to keep on dodging about like that all night, we made one more twist, and found ourselves right in front of Cattaro, where we were to land.

There was still light enough left to see the town, and a funny little place it was, all crowded together on a kind of doorstep between the cliff and the sea, with its houses all huddled up as if they were afraid of being shoved into the water; and above it a huge dark precipice went sheer up against the sky like a wall for hundreds and thousands of feet, so black and grim that I began to understand why the Montenegs. call their country Tserna-Gora (Black Mountain).*

* This is the native name of the country, 'Monte-Negro' being a literal translation of it.

Danilo was for starting off up the hills there and then, for he seemed as eager to get home as a fellow at school at the end of the Christmas half; but the general didn't seem to see it. First and foremost, Yury was too seedy to sit a horse, and could hardly be expected to *walk* twenty-five miles uphill in the dark; and then the general himself had some business to settle with the Austrian authorities of the place. So at last it was decided that Danilo was to set off at once with the heavy luggage, and get all ready for us at Tsettinje, and that we should follow next morning.

And so we did; for by that time Yury was quite fit again, after a good sleep and a good breakfast; and we got a horse for him, and the general and I walked. I wondered at first what was to be done with our portmanteaus; for, though Yury's had been strapped on to his horse (he being a pretty light weight), the general's and mine—both pretty heavy, too—were still to be disposed of. But when I asked him about it he laughed, and said there would be no trouble about *that;* and there wasn't, for when I got outside I found a Monteneg. *woman* with his portmanteau on her back, and another woman (a great strapping creature almost as big as a man, only rather round-shouldered and hunched-up, as if she were in the way of carrying heavy weights) just getting ready to shoulder mine!

I wanted to object, for I didn't take to the idea of letting a *woman* carry a big load while I carried nothing at all; but the old girl only grinned, and said in her queer mountain dialect: 'If little master like, I carry little master himself as well!'

I felt pretty small after *that*, as you may think; but I found out later on that it is quite the correct thing in these parts, for when I asked Stenka Radonitch (that's one of the chiefs here, a very good fellow, with whom I breakfasted this morning) how they got things up from the coast, he said they came on the backs of *donkeys* or of *women!*

Well, by half-past nine we were fairly under way, zigzagging up the mountain-road; and a nice road it was, upon my word—so narrow that we had to go single-file, and all strewn with great big stones one atop of the other, as if there had just been a landslip or an earthquake. The way Yury's horse picked its way over 'em was a caution; but once or twice, when it got pretty near the edge of the precipice, I could see that he did not half like it.

'Well,' said I, 'it's a good job for the Servian Patriarch that he left us at Constantinople and went home by way of the

Danube, for I don't think *he* would have taken kindly to this sort of thing.'

And the general laughed, and said he didn't think he would.

We were three mortal hours getting to the top of the first hill; and no wonder, with three thousand feet to climb, and such footing to do it on. And the best of the joke is, that the top of the mountain is in Montenegro, and the foot of it is in Austria; so, if tobogganing were in fashion here, a fellow might slide down over the frontier before he could stop, and be picked up by the border police for travelling without a passport!

When we got to the top what should we see but a great heap of snow, big enough to bury an elephant, lying in a hollow under a projecting rock ; and just as we came up to it we met a party of three German officers coming down, with two Monteneg. guides. The two guides began snowballing each other, and a ball hit me slap in the face; and so *I* made up a big ball, and let the fellow have it plump in the eye; and they both burst out laughing, and let fly at me back again; and then Yury jumped off his horse and joined in, and the old general threw off his cloak and went at it like a Trojan; and then the three officers took a hand, and we all peppered each other till there wasn't a breath left among the lot of us. And then they went *their* way and we went ours, and that was the first and last we saw of 'em. Queer sort of introduction, wasn't it?

After this we got on better, for now we were on a tolerably level bit of moor, which, if anything, went rather down than up; and we had a glorious view of the mountains all around, crest above crest, like a sea of frozen waves. By this time I was glad to put on my greatcoat, for though it had been pretty warm down below, up here it was cold enough for anything, and the wind that swept down from the snow-mountains right over this bare moor seemed fairly to cut you in two.

Presently we saw, a little way ahead, a small village, which the general said was Niegosch, the place that the Prince of Montenegro's ancestors came from, and from which his family is always called 'Petrovitch-Niegosch.' On the way there several Montenegs. passed us, and they all called out, 'Dobra fstretch' (A good meeting), which is the correct thing to say here when two people meet. I've got quite into the way of saying it myself, and the people seem awfully pleased when I do.

When we got up to the village, whom should we find there

but our two Montenegrinesses with the portmanteaus; for, though they carried weight and we carried none, they were first in after all. But the minute they saw us coming they were up and off again; and the general said they would take a short-cut by the mountain-paths, and distance us to Tsettinje, as they had done to Niegosch.

Here we made a halt (Yury being rather done-up), though it did not look a very hopeful stopping-place; for most of the houses were just made of loose stones piled on each other without any mortar, and roofed in with thatch—jolly cold berths in winter, I should say; and inside neither bed nor furniture of any sort, nothing but the bare earthen floor. But presently an old man came out of one of the cottages, and very civilly invited us in; and by his long dark robe and high black cap, shaped just like a tall hat with the brim knocked off, I guessed him to be the village priest; and so he was.

His house, though, was nothing to boast of; for it seemed just like the rest, except that it was a bit bigger, and had a sort of stone shelf or step, about a foot high, all round the walls, to serve as a bedplace. When we first went in we were half-stifled with smoke; and no wonder, for the house had neither fireplace nor chimney, and the fire was laid on a sort of stone platform in the middle of the floor, so that the smoke went out whichever way it liked, through the door and window and the chinks in the walls. But the old man was very kind to us, and he and his wife gave us a lot of milk and rye-bread, and some *castradina* (that's mutton pressed between two boards, you know, till all the juice is squeezed out of it and it's as dry and hard as an oak-log). They even wanted us to stay all night, but our guide said we'd better be going on again, because it looked like a storm; and, sure enough, it was looking rather sulky up to windward. So we said good-bye to the old gentleman and thanked him; and he gave us his blessing, and off we went.

And after that we got into such a maze of mountains as never was, going on and on as if it would never end. The Montenegs. have a legend, you know, that an angel was once flying across their country, carrying in a bag all the mountains that were to be distributed over Eastern Europe, when the bag burst, and they all tumbled into Montenegro.

It was ticklish work, for the path was just a ledge along the brink of a precipice; and once or twice, when we met some people coming the other way, it was rather a question who was to pass *outside*, and how he was to keep from falling over when he did. But the worst of it was still to come ; for now a few thin flakes of snow began to fall, and then they came faster and faster, till all the air was so thick with flying snow that you couldn't see the end of your nose !

The guide told us to keep close to him, and picked his way along in front, and Yury's horse followed him, and we followed *it* —all at a foot-pace, for, as you may think, there was no going fast among those precipices in a blinding snowstorm. Poor Yury was soon nothing more than a snow-image, and, remembering how delicate he is, I was very glad to hear the guide sing out 'Tsettinje !' just as we came over the top of a great high ridge as steep as a wall ; though, for all we could see of it, Tsettinje might just as well have been a thousand miles away.

But we got on better after that, for now it was all downhill ; and presently there came a lull in the storm, and, as the snow slackened, we caught a glimpse of a wide, bare plateau in front of us, just like the one at Niegosch, and in the middle a tall stone tower, with a lot of small houses clustering round it. In a few minutes more we were splashing and floundering through mud and half-melted snow along a straight, wide street, at the end of which was a big white house that I took for Prince Nikeeta's palace ; but the general told me it was only a hotel which the Prince had built for strangers.

And a funny place it was when we got to it. Upstairs there were gilt mirrors and velvet-covered chairs and sofas ; while downstairs, in the entrance-hall, pigs were rooting in heaps of rubbish, and hens and ducks strolling about as if the whole place belonged to them. But I can tell you that, after tramping for hours over these mountains in the teeth of a snowstorm, I wasn't in the humour to be particular ; and both Yury and I were very glad to get in and change our wet things in a snug little room upstairs, next-door to the general's, and have a rattling good dinner to warm us up.

But I must break off now, for here comes an aide-de-camp to say that the Prince has just got home from some place that he was visiting, and that we're to go and see him at once.

Nov. 6. Well, we have seen Prince Nikeeta, and very well worth seeing he is. He don't put on much style, for his ' palace ' is a meek little whitewashed cottage, nothing like as big as our hotel; but if his surroundings are not very grand, he himself makes up for it, for he is, if any man ever was, 'every inch a king.' And there are a good many inches of him, too, for he stands six feet four in his shoes, and has a chest like Hercules himself; and I can quite believe *now* all I've heard of his being the strongest man and the best shot in his kingdom.

He has a guard to match him, too, and no mistake; for every man-Jack of 'em's over six feet high, and the captain is *seven*. Each of them carries a long gun, a sword, two brace of pistols, and a couple of daggers a foot long; and when all these giants clashed their swords over our heads as we came up to the door (I suppose by way of doing us honour) I never felt so *small* in my life.

The rooms were very neatly furnished, but quite in a plain way; and Prince Nikeeta himself wore just the common Monteneg. dress, same as the Grand-Duke Michael used to be rigged out like an ordinary Circassian; in fact, he reminded me a good deal of Michael altogether, and he had just the same frank, pleasant way about him, that made you feel at home with him in a moment.

'I regret that your father is not with you, Monsieur Archer,' said he (*he* had heard of you too, you see), 'for I think he would find something worth looking at in this little kingdom of mine; but I hope you will pay me another visit some day, and that then he will be able to accompany you. I'm sorry that my wife is not well enough to receive you just now, and that my daughters are all away in Russia finishing their education; but they will be back soon, and then I must run away to the woods, for we shall have three pianos all going at once!'

And he laughed in such a jolly way that Yury and I couldn't help laughing too.

'So you came all the way from Russia by sea and were not sick!' he went on. 'Well, I *do* envy you that; for when I came back by steamer from France to Trieste I was sick all the time. If I ever have any more travelling to do I'll do it by land, for I could not stand such another voyage as that!'

It sounded so absurd to hear this great giant talk of being knocked over by sea-sickness that I laughed again, whether I would or not; but he didn't seem to mind a bit. In short, it all went off first-rate; and when we took leave of him, he said that if I wanted to make any excursions about the country, I had only to tell *him*—and I mean to do it, too!

THE BLACK MOUNTAINEERS. 213

But here comes a fellow to say that the mail's just going off, so I must shut up. A funny kind of mail it is, too ; for the letter-box is just an English biscuit-tin, with which a man trots down the mountain twice a week to the mail-steamer at Cattaro ; and as we get lots of biscuits at the hotel, I suppose they have a chance of a new letter-box pretty often.

Good-bye, daddy ; and please remember me very kindly to Count Bulatoff ; and I hope you and he will have a very successful trip.
—Your affectionate son,   H. ARCHER.

P.S.—There's a grand service at the church to-morrow, to which we are invited ; but I'm not fond of going that way, because the church-tower is hung all over with the heads of Turks killed in battle, and it looks rather nasty.* Ta-ta.

      * Happily these barbarities are now at an end.

CHAPTER XXIII.

BURIED IN THE SWAMP.

HEN he thus wished his father and the count a 'successful trip,' poor Harry little dreamed that their trip had been only too successful already.

Bulatoff had no wish to make a long stay with the Khan of Ala-Tau, for he was on thorns lest his audacious trick should even now be detected by some unforeseen chance; and Archer, though wholly ignorant of his friend's daring imposture, was equally impatient to complete their exploration ere the terrible northern winter set in. Thus both were agreeably surprised when, on the fourth morning of their stay, the Khan offered to furnish them with guides who should pilot them northward, by a short cut over the mountains, to the nearest of the military posts recently established along the Ili River by the Russians, in order to bridle the wild mountain tribes beyond it.

The two men assented at once (this being the very direction that they wished to take), and that same afternoon they set forth, with two native guides in addition to their Tartar henchman.

As they advanced, the gloomy hills around them seemed to grow higher and steeper and barer; but the count's keen eye did not fail to note the richness of the soil in the more sheltered valleys, and the signs of abundant mineral wealth in the formation and colour of the rocks around him.

'This would be a fine country, after all,' said he, 'if it were once opened up by good roads and planted with colonists, as I hope it will be before long, when we push a little farther to the east.'

'But might not our friend the Khan, and others of his class, be apt to object to that?' hinted Archer.

'Oh, *they* would be very easily disposed of,' said the count, with a pleasant smile. 'I don't mean by war, for it is a mere waste of valuable lives to make war upon such scum; all we need do is to give each of the tribes a few hundred roubles' worth of guns and ammunition, and then set them quarrelling among themselves, and in less than a year we could march over all their carcasses without firing a shot. It's just the same with those rogues in the Khiva Desert, too,' he went on, with the same easy self-satisfaction; 'instead of throwing away time and money in sending expeditions against them, what we *ought* to do is to stop up all the wells, and then the whole nation would either die of thirst or poison themselves with drinking the bad marsh-water. That would be the simplest way, if only we could be *quite* sure that it might not offend the public opinion of Western Europe.'

Archer made no reply (for, in truth, what reply *could* any one make to such a programme?), but he thought to himself:

'Well, this man and his friends used to rail at Krovolil's recklessness of human life; but Krovolil himself never went as far as *this!*'

The first night of their northward march passed off without any adventure, and the second likewise; but on the third morning one of the two Ala-Tau guides was nowhere to be found; and the other, in answer to Bulatoff's questions, explained that, finding the man beginning to fall lame, and likely to be a hindrance to their further progress, he had sent him back.

'He must have been a fool to *let* himself be sent back,' said Archer to the count, 'for of course it was all a dodge of this other fellow to get all the pay to himself.'

But the wary Russian, who had lived from his childhood in an atmosphere of constant intrigue and suspicion, saw more in the matter than this, and was for some time very grave and silent.

The rest of that day passed quietly enough, and so did also the ensuing night; but when morning came the other Ala-Tau man was missing in his turn!

'As I thought,' muttered the count. 'We are in a bad way!'

This was all he said, but no further explanation seemed to be needed either by Archer or by their Tartar guide, who growled, with an ominous shake of his bullet-head:

'This bodes us no good, my lords; let us push on quickly!'

On they pushed accordingly, and for the next three hours were too fully employed in forcing their way over the stones and briars of the vast rocky ridge before them to have any leisure for talking. But when they reached its summit and glanced round them, Bulatoff's face, which had looked very stern and thoughtful ever since the fatal discovery, suddenly lighted up.

'This is the very place that I wanted to reach!' he cried; 'for, if I am right, it is just here that the ancient caravan-road must have been. Do you see that bright streak below us! That's the Sari-Djaz, which falls into the Djangeh not far from here; and that pass yonder to the east, through which it flows, is the only gap in the great mountain-wall, for many a mile round, through which heavy loads could be carried with any chance of safety. Here, if anywhere, the place must be!'

And down the slope he went at a rapid rate, followed by his companions.

But as he neared the valley his face fell again, and with good reason. No road here, nor any sign of one; nothing but a foul, noisome, dismal swamp, where black slimy pools and broad sheets of festering mud alternated with forests of tall reeds and coarse wiry grass, the rank, unwholesome green of which betokened but too truly the fathomless depths of treacherous mire below. And beyond all this—an appropriate frame to that dreary picture—the turbid gray stream, to the overflowings of which this Eastern 'Slough of Despond' manifestly owed its existence, glistened faintly in the pale autumn sunlight.

But all at once, as the count's keen eye roamed over that disheartening prospect, a sudden sparkle told that it had caught sight of something which promised better fortune. Without a word he sprang from his horse and strode right down toward the brink of the swamp.

'My lord, my lord, thou art going wrong! *Here* lies the way toward the Ili,' cried the Tartar, pointing to a steep, narrow path that zigzagged up the broad, stony hillside to their left. 'Moreover, in yonder swamp there is no footing for man; it would swallow up the host of Sekundur Rumi!' (Alexander the Great).

'That shall be seen ere long,' said the Russian, still advancing.

His madness (if such it was) seemed to have infected Archer likewise; for at that moment the latter, after one quick glance over the morass, leaped to the ground in turn, and strode after him.

'They are mad, both one and the other!' muttered the Tartar, with a despairing shake of his round black head; 'and as well may one bid a waterfall halt in mid-plunge as try to stay a Western unbeliever when his mood is on him!'

Springing from grass-clump to grass-clump with a skill and success which nothing but long practice could have rendered possible, the bold Englishman had advanced (though not without more than one narrow escape) a considerable distance into the morass, when he suddenly stopped short and stood firm, as if finding some solid footing just below the miry and unstable surface.

'You're right, Feodor,' he cried; 'there *is* firm footing underneath; and if'——

Here a choking, gurgling gasp behind made him turn quickly round, and he saw with dismay his friend struggling waist-deep in the horrible slough, and evidently sinking deeper every moment!

'Spread out your arms!' roared Archer; and the count did so, thus checking for an instant the deadly action of the quagmire that was sucking him down. Meanwhile his English comrade got as near to him as was possible without a risk of slipping from the firm ground into the fatal pit that was engulfing Bulatoff, and flung to the latter one end of his stout belt, which the Russian just succeeded in clutching; while Archer, planting himself firmly on one knee, twisted his other hand in a thick tuft of tall, wiry grass beside him, and held on like grim death!

The struggle that followed was terrific, and for some moments it would have been hard to say whether Archer would drag the count *out* or the count drag Archer *in*. The lives of the two greatest travellers in the world, the future of a mighty discovery, the prosperity of an entire district, hung upon a leathern thong and a tuft of grass; but both held firm, and after a few seconds of frightful suspense, the Russian, drenched, dripping, covered with mud, and gasping for breath, stood on the firmer ground by his rescuer's side.

But ere either could speak, their eyes fell upon something which for the moment drove every other thought out of the minds of both.

In the final struggle a quantity of the grass which Archer had clutched so firmly had been torn away, disclosing beneath it the corner of a small white block of *hewn stone!*

Instantly both men were hard at work, tearing away the grass and weeds as eagerly as if unearthing a buried treasure; and in a trice they had laid bare a square block of stone nearly two feet high, bearing an unmistakable *Greek* inscription, so well preserved by its grassy screen that only a few letters were wanting, and the two friends easily read and translated it thus:

'CHEIRISOPHOS, SON OF SOSTRATOS, KING OF THE EAST-BACTRIANS, MADE THIS ROAD IN THE FIFTH YEAR OF HIS REIGN.'

'Oho!' cried the count, 'here's our friend Cheirisophos the Macedonian again, whose coin first made us acquainted in Moscow! Well, I thought by the marsh lying so level just here, while elsewhere it was all in lumps and pits, that there must be some sort of roadway under it; but I never bargained for such good luck as this. Why, *now* we shall not need to make a road here at all; it's ready-made for us, as soon as we choose to bank off the river and scrape away the mud. Well, Lyoff, our work is done; and you and I can make for the nearest Russian post as soon as we like.'

Hardly had he spoken, when there came a terrific crash, a stifled cry, and then the wild, half-human shriek in which a horse vents its agony of terror, blended with a furious clatter of trampling hoofs. A huge stone, falling from the overhanging cliff beneath which the Tartar had halted with the three horses, had struck the brave man dead on the spot, and the frightened beasts, breaking wildly away, had dashed madly off up the valley and vanished among the hills, carrying with them not only the supplies of the two forlorn men, but (as it seemed) their only chance of life as well!

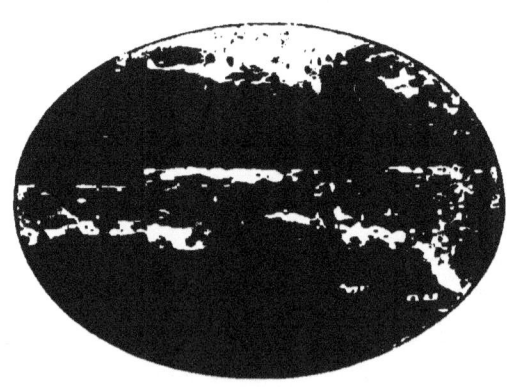

CHAPTER XXIV.

FAMINE.

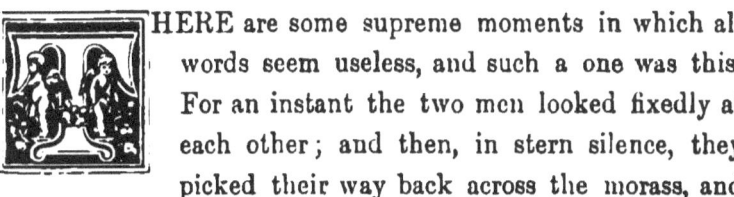HERE are some supreme moments in which all words seem useless, and such a one was this. For an instant the two men looked fixedly at each other; and then, in stern silence, they picked their way back across the morass, and halting only to take up the guns and pouches that they had left on the brink, went straight to the spot where their fallen comrade was lying.

They raised him, but he was quite dead; and then the two castaways (still without uttering a word) bore him away, and laid him gently down in a deep, narrow cleft, piling over him a sufficient quantity of heavy stones to secure him from being torn by the mountain vultures.

Then the count spoke for the first time.

'Let us light a fire and dry our clothes; we can't march with them swathed round us like this.'

It was soon done; and then the Russian said again, in the same dry, methodical tone:

'How much food is there in our pouches?'

'Just enough for to-day and to-morrow, cutting it close,' answered the Englishman, hastily examining.

'A day and a half,' muttered the other, glancing forward

as if measuring in his own mind the distance that remained to be done. 'Now, how long should you think a man ought to be able to keep on marching without any food at all?'

Had this iron man been discussing a move in a game of chess, in place of his only chance of escape from a horrible death, he could not have spoken more calmly.

'Well, I have known some Russian soldiers march without food for three days, and fight a battle on the fourth,' replied Archer with equal coolness; 'and I myself have often held out as long, though I can't say I felt in trim for much fighting at the end of it.'

'Well, say three days,' rejoined the count. 'That makes four days and a half before we break down; and the question is, Can we reach the nearest Russian outpost in that time?'

'And the answer is—No!' said Archer as quietly as ever.

'So I think; but we must try it, for it's our only chance. After all, we have two points in our favour: we've got our guns with us, and may shoot some game; and we might possibly fall in with a Russian scouting party, for there are always plenty of them about. Come along!'

And away went the doomed men, on their match against time with death.

As they advanced, the country around them seemed to grow wilder and lonelier with every mile; for they were now in the heart of that grim mountain-wilderness that borders Western China, and had on their left the bleak, pathless tableland where the dark waters of the Issik-kul* slumber in their rocky hollow more than five thousand feet

---

* *Kul* means lake; *Tau*, mountain; and *Darya*, river.

above the sea, and on their right the vast mountain-wall of
the Chinese border, above which the great white tower of
Khan Tengri reared itself twenty-four thousand feet against
the eastern sky.

The first day passed off well enough, for they had the
advantage of having made a good meal ere the disaster befell,
so that their strength was still unimpaired; and, borne up
by the excitement of this life-and-death struggle, they covered
a greater distance than usual.

But the night that followed was a sore trial even to these
hardy wanderers. As ill-luck would have it, their warm
native rugs had been carried off along with the runaway
horses; and at the great height which they had now attained,
the bitter cold of this bleak region pierced so keenly through
their unsheltered frames that, though they piled up a double
wall of stones to shield them from the wind, and huddled
together as closely as possible behind it, it was only sheer
exhaustion that enabled them to sleep at all. As it was,
they slept brokenly, and awoke unrefreshed.

The second day was like the first—a weary, unending
struggle over stony ridges and through tangled thickets,
which seemed to multiply interminably before them. The
second night was a little less intolerable than the one before
it, the two pilgrims having succeeded in finding a sheltered
hollow, and covering themselves from head to foot with a
huge pile of dead leaves; but even these reckless adventurers
could not call to mind without some emotion that their *last
morsel* of food was now consumed, and that they had still,
on the lowest estimate, more than seventy miles of this
ceaseless and exhausting hill-climbing to accomplish without
any nourishment whatever!

Just at first, however, the full horror of their situation did not make itself felt. The *first* day of absolute starvation is often a season of unwonted briskness and energy, though this unnatural buoyancy never fails to avenge itself later on by a dreadful reaction. The two men went along for a time as nimbly as if they had just started; and that day, too, they made a longer march than usual.

As they struggled on they watched eagerly for any sign of game; and though they found none, the eternal expectation served to keep up their flagging spirits. But they hoped and watched in vain. The only living thing to be seen was a solitary wild goat, far out of rifle-range, skipping gaily from crag to crag as if to mock their misery.

That night was colder than the last, and told sorely upon the two weary and starving men. When they rose next morning the first thing they did was to *tighten their belts;* and each knew by himself that the other must be already beginning to feel the first pangs of that frightful torment of which no one who has not actually felt it can form any idea—which begins with a mere sense of hollowness and sharpened appetite, but ends in such a rending agony as if a ravenous wolf were tearing one's very vitals.

As the next sun began to sink, even *their* stout hearts sank with it, weighed down by the tomb-like silence and lifeless desolation around them. In this mighty wilderness of gloomy thickets and black, frowning precipices — where they were but two mere specks in a boundless void—Nature showed herself in her sternest mood, stonily unmindful of their presence, cruelly indifferent to their despair.

But, in spite of all, the two brave men bore up, not only because it was death to give way, but also because (almost unconsciously to themselves) the rivalry of race was awake at last. The Russian was determined not to fail before the eyes of an Englishman, and the Englishman equally resolute not to be outdone in hardihood by a 'foreigner.'

But the match was no equal one after all. The gallant Russian bore up as bravely as man could do; but he lacked Archer's perfect training and iron endurance, and his recent life in the fashionable circles of Moscow was an ill preparation for the Eastern deserts. When they started again on the following day (their third without any food whatever) the Englishman noted with a sinking heart his comrade's dragging step and drooping head, and felt that this was the beginning of the end.

So it was indeed. Ere they had been an hour on the march (which was now pursued in gloomy and unbroken silence) a few thin flakes of snow came quivering down from the lowering sky; and then they flew thicker and faster and heavier, till it seemed as if the very sky were falling, and the two forlorn men were fain to creep in under a projecting rock for shelter—forced to sit still just when their only hope of life lay in pressing on with the utmost speed! Archer was not a man to give way lightly; but if ever he had prayed in his life, he did so as they sat crouching there, waiting in vain for the storm to cease.

It ceased at last, and forth they crept; but the added labour of struggling upward through the deep snow-drifts told fearfully on both men, and more especially on Bulatoff. Archer took the other gun from his comrade, who seemed hardly conscious of it; for his gait was now the slow, mechanical movement of a sleep-walker, and all at once he stopped short, tottered, threw his arms out blindly as if seeking support, and fell heavily to the earth!

The contact of the snow seemed to revive him, and he muttered faintly:

'It's all over with *me*, Lyoff—save yourself!'

'I'll be hanged if I do!' said Archer gruffly; and, spoken under such circumstances, these words, homely and almost rude as they were, had more true grandeur than many a 'fine saying' preserved by historians.

The count attempted to reply; but his voice failed, and he became unconscious.

'What's to be done *now?*' muttered Archer, looking round him in despair. 'God help us!'

The prayer seemed to be answered, for hardly was it spoken, when he heard, or thought he heard, a distant shout!

He shouted with all his might in reply, firing off his gun at the same time; and now there could be no doubt about it—there *was* an answering call. Regaining for an instant all his lost strength from sheer excitement, he actually lifted his senseless comrade on to his shoulders and struggled on toward the brow of the hill, which seemed farther away every time he looked at it.

Spurred on, however, by the sight of a thin wreath of smoke curling up from behind it, he fought his way desperately on, and reaching the summit, saw in a sheltered hollow below him a group of wild figures gathered round a fire. Their presence in such a place, at such a time, amply sufficed to tell *what* they must be; but Archer was past all thought of that now, and he went straight down toward them, as he would have gone, in his present mood, into the den of a hungry lion.

As they sprang up and ran to meet him his overtasked strength gave way at last, and his friend's body slipped from his nerveless hold on to the snow, while he himself only escaped falling beside it by propping himself against a stump. But his swimming eyes saw dimly that the savage-looking fellows who surrounded him were armed to the teeth and stained with fresh blood, and that among them was *one* face which he had thought to be long since buried for ever beneath the sullen waters of the Caspian Sea—the face of *Krocolil the Brigand!*

CHAPTER XXV.

AMONG WILD BEASTS.

HE shock of this astounding discovery steadied for an instant the worn-out man's reeling senses, and looking full at the amazed robbers (who were eyeing him as if they did not know what to make of him), he said boldly:

'Welcome, comrades! Give us food, for we are starving!'

The look of bewilderment deepened on the hang-dog visages around him, and Krovolil himself said, with a cruel and ominous smile:

'Do you know *who* we are, that you call us comrades?'

'Robbers, I suppose,' said Archer recklessly; 'but anyhow, you are the only men within reach, and my friend here is dying of hunger!'

A hoarse laugh circled through the savage band, and the 'Blood-shedder's' face lighted up with a glow of honest admiration of the only virtue that he could understand or appreciate—indomitable courage.

'They don't breed cowards where *you* come from, I see,' said he approvingly. 'Who are you?'

'An Englishman,' said the traveller.

'An Englishman!' echoed the robber-chief, looking closely at him. 'I know you now; you're the fellow who bound up my hand for me on the steamer when that cat tore it. I thought I knew your voice. Why, this is as good as a ballad! Bring him to the fire, you fellows, and give him some tea; it will be better for him than meat, after such a long starve.'

And in a trice Archer was seated by the cheering blaze, and swallowing draught after draught of the famous 'brick-tea' of Tartary, with small pieces of coarse bread steeped in it, the warmth of which comforted and strengthened his numbed and weary limbs as nothing else could have done.

But he was not left long in peace; for, as the robbers carried the helpless count forward in his turn, Krovolil cast a keen glance at his upturned face, and asked pointedly:

'This man looks like a *Russian;* is he the same whom I saw with you on the boat—Count Bulatoff?'

'He is,' said the Englishman, seeing that there was no help for it.

'Aha! the kinsman of that rascally general who hunted us down like rats!' shouted the savage leader, with ferocious joy. 'He shall die, and all the more because he is the Emperor's friend!'

'If you want to kill him, you must kill *me* first!' cried Archer, springing up and standing over the prostrate man.

But ere any one had time to speak or move (for the lesser ruffians were struck dumb with amazement at seeing this half-starved and defenceless man confront their terrible chief so boldly) Krovolil's quick eye caught sight of the Persian dagger in Bulatoff's belt, which, as will be remembered, had been given by the dying brigand to Yury, and passed on by him to his father.*

'Ha!' cried the robber-chief. 'I know that dagger! Where did *he* get it?'

'From his son, to whom it was given by a man whom he

* See chapter xi.

helped when dying of hunger among the mountains, as *we* are now.'

'And what became of the man who gave it?' asked Krovolil eagerly.

'He was too far gone to recover, and so he died.'

'Died?' repeated the 'Blood-shedder' sadly. 'Poor Loris! I thought it must be so; for had he been alive he would have found me, though the whole breadth of Russia lay between us!'

'Loris!' echoed the Englishman. 'Was he the man who used to dance the "Rattle" so wonderfully?'

'Ah! you know him, then?' cried the bandit, with a pleased smile. 'Where did you meet him?'

'I never met him myself, but I have heard of him from my friend Prince Shervashidze, who once danced a match with him in your presence.'

'Yes, I remember that—I let him go free because he danced so well,' said the brigand-captain, with a hearty, boyish laugh, his passing emotion at the news of his friend's death being already forgotten. 'Well, if this man and his son have been good to Loris in his need, no one shall hurt him. It's a pity, too, for we should have had grand sport torturing him to death; but I can't touch a man who was good to my old comrade.'

By this time Bulatoff, revived by the warmth of the fire, had come to himself again; and Archer, while aiding him to sit up and to swallow some tea and soaked bread, apprised him, in a cautious whisper, of their present situation as the guests or prisoners of the dreaded 'Blood-shedder.' To hear such a disclosure wholly unmoved was beyond even the iron-nerved count himself; but, whatever he might feel, he showed as little outward emotion as the rocks around him.

'So we have met again, Ataman' (captain), said he to Krovolil, as pleasantly as if this merciless cut-throat were his best friend. 'People may well think you can't be killed, for we all made sure you were drowned that time in the Caspian Sea.'

'Yes,' chuckled the robber, 'there again you were at fault. When the ship went down I thought that here was a good chance of escape for me, and as she was sinking I clutched a floating spar and drifted away into the darkness. When morning came I found myself so close to the shore that I easily reached it; and then I smashed my chains with a big stone, and away I went through the deserts. I got over them all right, as you see; and here I am at the head of a new band already.'

'You *do* seem to be lucky, indeed,' said the Russian, laughing; 'and we were lucky to fall in with you when we did, for we could not have kept up much longer, after tramping all the way from the Sari-Djaz Valley without food.'

'Did you really?' cried the 'Blood-shedder,' with unfeigned interest, while his savage followers exchanged looks of wondering admiration. 'Well, that's more than I ever did, and more than I should care to do, either. You two must be the sort of men whom, as we say, Death does not know by sight. Why, this English chum of yours was carrying you on his back when we first caught sight of you both.'

The count shot a glance at his friend that said more than any words; and then, taking the dagger out of his belt, he held it out to Krovolil, saying heartily:

'Before we go any farther, Ataman, let me hand this over to you. It seems that the man to whom it belonged was a follower of yours, so you have a better right to it than I have.'

The bandit's eyes sparkled, and he clutched the proffered weapon as eagerly as a child snatching at a new toy.

'Old Loris's dagger!' cried he; 'the very one with which he cut that old Greek's nose off in fun—he was always a merry lad! Fancy it coming back to me like this! Thank you, count; it is very good of you to give away such a fine weapon—one that *I* would never have parted with had it been mine. If ever I have a chance to do *you* a good turn, you shall see that I won't let it slip.'

'Well, it seems to me,' said the count, smiling, 'that you have repaid me in advance by saving my life; for, though it may not be worth very much, it's the only one I have, and I set some store by it. I may count myself doubly lucky, for I could never have expected to meet any one here at this season, and *you* least of all; for I should hardly have thought you could find anything to do in a place like this so late in the year.'

'You are right,' said Krovolil; 'and, in fact, we were just getting ready to move south for the winter, when there came a messenger to us from the Khan of Ala-Tau, who has put some business in our way more than once already, though we have not been here long; and he told us that some Russian envoys had come to him from the Czar with rich presents, and a letter from the Emperor himself, and that, having dismissed their train, they were travelling with but one attendant; and that he himself and his comrade had led them this road, by way of a short-cut to the nearest Russian fort, so that we had nothing to do but wait here till they came up, and then pounce upon 'em. Well, we did so, thinking such game worth trapping; and now, you see, *the rogues have not come after all!*'

CHAPTER XXVI.

CAUGHT IN HIS OWN TRAP.

T any other time Count Bulatoff would have been not a little amused at the tone of righteous indignation in which this double-dyed cutthroat denounced the unpunctuality of the expected travellers in coming to be killed; but this sudden disclosure of the foul and murderous treachery to which they had all but fallen victims blotted out for the moment every other thought. It was eminently characteristic, however, of this wily and unscrupulous man (himself a master of every form of stratagem and deceit) that his first feeling toward the author of that cruel and treacherous plot against his own life was one of instinctive *admiration.*

'That old Khan is not such a fool as I thought him,' said he to himself; 'he did not mean us to tell any tales of what we had seen in his country, and he has managed matters so that, if by any chance we *did* come through alive, he would get the full credit of having given us a kind reception, and if we were killed, all the blame would fall on the robbers, and *he,* of course, would know nothing about it. 'Pon my word, the old fat-head has some sense after all!'

During this talk Archer, rightly judging his friend able to deal with Krovolil unaided, had drawn a little apart, and was now busied in cleaning, with the help of one or two of the robbers (whom their formidable chief's friendly reception of him had made extremely civil), his gun and revolver, which had suffered somewhat from the damps of that dismal region. Hence he was still ignorant of the startling revelation just made; and the Russian, finding himself thus left free to deal with the matter as he thought fit, felt his subtle spirit rise to meet the emergency, and, practised as he was in seizing at a glance all the points of a difficult question, saw at once how this new discovery might be turned to account.

'Is it long since that messenger was here?' asked he, turning to Krovolil with an air of interest that manifestly pleased the young bandit.

'Why, he is here still!' cried the 'Blood-shedder.' 'You don't suppose we would let him come to us with a story like that, and then go away again as if he had only come to say good-morning. We kept him with us till his tale should be made good, and he is with us now.'

'Ah, indeed?' rejoined the count, so quietly that the keenest observer could not have penetrated the dreadful meaning which underlay that simple remark. 'Well, Ataman, you have saved my life when you might just as well have taken it, and you have been kind to me and my friend; and I really cannot stand by and see you and your men cheated into hunting on a false scent.'

'On a *false* scent, say you?' cried the young chief, with a sudden and ominous gleam in his large, bright eyes.

'Yes, indeed; for we ourselves have just come from Ala-Tau, where we stayed several days with the Khan; and I give you my word that when we left, no Russian envoys had arrived there, and none were expected!'

'Do you mean, then, that this messenger has *lied* to me?'

said the 'Blood-shedder' in a low, stern whisper, more deadly than the noisiest outburst of rage.

'It looks rather like it,' replied the other coldly. 'If you like you can ask my friend yonder; he will tell you the same story.'

In making this offer the worthy count knew well that he was quite safe; for, as has been seen, Archer's ignorance of the local dialect had kept him wholly innocent of the audacious trick played upon the Khan by his comrade. Thus, when Krovolil put the question to him, the Englishman answered, in perfect good faith, that no Russian envoys were expected at Ala-Tau so far as he knew, and that certainly none had been there during their stay.

Krovolil came back and sat down again by the fire without uttering a word; and the ominous pause that followed bore hard upon the strong nerves of Bulatoff himself.

'Well, Ataman,' said the count at length, 'what do you say *now*?'

'*Some one* has been deceiving me,' replied the bandit, 'and when I find him out'——

'You will punish him as he deserves; is it not so?' rejoined Bulatoff, with a composure which, under the circumstances, might fairly have earned him the Cross of St George. 'Now, I'll just tell you *my* idea of this business; and a sharp fellow like you will soon see whether I am right or not. To begin with, is this Ala-Tau man here on the spot?'

'No; he is at our other camp, three versts (about two miles) away.'

'Well, anyhow, you can tell me if he's not a tall, lean, raw-boned fellow, with a short, black beard just turning gray, a scar on his right cheek, and a slight cast in his left eye?'

'That's he, point for point,' said the 'Blood-shedder,' looking surprised.

P

'As I thought,' rejoined the Russian, with a cold smile. 'Well, it's a pretty clear case. This fellow is our own runaway guide, who deserted us on the first night of our journey northward from Ala-Tau. The Khan, being doubtless angry at getting nothing more out of us than the few little trumpery trinkets that we could spare him from our stock, and not having the courage to attack us openly, must have given him secret instructions to betray us into *your* hands, knowing what short work you make of your enemies; and then, in order to magnify his service in your eyes, and to secure himself a good share of whatever plunder might be got from us, this precious messenger took it into his head to make out that *we* were ambassadors from the Emperor. But, unluckily for himself, he forgot that a man of your shrewdness and experience would never be fool enough to think that two half-starved men in rags, wandering all alone among the hills on foot, without even food to keep them alive, could be envoys sent all the way here by the Czar with gifts and letters from himself!'

These last words seemed quite a conclusive argument to the ignorant ruffian, who, with all his cunning, knew but little of the world, having had, as may be supposed, few chances to see anything of it.

Bulatoff noted the effect of his words with no small inward relief; for it was now, plainly enough, a struggle to the death between them and their treacherous Ala-Tau guide. Either he or they must perish, and in such a case it was obviously of the last importance to discredit his tale in advance.

'If this is so '—— began Krovolil in a voice like the growl of a rising storm; but a warning gesture from the count stopped him short.

'Gently, Ataman, gently,' whispered the Russian, laying

his hand on the robber's shoulder as familiarly as if this murderous savage were his sworn friend and brother. 'I don't want my comrade yonder to know anything of this, for all these English are hot-headed, slap-dash fellows; and if he once knew what this Ala-Tau rogue had done, he would be likely enough, the moment he caught sight of him, to strike him dead on the spot; and *that* would be a pity, wouldn't it?'

The frightful significance of this final hint was not lost upon Krovolil, whose wolfish grin showed how fully it harmonised with his own innate cruelty. In fact, throughout the whole of this extraordinary interview the untaught brigand was a mere child in the hands of the subtle and cold-blooded schemer, who felt the same pleasure in thus overmatching the rude cunning of barbarism with the disciplined craft of civilisation which a great sculptor feels in evolving from a shapeless mass of rough stone his own perfect thought.

'Now,' resumed the count, 'I'll just tell you how you can find out whether I have spoken the truth or not. You already know for yourself that we are *not* the Czar's envoys; so all that you have to do is to bring me face to face with this knave of a messenger, and if he recognises *me* as one of the men whom he guided, and whom he announced to you as ambassadors from the Emperor, his falsehood is exposed at once.'

'And then,' said Krovolil, with a savage emphasis which made even the Russian's iron nerves tingle, 'we shall have as good sport out of *him* as we meant to have out of *you!*'

There was a moment's silence, and then Bulatoff added:

'And now that that's settled, Ataman, I should be glad,

with your permission, to sleep a bit, for I am really so tired that I can hardly keep my eyes open.'

Archer came up at that moment with the same request, and not without reason; for, now that their devouring hunger had been appeased and their frozen limbs warmed, all the accumulated weariness of the five terrible days seemed to swoop down upon them at once, and a few minutes later they were sleeping as if they would never wake again.

It was well on in the afternoon when they were aroused by their new comrades, who were hastily cooking a wild goat that they had killed, a share of which they offered to the travellers; and then, the meal over, they all set out together for the other camp.

The count, who walked by Krovolil's side, saw by the fierce looks of the other bandits that all were fully aware of what had passed between him and their chief, and just in the very mood in which he wished to have them—eager for a victim on whom to avenge their disappointed rapacity, and caring little who that victim might be.

Short as the march was, it told heavily upon the two worn-out travellers; but, resolute to show no sign of weakness before the ruffians around them, they bore up manfully till at length they reached the other camp. Its site was chosen with considerable skill, on the brow of a steep and stony ridge, along the side of which all the brushwood had been carefully cut away, so as to leave any assailant fully exposed to the fire of the defenders from the dense thickets above. The rear of the position was protected by a vast overhanging cliff, and its flank by a terrific precipice.

The two guests found, to their surprise, a light hut, similar to those tenanted by the brigands themselves, already run up for *them* by order of the young chief, who had sent off one of his men for that purpose earlier in the day; but this hospitable care, however reassuring with regard to *one* cause of anxiety, suggested to the keen wits of our heroes another almost as bad.

Archer and his friend settled themselves at once in their new quarters; but hardly were they installed, when a man came in haste to call Bulatoff to the presence of the chief. The count instantly rose and went out, saying carelessly, 'I suppose he wants to ask me some more questions about Ala-Tau;' while Archer, little guessing the fell errand on which his comrade had gone, lay down again, and was soon asleep.

But all at once he was aroused by a fearful cry, so terrific, so full of mortal agony and despair, that it might almost have broken the slumber of the grave. As the Englishman started up the cry was repeated, evidently at no great distance; and bursting headlong out of the hut, he beheld a sight that made his blood run cold.

Not twenty paces from where he stood, in the blood-red glow of sunset, a stunted tree grew right out from the very brink of the precipice, so as actually to overhang the abyss; and suspended from one of its branches by a stout cord, made fast under his armpits, was a bound and helpless man, in whom, distorted as his face was by mortal terror, Archer at once recognised his traitor-guide from Ala-Tau. A second glance showed him a long, sharp knife fastened to a lower bough in such a way that every movement of the poor wretch's body, as the wind swayed it to and fro, sawed the rope backwards and forwards across the edge of the blade, *slowly severing the cord strand by strand.*

The brave Englishman was about to spring forward to the rescue, at whatever risk to himself; but ere he could do so the end came. The rope parted with a sharp snap, and the doomed wretch, with one last wild and horrible shriek, vanished for ever into the black gulf below. In the gloomy silence that followed the death-cry, there was faintly heard the muffled reverberation of a heavy body dashed from ledge to ledge down a seemingly fathomless abyss—and then all was still.

'I'm sorry that fool should have disturbed you with his yelping,' said Krovolil, coming up with a laugh still on his face. 'I had gagged him to keep him quiet, but the gag must have got loose somehow; and he *did* make a fine noise just at the last, didn't he?'

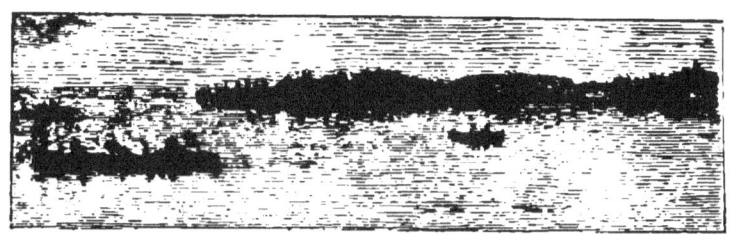

CHAPTER XXVII.

A TRIP THROUGH MONTENEGRO.

AND what were the two boys about all this time? Let Harry speak for himself.

ON LAKE SCUTARI, *Nov.* 23, 1871.

DEAR DAD,—Here we are right at the other end of nowhere (as old Kingsley says), in a queer sort of No Man's Land that's neither fish, flesh, nor red-herring— neither Turkey, Austria, Montenegro, nor anything else. The Prince told me, you know, to tell him whenever I wanted to make any trips about the country; and, sure enough, I've taken him at his word, for with him to help me forward and Prince Danilo to show me about, I've gone slap from one end of the kingdom to the other.

The more I see of this country the more I like it. It's just like going back hundreds and hundreds of years, to the old times that dear old Walter Scott tells of, and a good deal farther, too. I once heard some old professor say that any man who wanted to understand Homer thoroughly had only to make a tour in Montenegro; and he never spoke a truer word in his life, for it's just Homer all over again. Every chief has his own little batch of followers, same as those kings in the *Iliad;* and strangers turn up suddenly, and make themselves quite at home, just as that sly old file Ulysses did whenever he happened on a place where there were lots of fat oxen and sheep; and the king walks about among his people quite hail-fellow-well-met, and any one can go up and talk to him, like those Phœacian chaps with old Alcinous; and as for Princess What's-her-name bringing back the clothes from the wash, you can see that here any day you like; and the shepherds tend their flocks, weapon in hand, like that 'godlike swine-herd' who hung out in Ithaca; and when a fellow hasn't got cattle enough of his own, he goes out and steals a lot.

I wish, though, these jolly, good-natured fellows were not so horribly cruel. I've told you about the Turks' heads hanging all over the church-tower like apples on a tree; and down on the lake here, there's a military hospital full of the wounded Turkish prisoners taken in this last border war of theirs. Well, the first time I went into it I thought it would have turned me sick, for every man of them had had his ears and nose cut off, and the sight of their faces—ugh! I haven't got over it yet. Isn't it horrid? It quite spoils one's pleasure in being among them. Every time I shake hands with one of 'em I catch myself wondering how many heads that hand has chopped off; and it doesn't sound very nice to hear some bright-eyed, curly-headed little fellow, with a face like one of Chantrey's 'Sleeping Infants' at Lichfield, singing at the top of his voice:

> 'My name is Spiro Markovitch; I am a *pushko* * bold;
> My sword's inlaid with silver, my pistols tipped with gold;
> The Turks have killed my father—but with my father's gun
> I'll kill the Turks, and hang their heads to blacken in the sun!'

Indeed, the children here seem to be quite as warlike as the men. At Tsettinje the school was next door to our hotel, and the general and I went in to see it one day, and they showed us a bright little chap of eleven as the smartest pupil in the whole school; and the general and I had a talk with him, and he told us that his name was Saave Jurovitch, and that he was going to work hard and get to the very top of the school; and I was just thinking what a model boy he must be, when he went on, 'For when I get to the top, you know, I'll be able to leave school and become a warrior, and wear pistols and daggers in my girdle like Uncle Yanko (John), and cut off Turks' heads, as *they* cut off the head of my father!'

I didn't ask him any more questions after *that*, I can tell you.

But these Montenegs. are really very fine fellows in spite of it all. Isn't it grand to think of this little bit of a country, only sixty miles by thirty-five, having held out for more than four hundred years against the whole power of Turkey, and never been conquered yet, while all the rest of Servia (for the general says

---

* Rifleman—literally, 'man with a gun.'

they *are* Serbs by race) has been tramped flat by 'the hoof of the unspeakable Turk,' as old Carlyle used to say ? (Do you remember that night when we had tea with him, and how he blazed up at your first mention of the Turks, and said he would 'gladly see every rogue of them pitchforked out of the world by Russian bayonets'?) They seem to hate the Austrians, though, almost as much as they do the Turks ; but, queerly enough, the only money in the country is Austrian coinage, for they have never coined any of their own.

As for Prince Nikeeta himself, he 's as good a fellow as ever stepped in *opantchi* (native sandals), and does his very best to civilise and educate these wild subjects of his; and I'm sure I wish him all success, though it strikes me he'll have rather a tough job of it. Yury and I dined the other day with him and the bishop—a fine-looking old graybeard in a long violet robe and high black cap—who seemed quite pleased when he heard I'd been at Moscow (where the Monteneg. bishops all go to be consecrated, you know), and asked me all sorts of questions about it; and he offered me some cigars, and when I told him I didn't smoke he stared, and said he thought everybody did.

Then when dinner was done, up got the bishop, and told Yury and me that he'd got something to show us which we had not seen yet ; and he marched us off to the back of the church, and opened a small, narrow, wicked-looking door in the side of the hill, just like that place in the *Pilgrim's Progress*, you know, which the shepherds showed to Christian and Hopeful. Inside it was a horrid black hole right in the heart of the rock, pitch-dark, and as wet and cold as could be, with not a sound to break the silence except the tick, tick, tick of great drops of water falling from the roof ; and he told us that this was the dungeon in which they used to keep their prisoners—fancy that ! I suppose I must have looked pretty black at the mere idea of such a thing, for he went on directly to say that they never put any one there *now*—and I should rather hope they didn't.

Then the bishop took us into a sort of little chapel tacked on to the church, and showed us the robes of all the prince-bishops (*Vladikas*, I think they call 'em) who had reigned over Montenegro—all splendidly embroidered and covered with great pearls and sapphires, worth I don't know how much money ; and he told us tales of their feats in war with a relish that seemed rather queer in a churchman. But I found out later on that the bishop himself had been a soldier too, and had done as much fighting as any of 'em, though he didn't care to say much about it.

In fact, every man in Montenegro is a soldier; and though the *pushki* are only by way of being 25,000 strong, they can make 'em 100,000 at a pinch any day they like. On the way down here Danilo told me that they have a law in this country, handed down from the days of the very first prince, which says, 'The man who takes not up his arms at once when his country is attacked, his weapons shall be taken from him, and never may he wear them more. Never more may he hold any place of honour in his country's service, or march in the ranks of the sons of the Black Mountain; and in place of a warrior's dress, he shall be doomed to wear for evermore the apron of a woman, that all who see it may know that he hath not the heart of a man!' But when I asked if such a thing had ever happened he laughed, and said that he had never heard of it, and that he did not think he ever should.

And now to tell you how we got here. The Prince has a country-house on the shore of the lake, and he told us the other day that, if we cared to see it, our friend Danilo, his cousin, was going down there, and we could go too. Of course we jumped at it, and the general (who had to have a talk with some of the border chiefs about something or other) thought it a good chance for *him* to go too; so off we all went together.

It was almost as hard work to climb down to the lake as it had been to climb up to Tsettinje. First we went up, and then down, and then up again and down again, as if we should never be done; and though the distance was nothing to speak of, we had to halt for the night on the way, for there were one or two places where Yury's horse couldn't pass, and he had to scramble up and down the rocks on foot till he was quite tired out.

As we went along we heard a kind of howl overhead every now and then, though no one was in sight; and Danilo told us that the mountain-men signal to each other like that from hilltop to hilltop whenever a stranger is passing, so that, friend or enemy, they may be on the lookout for him; and he said that the call could be heard miles away, just like that Australian 'coo-ee' that you used to talk of. Anyhow, when we got to the village where we were to halt they seemed to know all about us, and a lot of 'em came and banged off their guns close to our heads by way of welcome ; and it just struck me that if one of them had happened to load with *ball* by mistake, it wouldn't be very pleasant.

They gave us a rattling good supper of *skoranza* (salt-fish), ryebread and honey, lots of dried fruit—for they grow no end of grapes and figs along the lake—and potatoes, which I hardly expected to find here. But I'm told that one of the Monteneg. bishops introduced them into these parts even before they were started in Germany, and that the people, in their gratitude, made him a saint ! But the funniest part of the whole business was that when I gave one of the children some sweet biscuits that we had brought from the hotel, all the household came and kissed me, men as well as women ; and Danilo says it's their regular way of thanking you. Queer notion, ain't it ?'

The rest of the way to the lake was all plain sailing, right down a sloping valley, up which the Turks used to come when they invaded the country, and down which, I'll be bound, they came pretty often a good deal faster than they went. After all these rocks and snows and precipices, the smooth lake and the vineyards and orchards all round it looked very pretty, if it hadn't been for the smoke of a newly-burned village going up a little farther along the shore.

We've been here three days now, and a very jolly time we're having. Every morning Yury and I have a big swim in the lake, and in the afternoon we go fishing ; only the general won't let us go far out, for fear of being drifted down to the Turkish end of the lake, and being killed or carried off for slaves by the Albanian robbers, which would not be very nice. (We are so near the border here that we can see quite plain, every now and then, a gang of Albanians, in their white kilts and red caps, scurrying off on some mischief or other ; and I can see by the faces of our Montenegs. that they're just hungering to be at 'em.) Then in the evenings the Montenegs. amuse us with songs and native dances, and telling of stories, just as those fellows in Homer used to do when they had no fighting to amuse them.

Nov. 24. I've just got your last from Meshid, which was forwarded here from the Caucasus. You *have* had some famous adventures, and no mistake. Fancy Krovolil being drowned ! I should have thought he was safe enough from *that,* anyhow.

The same man who brought your letter here brought a message to the general that the Prince wants him at once (some political bother, I suppose), and he has just started back to Tsettinje. We shall have it all to ourselves now, for Danilo's off hunting somewhere; but he's to be back to-night, and the general's to be back the day after to-morrow, and we can hardly get into any scrape before then.—And so believe me, your affectionate son,

H. ARCHER.

General Naprashkin was a shrewd and experienced man, and very seldom made a mistake of any kind; but he never made a worse one in his life than when he left these two madcap boys behind him *unattended*.

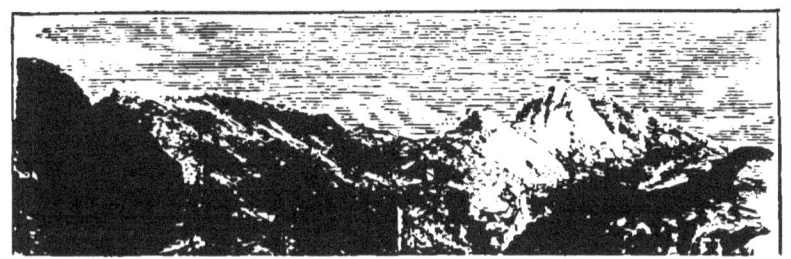

CHAPTER XXVIII.

MISSING.

EASONED as Livingstone Archer and his brother-explorer were to every form of horror, the deserter's hideous fate, with its new and frightful proof of the fiendish cruelty of this incarnate demon in whose power they were was too much even for *them*. Count Bulatoff himself, with all his ruthless cynicism, tried in vain to sleep when he came back to the hut; and both alike felt that all the terrors of the famine-haunted wandering from which their terrible host had rescued them were far less appalling than this.

But there was no help for it. The two observant travellers had already noted, with secret dismay, that this strange being (who appeared to unite the frank impulsiveness of a child to the bloodthirsty ferocity of an assassin) seemed to have conceived a sudden friendship for them both, which, though securing them against the stroke of death for the present, menaced them with almost equal peril in the future; and it was not without some inward emotion that the defenceless men heard Krovolil announce on the following morning— with a look and tone as bright and joyous as if all the horrors of the past night were but a dream—that now they were only waiting for a caravan (the last of the season) which was said to be on its way to pass the mountains not far from that spot; and as soon as it had been surprised and plundered, he and his men would go and establish themselves on the other side of the mountains for the winter, carrying their two guests along with them!

Here was a dilemma!

On one side lay a prospect of prolonged imprisonment (for it would be nothing less) amid a gang of the worst scoundrels on the face of the earth, and at the mercy of a human tiger who, the moment they happened to displease him, would certainly doom them to a worse death—if worse there could be—than that by which the wretched traitor had just perished before their eyes. On the other side was an all-too-probable chance of being killed in some obscure skirmish with a Russian detachment, or with the natives of the district (who would, of course, be against these plunderers to a man), leaving the magnificent success which they had just achieved unknown and useless for ever.

Well might the Russian's stout heart sink within him as he (while making a show of extreme satisfaction at Krovolil's announcement) tasked his ready brain to the utmost for some way of escape from this horrible dilemma, and tasked it in vain. But all at once, as his restless eyes roved despairingly round him, they caught sight of something which gave to his subtle and ever-plotting genius the very clue that it needed.

By this time the whole band of scoundrels were mustered around him, and in their ranks might be seen every varied type of humanity native to this wild region.

Foremost of the gang was a thick-set, red-bearded, low-browed Russian peasant, who, steeped as he was in crime and bloodshed, still wore on his brawny neck the little wooden cross hung round it by his mother when he was yet an innocent child. Beside him appeared the round, flat, muffin-like-face and narrow, oblique eye of a Tartar, flanked by a big, hook-nosed, swarthy Bokhariote, smoothing his long, black moustache with a dandified air that suited very ill with his ragged, filthy *caftan*, once green, but now showing every colour of the rainbow, with a softening haze of dirt shed gracefully over all. Then followed a lean, sinewy, keen-eyed Cossack deserter; and after him a squat, long-armed, ape-like Kalmuck, in a little pointed cap, with a face resembling nothing so much as a half-baked bun with two crushed raisins stuck in the middle of it. Next on the list figured a dark, lanky, high-cheeked Turkoman, in a high, black sheepskin cap; and then came a Kirghiz of the true desert type, whose sharp, fleshless face, hooked nose, and keen, restless eye gave him the look of a huge vulture suddenly changed into a man. Last but not least in this parade of nationalities was a hulking Bashkir, whose broad, puffy face and thick black hair were irresistibly suggestive of an overboiled black-currant dumpling.

But amid this great museum of international rascality there was *one* face which instantly riveted the wary count's attention—that of a gaunt, large-boned, wiry-looking fellow, who stood a little behind the rest.

The man's dress would have been enough of itself to attract attention, for it was that of an Albanian mountaineer —a strange sight indeed out here on the border of China, separated by the breadth of half Asia from the land to which it belonged. But it was his *face*, not his garb, that had drawn the shrewd Russian's watchful eye to him; and, in truth, that face, though anything but attractive, was one which could not easily be passed over unnoticed. Beneath a low, retreating forehead the small, deep-set, crafty eyes peered out with the half-cowed, half-ferocious look of a trapped beast of prey; and there was a sneaking, slouching air about the whole man seldom, if ever, seen among the fierce and swaggering highlanders of his lawless race.

The first sight of that scoundrelly visage inspired Count Bulatoff with a scheme worthy of the sharpest diplomat in the Russian Cabinet.

'Well, Ataman,' cried he, turning to Krovolil with a smile, as if replying to what the robber-chief had just said, 'it's very wise of you to shift your camp to the south, and get the hills between you and the Russian garrisons on the Ili, for perhaps you *are* just a little too close to them here.'

'Do you think I'm *afraid* of them, then?' asked the 'Blood-shedder' quickly.

'No; I'm not quite such a fool as that,' laughed the count. 'It seems to be rather *they* who are afraid of *you*, for I suppose you know that they have set a price of five hundred gold imperials * on your head, and promised a free pardon to any man who will give you up.'

As he spoke Bulatoff passed his hand quickly across his face, as if brushing the morning damp from his hair and eyelashes; but between his fingers he shot a keen glance at the low-browed Albanian, and the greedy glitter in the ruffian's cunning, rat-like eyes showed that the last words had produced the desired effect upon *him*.

'Let them offer what they like!' said Krovolil scornfully; 'the man who earns *that* reward will have to work well for it. But do they not believe me dead, then?'

'Apparently not,' replied the Russian, laughing again; 'and really, considering how often you have come to life again after being supposed dead, you can hardly expect that

---

* The imperial being worth five roubles, this would be nearly £400.

they should. But, as you say, the man who earns that reward will have to work well for it; and he will have to make haste about it, too; for, as you are going to move southward in three or four days at the latest, he has no time to lose.'

At these last words Bulatoff stole a second glance at the Albanian's face, and what he read in it told him all that he wished to know.

The whole of that day was devoted to hunting (it being now high time to lay in a stock of food for their southward march, which was to begin as soon as the expected caravan had been entrapped and plundered), and the entire band took part in it, with the exception of a handful of men left behind to guard the camp and the two guests, who were still too weak for such violent exertion, and perhaps not wholly trusted by Krovolil to refrain from attempting an escape.

To their guards the two men looked the very picture of listless contentment; but Archer, well practised by this time in reading the almost imperceptible changes of his friend's unrevealing face, was impressed by the strange air of *expectation* which deepened on it as the time of the hunters' return drew near, just as if the Russian were awaiting the news of some event which he had long since foreseen.

At length the figures of the foremost hunters were seen to rise against the bright evening.sky on the crest of the ridge, and move slowly along it toward the camp; but though the load which they carried told of successful sport, their agitated gestures and gloomy looks were more suggestive of some recent disaster.

'Brothers,' cried the first man—a tall Kirghiz—as his comrades of the camp came forward to meet him, 'assuredly it was beneath an unlucky star that Mehemet the Albanian

Q

went forth this day. Who could think that a man born among precipices would have ended by falling over one?'

'And *hath* he done so?' cried half-a-dozen voices at once.

'Even so. When we gathered to return to the camp he was not among us; and when we called his name none answered. Then we went forth to seek him, and lo! on the edge of a precipice we found a long mark in the soft earth, as if one had slid forward over the brink, and on a briar that grew out from the edge of the gulf hung our comrade's cap; and that was all.'

Then the Englishman looked in his friend's face, and saw that *this* was the news which he had been expecting, and that, for some unknown reason, it gave him special satisfaction.

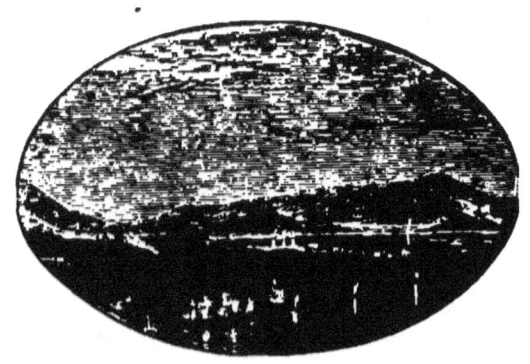

CHAPTER XXIX.

BURIED WITHOUT A GRAVE.

HE news of the Albanian's fearful death had no effect upon Krovolil, who merely remarked, with a smile, that 'it was lucky it had not been one of the better hunters,' and then proceeded to inspect the game brought back by his followers, to which he himself contributed no small share.

Half-an-hour later—having comforted his weary comrades with a cheering hint that 'by that time next day they might hope to be cutting the throats of the caravan-traders'—this strange being was seated like an old friend between his two guests at the camp-fire, and singing, in a voice as clear and sweet as the carol of a skylark, a simple Cossack song which he had learned from one of his band:

> 'Thou wilt grow into a warrior,
>   Ride with spear and brand;
> I will totter forth to bless thee—
>   Thou wilt wave thy hand.
> Bitter tears, all unregarded,
>   Then will dim mine eye;
> Sleep while yet thou know'st not sorrow—
>   Lulla-lullaby!'

But while the savages around him were listening in wondering delight, and even the two travellers, sincerely as they loathed him, were beginning to feel strangely moved, the 'Blood-shedder' suddenly raised his head, and his eye glittered like a hawk's when about to pounce on its prey.

Following the direction of his look, the explorers saw the long, supple body of a black snake (one of the deadliest in all Asia) gliding out from beneath a huge boulder not ten paces away.

'Watch now, and I'll show you some fun!' said Krovolil to them; and rising to his feet, he stepped forward and planted himself right in the serpent's path.

Finding its way thus barred, the snake reared itself up with a sharp hiss, and seemed about to spring upon him; but the bandit, without showing the slightest fear, deliberately bent down till his face was within a few inches of the quivering fangs, one touch of which was death, and looked fixedly into the small, green, glittering eyes.

Instantly the cruel light seemed to die out of them; a sudden spasm quivered through every fibre of the lithe, sinewy body; the threatening head drooped, and the snake lay limp and powerless on the earth; while Krovolil, having crushed with one fierce stamp the flat, slimy head, proceeded to pound the carcass beneath his feet, as if the mere feeling of crushing and mangling this still living creature filled him with a strange and horrible enjoyment.

As the young Ataman resumed his place the clamorous talk and merriment of his wild followers—suspended for an instant to watch their chief's exploit—broke forth again more noisily than ever. But all at once, jest and song, talk and laughter, were alike hushed, and a chill, creeping terror seemed to fall over the whole of that riotous band as a mighty shadow was seen hovering far overhead and slowly descending toward them.

Archer and the count looked on in some surprise; for, so far as *they* could see, this universal terror, though it seemed to have infected even Krovolil himself (who had till then appeared as utterly proof against fear as against pity), had absolutely no cause whatever, the object of all this panic being simply a mountain-eagle of unusual size hovering above their heads on its outspread wings.

But the sight of a whole Russian army closing round them with levelled bayonets could not have been more appalling to these reckless savages, steeped to the very finger-tips in violence and murder. Many of them actually grovelled on the earth, and the rest crouched and huddled together like frightened children. Several of the Russians were seen to make the sign of the cross with a trembling hand; and more than one bearded lip, long familiar with the foulest curses, faltered a half-forgotten prayer, while half-a-dozen hoarse voices muttered in tones tremulous with horror:

'The Simoorgh! the Simoorgh!'

Both travellers had sprung to their feet at the first alarm, expecting an attack of some kind. Krovolil himself rose likewise; but it did not escape Archer's observant eye that the brigand did so with the slow, mechanical movement of one yielding reluctantly to some overwhelming force, rather than following the impulse of his own free-will. All the rest were by this time prostrate on the earth.

On the eagle's first appearance the Englishman had instinctively stretched a hand toward his gun; but his growing interest in the weird tableau before him overcame even the thoroughly British impulse to bring down this pirate of the air with one shot, and he stood watching in silence to see how this strange scene would end.

Downward came the mighty bird in lessening circles, and as it neared them Archer and his friend, while admiring the grand proportions of its vast shadowy wings and giant body (completely black, save a small patch of snow-white plumage on the breast), looked keenly for anything in its appearance that could explain the general and overwhelming terror produced by its coming; but they could find nothing whatever.

Their perplexity, however, did not last long; for, from the muttered exclamations of dismay that broke from the terrified ruffians, our heroes soon gathered that the approaching bird was supposed by *them* to be no eagle, but an evil spirit that haunted these mountains, which was always known by its jet-black plumage and snow-white breast. It was only seen at long intervals, and never without bringing evil to those who beheld it, while any man round whom it circled in its flight was inevitably doomed to a speedy and frightful death.

The boldest and least superstitious man on earth is seldom wholly proof against a sudden outburst of superstitious terror on the part of other men, however firm in his conviction that such terrors are utterly groundless and absurd; and even these two brave, experienced, clear-headed men (who despised, as heartily as any one living, the childish bugbears of ignorance) felt, in their own despite, the chilling influence of a scene every accessory of which tended to deepen its gloomy impressiveness. The grim precipices all around them; the frightful chasm that yawned at their very feet, down which they had so lately seen a fellow-creature plunged shrieking to destruction; the blood-red glare of the sinking sun, breaking stormily through the ghostly shadows that were already darkening the sky; the strange

The eagle hung poised for an instant on its expanded wings.

PAGE 257.

terror that had so suddenly palsied these fierce and reckless
cut-throats; the broadening and deepening of the vast black
shadow above them; the eagle's unaccountable departure
from the wonted habits of its wild nature, which would
have led it to shun rather than to seek the unaccustomed
presence of so many human beings in that lonely place;
the tomb-like silence and encompassing desolation—all com-
bined to chill the bold hearts of the two adventurous men
with a creeping horror which they could neither explain nor
resist.

A few feet above the ground the eagle hung poised for
an instant on its expanded wings. Then it made a wide
sweep right round the prostrate band, and having done so,
flew straight across the ring to Krovolil, as if instinctively
drawn to a creature more pitiless and cruel than itself.
Passing so close to him as actually to brush him with its
wing, it *circled round him*, and then, shooting up again like
an arrow, vanished ghost-like into the fast-falling gloom of
night!

'I care not!' cried the 'Blood-shedder' defiantly. 'My
fortune has been told me already by a *koldoon* (sorcerer)
of my own country, and he said that no hand of man shall
ever take my life, and that no hand of man shall ever dig
my grave. Let all the eagles of the hills come and fly round
me if they like—I care nothing for it!'

And his fellow-ruffians, slowly raising themselves from
the earth, listened to his wild words in shuddering silence.

What Krovolil really thought of the strange events of
that evening no one could say, for that night he was seen
no more. Contrary to his custom, he at once shut himself
up in his own hut, and took his evening meal in gloomy

solitude, which the boldest of his wild followers did not dare to disturb.

But upon the rest of the gang the crushing effect of that weird portent was too tremendously manifest to leave any room for doubt. One and all wore the listless air of men who, feeling themselves sentenced to death, took no heed of what was passing around them, and would hardly take the trouble to speak or stir. So low, indeed, did their childish superstition sink these strong and savage outlaws that Bulatoff actually heard one of them trying to keep up the failing courage of himself and his comrades (apparently with not much success) by pointing out that, after all, the spirit of evil had really circled round no one but Krovolil himself; for, the rest of them having been flat on the ground, the fatal circuit had been made, not *around* them, but *above!*

The next morning Krovolil and most of his men went out hunting again, leaving, as before, a few of their number to guard the camp. But so utterly cowed were the latter by the fearful omen of the past night that, had the two prisoners known which way to go, they might have escaped there and then, without any one even attempting to hinder them.

Archer hinted as much to the count; but the wary Russian (who again wore that strangely *expectant* air that his friend had noticed on the previous day) answered guardedly that they would be always in danger of falling in with some of the hunters, and that it was best to run no risk. This excuse, however, plausible as it was, did not impose upon the shrewd Englishman, who felt sure that his comrade had some *other* reason for holding back, which he did not choose to tell.

The same gloom which weighed down the brigands who remained behind seemed to haunt likewise those who went forth; and their chase that day was singularly unsuccessful. The best hunters among them only scared their game instead of running it down, and missed their mark again and again when it was quite plain before them. All this, though really due to their own shaken nerves, was of course set down to supernatural agency; and they came back toward sunset, all but empty-handed, with the firm conviction that they were one and all under a curse, against which it was vain to struggle.

This cheering conviction was not a little strengthened when, just about nightfall, a native scout in Krovolil's pay came in with the news that the caravan which they were waiting to attack had taken another road and escaped them—a piece of intelligence which produced such excitement in the camp that, when our heroes were left alone in their hut, Bulatoff said gravely:

'If we don't escape at once, Lyoff, one of two things will happen; either we shall be carried south beyond the reach of help by these fellows—who have nothing more to keep them here now—or else, in their excitement at missing that caravan and being haunted (as they think) by an evil spirit, they'll take it into their heads that *we* have brought them ill-luck, and murder us both on the spot!'

'Very likely,' said Archer as composedly as ever; 'but I don't quite see how we *are* to escape, unless we were to slip off while the bulk of the gang are out hunting, as I proposed to-day.'

'Why not wait till they are asleep, and then kill them all?' suggested the Russian as coolly as if he were speaking of shooting partridges.

The Englishman's sun-browned face glowed like heated iron, and he answered, more fiercely than he had ever yet spoken to his friend :

'*You* may, if you like; that sort of thing is not in my line. Anything that befits a *man* I am ready to do, but I have no gift for treacherous and cowardly murder!'

But the cool count, not a whit discomposed by his vehemence, replied as calmly as before:

'Don't let us quarrel about it, Lyoff; we have each our own way of thinking, and this is no time to dispute which way is the best. What we have to do *now* is to help each other to get free from the clutches of these rascals.'

But this, as has been seen, was much easier said than done.

The first thing our heroes heard next morning was Krovolil's voice, so changed from its usual tones that both men felt at once that some great crisis had come; and, hurrying out, they found the 'Blood-shedder' standing amid a trembling circle of his men, who had drawn back from him on every side, as if either fearing violence at his hand, or moved by a deeper and darker terror to shrink away from one whom Heaven itself had doomed.

But, in truth, they had good cause to shrink back; for the aspect of the robber-chief was that of a man absolutely driven to desperation. His lips quivered, his eyes glared, his face was unnaturally flushed, and in every word that he uttered there was a tremor of ill-suppressed fury which showed that the slightest opposition would suffice to goad him into some fearful outburst of rage, which would be certain death to every living thing within reach.

'Don't prate to *me* of omens and warnings!' he roared in a voice less like the speech of a man than like the inarticulate yell of a wild beast; 'the only curse that rests upon me is the curse of being cumbered with a pack of frightened fools that are afraid of their own shadow. I'll soon show you how much *I* care for your babyish fancies! When we go forth to hunt to-day, I will go one way with these two strangers (for the eagle circled round *them* as well as round me, and so, on your own showing, we are all three under the same doom), and the rest of you can go another way by yourselves; and *then* we will see which of us has the best luck!'

Archer did not see the ominous glitter that lighted up the count's keen blue eyes at these last words; but he *did* see at once what an unhoped-for chance of escape this strange plan offered to them both, and sternly resolved that he would not be slack to seize it.

No one dared reply to Krovolil's challenge, and the bandits finished their morning meal in gloomy silence, while the robber-chief and his two newly-chosen comrades hastily got through theirs. This done, the main body of the brigands (having left, as usual, a few men to guard the camp) filed off, noiselessly as shadows, in the same direction as on the previous day; and Krovolil, leading his two guests down the ridge that they had ascended on the memorable day of their arrival, turned suddenly away to the left, and struck off through the pathless wilderness of dark rocky hills beyond, at a pace which even his active companions found it hard to equal.

'We shall have warm work of it if he goes at this pace all day,' said Bulatoff in a low voice, 'for the air is as close as an oven.'

It was indeed, without any apparent reason, the sun being completely hidden by a gray, sullen haze that brooded over the whole sky. Not a breath of wind was stirring; no leaf rustled, no grass blade shook. All was ominously and terribly still.

'Seems to me there's a storm coming,' muttered Archer, 'and I only hope it will hold off till we get back.'

But at that moment Krovolil faced round upon them with eyes like live-coals.

'Silence!' he hissed. 'Do you want to scare our game?'

Both men were somewhat startled, for there was no game whatever in sight; and even had there been any, the whisper in which they had spoken could not have been heard ten yards away. But, as may be supposed, they had no inclination to contest the point with him just then; and thenceforth they moved onward in perfect silence.

All at once the tomb-like stillness was broken by a strange, dull, far-off sound, not unlike distant thunder, had thunder been possible in that place at that season. A cannon it could not be, for the sound was too gradual and too prolonged; and it seemed not so much like thunder as like the harsh, grating rumble of a ponderous wheel—a strange sound indeed in a region where no wheel had passed since time began.

The count and his friend exchanged looks of visible disquiet; but Krovolil, who seemed either not to hear or not to heed the mysterious noise, pressed on at the same headlong rate as ever, straining his eyes forward with a fixed, never-changing stare, as if watching something which no one else could see.

Closer and closer became the air; darker and darker grew the sky. Before the vague menace of these weird phenomena and the wild behaviour of their grim guide even the brave Englishman felt uneasy without knowing why, and the cynical count himself began to look grave.

Suddenly the mysterious sound came again, still faint and

far away, but perceptibly louder and sharper than before.
This time Krovolil evidently heard it, for he raised his head
as if listening; but not for a moment did he slacken his
headlong advance or change the fixed and ghastly stare of
his haggard eyes.

Where had Archer seen such eyes before, and with just
such a look in them as this?

And then it flashed upon him that, on his last visit to
London, the picture of the year had been a large painting of
'Orestes pursued by the Furies,' wrought out with such
terrific force and reality as to scare into a fainting-fit one of
the ladies who went with him to see it. The tortured face
of the hunted man had haunted Archer's memory for many
a day after; and now that face was before him, in all its
horrors.

'He may well be haunted,' said the brave Englishman to
himself, with a half-unconscious shudder, 'after all that he
has done.'

All at once Krovolil stopped short—not a little to the
relief of his panting followers, whose strength was not yet
sufficiently restored for such a break-neck rush over hill and
dale—and, standing motionless a little way in front of them,
gazed wildly around him.

The creeping dimness above them was fast deepening into
absolute gloom, the sky being doubly darkened just then by
a strange, smoke-like vapour that hovered along the crests of
the hills, and appeared to be slowly descending toward them;
and Archer saw, with a sudden quiver of his strong nerves
which he would have been very loth to own, that it had, or
seemed to have, the shadowy outline of a monstrous *eagle!*

It was plain that Krovolil had noticed it likewise, for he
was seen to shake his clenched hand at the terrible shadow

with a gesture of fierce defiance. But scarcely had he done so, when he faced sharply round, and, pointing straight before him, shouted with an air of frantic excitement:

'There goes our game! I'll have it! Come on!'

And away he flew like a whirlwind, dashing over loose rocks, leaping fallen trees, and clearing perilous chasms at a bound, with a recklessness which made his escape from death or severe hurt little short of a miracle.

It seemed as if his frenzy had infected the two others as well, for, though no game whatever was to be seen, they instantly darted away after him in the same frantic fashion, echoing his wild cries, and filled with a kind of mad eagerness for they knew not what.

In this headlong manner they had gone hurrying onward for some distance—still keeping Krovolil well in sight, though to come up with him was impossible even for *them*— when, all of a sudden, the bandit-chief was seen to come to a dead halt, as before, a little way in front of them.

Ere they could get up to him he had unslung his rifle, and bringing it to his shoulder with the speed of thought, aimed right at a spot about thirty yards beyond him, and let fly. Then, flinging down his gun, he waved his hand with a triumphant shout, like a hunter who has just brought down his game.

There was no game there.

Archer and the count looked at each other—a look that said more than any words.

'There!' shouted Krovolil, uplifting his face toward the darkening sky as if he would defy Heaven itself. 'Eagle or spirit, I laugh you to scorn! Do you think to terrify *me* with shadows? Come what may, I stand firm—ay, firm as the very earth under my feet!'

Hardly was the rash challenge uttered, when the same strange and ominous sound that had been heard twice already came once more—and this time in a rending, crashing, grinding uproar beneath their very feet. The eagle-shaped cloud swept up over the sky, shrouding the whole scene in a cheerless and ghostly twilight; the earth shook; the wooded hill-tops trembled; the thunder of falling crags was heard far and wide around them; and the two men sank dizzily to the ground.

But even in falling they saw dimly, but with a thrill of horror never to be forgotten, the earth open within a few paces of them, and Krovolil (with the look of defiance still on his face) *vanish into it!*

When they rose to their feet again the unearthly darkness had begun to melt away, and they could see plainly that the path in front of them—along which they had just been hurrying with such headlong speed—was now buried deep beneath a mighty mass of fallen rocks and up-torn trees, rent from the mountain-side by the shock of the earthquake. But of Krovolil not a trace was to be found. The earth had closed again where he disappeared, and he was gone as if he had never been.

CHAPTER XXX.

LOST ON THE MOUNTAINS.

'E'S gone at last, thank Heaven!' cried the Russian, drawing a long, deep breath of intense relief.

'Poor wretch! May God have mercy on him!' said the Englishman solemnly.

Both utterances were thoroughly characteristic; and it was even more so that the count instantly added, with perfect composure:

'And now, Lyoff, as we seem to be our own masters again, we had better continue our march towards the forts on the Ili, which the late Mr Krovolil so unseasonably interrupted.'

'If we can find our way there,' said Archer meaningly.

'Pooh! that ought not to be a very difficult matter. If we keep on heading to the north-west we *must* strike the Ili sooner or later; and, once there, it won't take long to reach one of the forts. The only pity is, that we should have been going *away* from it all this time.'

'Yes,' cried Archer, 'we're a good ten miles farther off than when we started this morning. But at all events,' he added, slapping his well-filled provision-bag with an air of satisfaction, 'we're better provided now than on our *first* march that way.

Now, let us take our bearings. Which way does the camp lie?'

'Just about due west, I should say,' replied his friend.

'Then we had better keep well to the north, so as to be sure of not falling in with any of the worthy gentlemen belonging to it.'

'Quite right; and, in my opinion, we had better head up this valley to the left, as soon as we have had some food.'

And in a trice the two indomitable men, unshaken by all the horrors through which they had passed, were setting off on a fresh march through this frightful wilderness as coolly as if only going for a stroll about the streets of Moscow.

By this time the sky was fast clearing, the atmospheric convulsion having now spent itself; and when the sun reappeared they saw with some surprise that it was still high in the sky, the whole of this weird drama having wrought itself out in the space of a very few hours.

But though they had now light to guide them, their advance was neither rapid nor easy. No one who has not actually tried it can form any idea of the overwhelming labour of a march on foot (especially when weighted with a gun and bag) through a region where the way lies now up a precipitous cliff, and now through a waist-deep and ice-cold torrent—at one time crossing endless heaps of loose stones, with a stumble and a bruise at every step, and at another time plunging suddenly into a black tangle of spiky thorns and matted briars, supple as whip-cord and strong as iron wire.

But, as if all this were not enough, our heroes were forced to make circuit after circuit in order to avoid the chaos of rocks, bushes, stones, shattered trees, and masses of loose earth and gravel with which the earthquake seemed to have blocked their way at every turn; and hence, though they kept pressing on (in spite of the severe fatigue of the morning) as gallantly as men could do, yet when night came to check their progress they were barely eight miles on their way toward life and safety.

'We must just do better to-morrow, that's all,' said Archer as cheerily as he could. 'It won't do to light a fire, though, for we must be close to the haunts of these rogues now, and some of 'em might catch sight of it; so we'll just have to keep as warm as we can without one.'

This was but poor comfort in such a place and at such a season; but, in spite of the cold, the weary men slept till daybreak, from sheer exhaustion.

'Your Excellency, the coffee is here!' cried Archer, mimicking the call with which the count's Russian lackey used to rouse them at Borjom.

'I only wish it was!' said Bulatoff, with a rueful grin, as he stretched his benumbed limbs painfully and tried in vain to still the castanet-like chattering of his teeth.

'Well, as the Russian Government has not built a hotel here yet, we must just be content with a cold breakfast for once,' replied the other, with a jolly English laugh; 'and now we'll be off again. We can't well be much more than one day's march from the Ili *now*, any way.'

Off they went accordingly; and, glad of any exertion to warm their frozen limbs, they tramped along briskly, to all appearance quite unmoved by the thought that they had nothing to guide them beyond a vague guess at the right direction (for the hidden sun gave them no aid whatever), and that they were, in fact, as completely lost amid these wild and perilous mountains as when they made their first start from the fatal valley of Sari-Djaz, after the death of their Tartar guide.

'I *hope* we are going right,' muttered the count at length, 'but I wish I could be quite sure. If only the sun would come out a bit!'

But this was just what the sun seemed bent upon *not* doing; and for half-an-hour more they struggled on in silence, in the same direction as before.

All at once Archer waved his hand with a joyous shout toward a tall, grim, mitre-shaped crag which stood up like a tower at the angle of a bold wooded ridge a little way in front of them.

'I know that rock!' he cried. 'I camped at the foot of it three years ago, when I crossed these hills to hunt for the ruins of King Cheirisophos's town. I know where we are now, and we'll be all right after this, for there's a valley running from there right down to the Upper Ili and the Russian outposts! Fancy being among Christian folk again after all this! And just think what a welcome they'll give us when we get there! Hurrah!'

Hardly were the words spoken, when out from behind the cliff on their left came suddenly upon them seven or eight wild-looking figures, armed to the teeth, in whom our heroes recognised at a glance some of their late comrades of Krovolil's band.

'Here they are!' cried three or four voices at once; 'and now we shall know all about it. Whither are you going, strangers; and where is our chief?'

Ere Bulatoff could answer (as he intended) with some neat little lie ready-made for the occasion, the Englishman broke in bluntly:

'Your chief will never come back; he has died, as he said he would, *untouched by the hand of man !*'

And then, in a few simple words, he told the fate of the 'Blood-shedder.'

'He lies!' roared a savage-looking Russian fiercely. 'Would this fellow have us believe that the curse has smitten but one man out of three, and spared the other two? They have murdered our captain themselves, brothers. Down with the dogs!'

'Ay, down with them!' yelled a lean, wolfish Tartar, 'or else the curse that rests on them will fall on us likewise. Kill them both!'

But the two travellers had unslung their rifles at the first alarm, and were quite ready for this attack, sudden as it was. There was a flash and a crack, and two of the ruffians fell disabled to the earth; while our heroes, felling two more with their clubbed guns, broke through the rest with a sudden rush, and darted away, with the speed of hunted deer, toward the tower-like crag to which Archer had pointed.

With all their haste, however, they were not a whit too soon, for as they ran they caught sight of another and a larger group of brigands coming racing toward the spot, as if drawn by the sound of the firing. It was plain the whole robber-band were astir in quest of their missing chief, and that the two bold adventurers were lost if they could not at once find some sure place of refuge.

But, happily for them, such a refuge was before their very eyes.

On the side facing the valley the rock went sheer down in a vast black precipice of more than a hundred feet; but where it joined the main ridge the ascent was nothing more than a very steep slope till within about twenty feet of the top; and between the two crests of its mitre-shaped summit lay a dark cleft, wide and deep enough to shelter a dozen men in place of two. Could they but reach *it* they were safe.

But *would* they ever reach it? It seemed more than doubtful, for the robbers were coming on like hungry wolves in sight of their prey, making the silent valley ring with their yells, while every echo of the surrounding rocks answered the crack, crack, crack of the guns that sent bullet after bullet whizzing around the fugitives.

But, whatever the authors of penny-romances may say, it is *not* the easiest thing in the world to hit a swiftly-moving object while running at full speed one's self; and, though both were spattered again and again with the earth and gravel dashed up from beneath their very feet by the flying bullets, they reached the foot of the ridge unhurt, and flew up it at a pace which few men could have equalled even on level ground.

But by this time the pursuers (who were far fresher than the pursued) had got perilously near; and Archer saw that something must be done to check them, or all was lost.

'Get behind this stone, and we'll give 'em a shot!' panted he, seizing the count's arm with one hand, while he drew his revolver with the other.

The boulder was large enough to hide them both, and the pursuing ruffians, supposing them to be still retreating up the slope, came yelling on at their utmost speed, fearing no return fire; for they knew that the two fugitives had had no time to load their discharged guns, and they had no idea that both were armed with revolvers.

Foremost of the murderous gang was the fierce-looking Russian who had been the first to clamour for the blood of the two strangers. He had just reached the foot of the slope when the English revolver cracked, and he fell dead without a cry.

Just behind him came two Tartars in a line, one close behind the other. Bulatoff fired in turn, and brought down both with one shot.

'Very pretty practice,' remarked he, with a quiet smile. 'I have always been curious to know if one of these bullets would go through two men at once, and now I am quite satisfied.'

Once more the Englishman's blood boiled at the cold cruelty of his iron-hearted comrade; but this was no time for disputes. As the brigands, dismayed by this sudden havoc, hung back irresolutely, the hunted men, with one desperate rush, gained the edge of the thickets above, and vanished amid the sheltering leaves.

To reach the crest of the hill from thence was easy; but their perils were not over yet. For a space of full twenty yards from the crag itself all the brushwood along the summit of the ridge had been cut clean away; and as they darted across this open space in full view of their enemies beneath, their figures, boldly outlined against the sky, made a fatally plain mark, as was shown by the instant crash of a volley from below.

The Russian staggered—a bullet had passed through his cap and had grazed his head. A spot of blood on Archer's jacket showed where a ball had slightly wounded his shoulder, and several more flattened on the stones within a few inches of them both. But in another moment they had put a projecting angle of the crag between them and their foes, and clambering nimbly up a narrow, chimney-like cleft behind it, dropped down into the sheltered hollow beyond.

'Den!' shouted Archer, like an English schoolboy playing a game of 'prisoner's base.'

'We have won the race,' laughed his friend, 'and so we may as well have our breakfast; for, now that I come to think of it, we have not eaten yet to-day.'

'No more we have, by-the-by,' cried Archer. 'I was in such a hurry to warm myself by tramping off at once that I forgot all about it.'

And these iron men settled down to their breakfast on the brink of that frightful precipice, with merciless foes hungering for their life all around, as composedly as if they were in a London hotel.

By this time the whole gang of brigands had reached the foot of the crag; and while some of them scrambled up the ridge under cover of the bushes, the rest opened a spattering fire from below upon the natural watch-tower that held their intended victims.

'Very kind of these fellows to give us salt with our bread,' said Bulatoff, with a grim chuckle, as he blew off the dust which a well-aimed bullet, striking the edge of the rock behind which he sat, had spattered over the piece of bread in his hand.

But Archer made no reply, and a very grave look began to steal over his bold, brown face.

'How now, Lyoff?' cried the count. 'What is there to look glum about? They can't get at us, and we have plenty of food.'

'But not plenty of *water!*' answered the Englishman, with meaning emphasis. 'We have not a drop beyond what is in our flasks, and when that is done, *what then?*'

'True,' said the other, looking grave in his turn. 'It's a pity this new hotel of ours has not a *cistern* in addition to its other advantages. However, let us finish breakfast first, and then we'll consider what is to be done.'

In truth, their position needed the most careful consideration that they were able to give it; for never yet had they been in such peril as now. Beset on every side by murderous savages, with a limited stock of food and ammunition, a scanty supply of water, and not the faintest hope of mercy should fortune go against them, they were indeed in evil case.

Nor was this all. Their very lives depended on keeping a constant watch lest the unseen foes, who were now pelting them with bullets from the thicket in front, should storm their little fortress with a sudden rush; and yet, should either of them, while doing so, expose himself for one moment to the deadly aim of the marksmen who were firing at them behind as well as before, it would be certain death.

Nor could the besieged men even comfort themselves, in this desperate strait, with the forlorn hope that the bandits might tire of the siege and abandon it of their own freewill. The Tartar brigand had spoken the secret belief of his comrades as well as his own in declaring that unless the two doomed men were put to death, the curse that clung to *them* would extend its fatal ban over the whole gang of cut-throats; and such a conviction in the minds of these ferocious and ignorant savages was an ample warrant both that they would persevere in their attack to the bitter end, and that the ill-fated travellers, if overcome, might as well ask mercy from the hungry vultures that were already circling restlessly overhead and watching greedily for their expected prey.

At that very moment—as if to heighten the bitterness of death itself—there came to them a sudden glimpse of the haven of rest and safety that lay so near them, yet so utterly beyond their reach. Far down the valley to their left they caught sight of a glittering streak, and knew it to be the stream of the Ili, on which stood the Russian forts that they had hoped to reach. There it was full in view; and here were they, doomed to die a cruel death with it actually before their eyes.

'There lies help, if we could only reach it,' said Archer grimly.

'Or if *it* could reach *us*,' rejoined the count; 'but it seems to be a long while coming.'

'*Coming!*' echoed the Englishman, looking fixedly at him. 'Why, what do you expect?'

Ere the count could reply the question answered itself.

Through the black, narrow, tunnel-like mouth of one of the rocky glens that opened every here and there into the wider valley came filing out, rank on rank, a detachment of *Russian soldiers*, in the van of which, as if playing the part of guide, Archer's powerful spy-glass showed him a man in Albanian dress—no other, in fact, than the traitor Mehemet, whose pretended death (as Bulatoff had guessed all along) was merely a trick to pave the way for his betrayal of his comrades.

CHAPTER XXXI.

NEWS FROM EUROPE.

OR some moments neither of the two men spoke a word; for, weakened as they were by so many sufferings, this sudden reaction from seemingly utter despair to overwhelming hope was almost more than they could bear.

'Now, Lyoff,' said the Russian at length, 'here's help coming at last, and *we* must take our part in the work too. Those fellows yonder among the bushes won't have seen the soldiers yet, for we can only just see them ourselves from up here; and what we have to do now is to occupy the attention of the rogues, and keep them from finding out what is coming upon them. It's only those who are up here on the ridge that we need care about; for as to the others down below, they'll never see the soldiers till they feel 'em.'

In accordance with this plan, the wily count stepped forward and shouted to the ambushed robbers, through a crack in the sheltering rock:

'Now, you sneaking dogs! we have had our breakfast, and we are all ready for you!'

This insulting defiance, and the utter contempt implied in this cool making of a leisurely meal in the very face of all that the assailants could do, stung the savage outlaws to fury, and they answered with a fierce yell and a shower of bullets; to which the count replied by discharging his gun at them as fast as he could load it, accompanying every shot with a burst of those pointed and forcible terms of abuse in which the Russian language is so proverbially rich.

In this his English comrade (who began to enter into the humour of this strange scene) seconded him stoutly; but, while thus helping to keep the robbers in play, Archer shot a keen glance down the farther valley ever and anon, to watch the advance of the rescuers, which seemed fearfully slow to the doomed men whose lives hung upon it.

Foot by foot the coming detachment moved on; but it was still a terribly long way off, when Archer saw its march halt suddenly, while two men in front of it (whom the glass showed to be an officer and the Albanian guide) seemed to hold a hasty conference apart.

It was plain, from their repeated pointing toward the ridge which was the scene of action, that the speakers saw and understood what was passing there; and the result of their conference was soon apparent in the sudden dividing of the Russian detachment, one half of which vanished into a dark, narrow, wooded gorge on the left, while the other continued its advance up the valley.

'Good!' said the count when this was reported to him; 'our men are going to surround them—just what we want!'

But at that moment Archer's cap was struck from his head by a shot from below; and, thus warned that he had not kept sufficiently under cover, he drew hastily back behind his rock.

When he ventured to peer forth again, he did so in the joyful expectation of seeing the Russian soldiers close at hand. He looked—started—rubbed his eyes as if thinking

that they must have played him false—and then looked
again, with a slowly deepening expression of astonishment
and dismay.

The soldiers were *gone*—gone like a dream!

Archer carefully wiped the lenses of his glass, and swept
with it the whole length and breadth of the defile; but no
—not one soldier was anywhere to be seen!

All at once, however, he thought he saw something moving
in the depths of a dry, stony torrent-bed that zigzagged
along one side of the valley; and, looking fixedly at it, he
at length made out a line of prostrate figures worming their
way, one behind the other, along the deep, narrow channel,
nearer and nearer to the unconscious robbers. So cautiously
and silently did they glide onward that, even while looking
right down upon them, he had hard work to assure himself
that they were really there.

'Very prettily done,' said the Englishman approvingly;
'these fellows know how to skirmish, and no mistake!'

But just then Bulatoff lifted his head quickly, and began
to sniff the air like a hunted stag.

'Don't you smell *burning?*' cried he. 'I'll be bound our
men have set the thickets on fire, to drive these fellows
out!'

The thick gust of hot, stifling smoke that came rushing
up over the brow of the hill as the words were spoken gave
them a full and terrible confirmation; and the two brave
men felt their hearts sink, for if they sprang up to escape
they would be shot dead by the watchful marksmen below,
and to remain there a moment longer was to run the
imminent risk of being stifled or burned alive.

Ere they could speak or move, a hot blast of thick black
smoke made all around as dark as night; but through this

unnatural gloom broke a fierce red glare, as the fire overleaped the crest of the ridge and surged up along it like a wave, till all was one whirl of roaring, leaping flames, the scorching heat of which seemed able to melt the solid rock itself.

But for the sheltering rock-wall between them and this sevenfold furnace (against which the narrow clearing was no protection) the two adventurous travellers must have perished there and then. As it was, they were fain to throw themselves flat on the ground, press their burning faces into a cleft of the rock, and, covering their heads as best they might, await the issue of this last and fiercest onset of death.

But how long could they sustain it? Their eyes smarted as if filled with pepper, their skin seemed cracking with the blistering heat, and every breath that they drew was a convulsive gasp, which seemed to tear their labouring lungs asunder.

All their sufferings, however, could not make these practised warriors deaf to the sounds of battle that now broke forth below. Amid the roar and rumble of the flames, the sharp snapping of dry twigs, the hiss and crackle of freshly-kindled boughs, the thundering crash of falling trees and loosened rocks, there mingled for a few fierce moments a wild clamour of shouts, groans, yells, hoarse words of command, and the sharp reports of muskets and rifles; and then came a dead, ominous silence.

Little by little the heat became less intense, the devouring flames sank from sheer lack of fuel, and a sudden change of wind beat back the stifling smoke; and at length the two heroes crept forth from their lair, and as they appeared on the summit of the crag, were greeted by the victorious

Russians below with a lusty cheer, which their parched and gasping lips vainly strove to answer.

The wanderers were safe at last, for every man of the murderous gang had perished; and their journey to the fort with their rescuers was both short and easy. Captain Martchenkoff, the officer in command, was not a little surprised to learn *whom* he had saved, and said warmly:

'I never expected, when I came out to punish these rogues who have been annoying the district, the good fortune of rescuing your Excellency from their clutches. As soon as we get to the fort I'll send off a courier to Vernoë, our nearest telegraph station here, to give his Imperial Majesty the news of your safety, about which he must certainly have been anxious.'

'Many thanks, captain,' said the count; 'and, with your leave, I'll write the message myself, so as to lose no time in announcing to his Majesty the complete success of our mission.'

He was just pencilling the last words of the despatch, when Captain Martchenkoff's eye happened to light on the Albanian renegade, who was slouching along in the rear of the party.

'Well,' said he coolly, 'as this fellow is not likely to be of any further use to us, I suppose we may as well hang him.'

'A very good thought!' cried Bulatoff approvingly. 'I'm glad you happened to recollect it, for *I* had forgotten all about him. Might I ask you to do it at once, as I am rather in a hurry to get on to the fort?'

'What!' broke in Archer sternly; 'do you talk of hanging a man to whom you promised a free pardon, and who

gave himself up to you on that understanding? You may
say, perhaps, that I have no right to interfere; but, right or
no right, I won't stand by and see it done!'

Had any ordinary foreigner ventured on this presumptuous
interference, the Russian officer would have made short work
of him; but Livingstone Archer, honorary member of the
Russian Imperial Geographical Society, whom the Czar himself had coupled in a special mission with a personal friend of
his own, was not to be so summarily dealt with.

'Surely, Monsieur Archer,' remonstrated the captain, 'you
do not think the life of such a miserable scoundrel worth
making any fuss about. Besides, you must remember that
the pardon of which you speak was promised to him on condi-
tion of his putting Krovolil into our hands, and that he has
not done it.'

'But he has given you the information that *would* have
done it, if Krovolil had not been killed in the meantime,'
retorted the Englishman; 'and, at all events, he has enabled
you to destroy all the rest of the gang. I should be very
sorry to have any quarrel with you, after what you have just
done for us; but I protest against this man's execution as
nothing short of a murder, and if it is carried out I shall
take it on my own responsibility to report the matter direct
to the Emperor himself.'

This was a settler; and the young captain (though far
from guessing how important the despised traitor's life was
soon to be) gave up the contested point at once, not without
a slight smile of wondering amusement at the Englishman's
earnestness over such a *trifle*.

On reaching the fort (one of those meek little mounds of
dried mud encircled with a ditch, and with two or three tiny

S

guns sticking to it like flies on treacle, which stud the whole breadth of Central Asia from the Sea of Aral to the Chinese border) the two worn-out travellers slept for twelve hours at a stretch, and felt greatly refreshed by it; but even more reviving to Count Bulatoff was the arrival, on the second evening, of a telegram from the Czar himself, acknowledging his services in the most flattering terms, and conferring upon him the Star of St Alexander Nevski, the most coveted of all Russian distinctions next to the Cross of St George.

'Well done, Feodor!' cried Archer heartily. 'I'm glad they know what you are worth.'

'They ought to give *you* something too, though,' said the count; 'and I have no doubt they will, when we get back.'

Two more days passed, however, ere they could fully shake off—hardy as they were—the effects of their recent sufferings; and all this while both avoided, as if by tacit consent, any allusion to their late experiences.

At length, as they were strolling along the river-bank on the fourth evening, to watch the ugly little Tartars of the district fishing or towing their heavy barges, the Englishman said abruptly:

'You kept it pretty close about that Albanian; *I* quite believed him dead.'

'I knew that what I said about the reward would be enough for *him*, but I thought you might perhaps have some scruple about that too,' replied the count, with a slight sneer. 'It is just as well, though, that *he* knows nothing of this "curse" which is supposed to hang over us; for, if the story got abroad, these soldiers, who are now so eager to serve us, would run from us as if we had the plague!'

'Well,' said Archer gravely, 'I have none of that superstition about *me*, as you know; but I must say I'd give something for any satisfactory explanation of some of the things we've been seeing lately—for instance, the strange behaviour of that eagle, and the kind of mad fit that took us both as we were following Krovolil.'

'Nothing at all out of the way in that,' rejoined his friend quietly. 'A hungry eagle, espying several scores of men lying on the ground, might well hover round them to see if they were dead and eatable. Krovolil's sudden madness is not surprising, for I don't think he was ever quite sane; and considering how the atmospheric conditions attending an earthquake are wont to affect even the strongest nerves, I don't think the effect produced upon *us* was at all strange, especially with the presence and example of an actual madman superadded. But who comes here in such a hurry? Captain Martchenkoff?'

'This telegram has just come in,' said the captain, 'and I hope it may contain some reason for congratulating your Excellency anew.'

Bulatoff opened the missive, glanced over it, stared blankly at it for an instant, as if hardly understanding what was written there, and then his sun-browned face whitened to the very lips, and his hands clenched themselves convulsively till the fingers met through the paper.

Without a word he handed the message to Archer, who read it in turn, and bit his lips till they bled.

'We must start for home at once!' said the count in a voice that was not his own.

'We will!' said the Englishman; and they did so that very night, taking with them—to the unbounded amazement of the whole garrison—the Albanian traitor whom Bulatoff had been so eager to hang only a few days before.

CHAPTER XXXII.

DRIFTING TO THEIR DOOM.

HEN General Naprashkin (as already related) set off for Tsettinje at a moment's notice, leaving his nephew and Harry Archer in their new quarters on the Scutari Lake, he felt less anxious about them than usual, knowing that the absent Prince Danilo was to rejoin them that very evening. That the boys could get into any serious scrape during the three or four intervening hours seemed hardly possible; and still less could the worthy general foresee such a phenomenon as Yury leading Harry into danger, instead of Harry leading Yury. Yet both these seeming impossibilities were to come to pass that very day.

For about an hour after the general's departure the two lads, who had been climbing, swimming, or walking about all the morning, were content to sit still and turn over a book of Montenegrin views which they had found in the Prince's library. But after a time Harry's English restlessness began to assert itself once more.

'I say!' cried he, jumping up, 'we can't sit here all afternoon. What shall we do?'

'Let us go fishing,' suggested Yury; 'the sun has clouded over a bit, and we'll have a chance of a good catch.'

'I'm your man, sir,' cried his comrade briskly. 'Come along!'

The boys were usually accompanied on their fishing excursions by a steady old native servant belonging to the household, who knew the whole lake by heart; and had he been with them on the present occasion, the coming tragedy would never have been. But unluckily for them (though perhaps fortunately for himself) old Juro happened to be out of the way just at that moment, and the impatient boys were in no humour to wait for him.

The boat was launched in a trice, and away they went; but, contrary to Yury's expectation, their sport was not very successful, and the young noble began to grow impatient.

'We must go farther out,' he cried; 'you remember what a lot we caught out yonder the day before yesterday. Come on; get her head round.'

'But did not your uncle say,' objected Harry, with a prudence quite miraculous in *him*, 'that we must not go far from the shore, for fear we should drift down to the Albanian side?'

'Of course we must not go *too* far out,' replied Yury snappishly; 'but if we go just as far as we have gone before, there is no harm in *that*, is there?'

Harry looked doubtful; but his companion (who had slept badly for the last night or two, and was nervously excited in consequence) was in no mood to hear any remonstrance. The English boy yielded against his better judgment (though little dreaming what fearful consequences were to follow that ill-judged concession), and away went the boat toward the centre of the lake.

Here their luck changed at once, and the sport went on briskly enough to satisfy Yury himself; nor was it till they had been at work more than half-an-hour that Harry at length happened to look back toward the house which they had left, and was not a little startled to see how far away from it they now were.

'Look out, Yury! We're *drifting!*' shouted he, seizing his oar. 'Get to your oar, man—quick!'

Repenting too late of his fatal rashness, the young count bent to his oar with a will; and for some time they rowed hard in utter silence, glancing up uneasily ever and anon at the fast-darkening sky; for by this time the rising clouds, which had already begun to dim the sunshine when they started, were rapidly blotting it out altogether—betokening but too surely the approach of one of those sudden and furious storms for which this highland lake is so ominously famous.

The two lads pulled with all their might, for both alike felt more and more strongly the apprehension which neither cared to utter aloud—namely, that the storm might burst upon them ere they could get back to the shore. But though the sky grew blacker and blacker every moment, the bursting of the squall was still delayed; and Harry Archer was beginning to hope that they might, after all, reach land ere it came, when a gray, ghostly dimness seemed to rush down over the whole landscape—a weird, ominous moan swept through the still air, swelling suddenly into a deep, hoarse roar—there came a shock that made every plank quiver, sending Yury sprawling in the bottom of the boat, and hurling his comrade with crushing force against her side. The waves came hissing and foaming in over the gunwale, and for one instant even the brave young Wintonian gave himself up for lost, expecting that a moment more would find them both struggling for their lives in the raging waters.

But the end was not yet. The boat righted herself suddenly, and, though half-full of water, still kept afloat; while Harry, heedless of the blood that poured down his face from a deep gash in the forehead, sprang up and began to bale her out with all his might and main, vigorously seconded by Yury, who used his cap as a baler. Meanwhile the storm whirled them wildly away before it, whither they knew not; for, what with the driving mist and the pelting rain (which beat against their faces like the strokes of a whip), they could not see a yard beyond them.

At last the storm began to abate, and the setting sun broke through the parting clouds; but the light, when it came, served only to show that their position was even more desperate than they had thought it. They had been driven right down the lake, far beyond the border-line of Montenegro, and were already close to that fatal Albanian shore against which they had so often been warned, where every man was a mortal foe, who would hail with joy a chance of murdering them both.

Harry Archer's keen eye quickly perceived that they had been driven by the squall into the track of a cross-current, which was every moment sweeping them nearer and nearer to the low, bush-clad beach where death or bondage worse than death awaited them; and he saw at once that their only hope (if such it could be called) now lay in their oars. But one glance toward them showed that Yury's oar was gone—carried away, no doubt, when the boat careened under the first rush of the storm—and that they were thus left utterly helpless!

The brave English boy was far too manly and generous to reproach his unlucky comrade, whose rash and obstinate folly had been the sole cause of the fearful disaster that now threatened destruction to them both. But Yury himself bitterly realised what he had done, and said penitently:

'It's all my fault, Henri. If I had listened to you, we should never have been in this trouble at all; and now, in trying to save *me*, you have destroyed yourself.'

'Well, it's no use bothering ourselves about that *now*,' said Harry bluntly; 'the thing is to get out of this scrape. We can't manage the boat with one oar, that's certain; so the only way now is to run her aground, jump ashore, and then make a dash for home along the beach. If we don't meet any Albanians on the way, we may do it yet.'

Desperate as this plan was, it seemed to be the only one left them; but they were not destined to have a chance of trying it. At that very moment a man issued from the thickets in front of them—then a second—a third—a fourth; and poor Harry recognised at a glance the white kilts and scarlet caps * of the savage Albanians!

Quick as thought our hero flung himself down in the bottom of the boat, dragging his friend along with him.

'Lie close!' he whispered. 'If they haven't seen us yet they may think it's only a boat got adrift, and not trouble about it.'

But the bold stratagem came too late. Unseen by their victims, the fierce marauders had long been watching from their ambush, with cruel glee, the approach of the doomed castaways; and in another moment the savages came dashing through the shallow water like wolves rushing on a wounded deer, and sprang upon them with a yell of ferocious triumph.

That yell was answered by a cry from the far-off house

* The true Albanian head-dress is a shawl wound turban-wise round the head; but the red 'fez' is now generally substituted.

Sprang upon them with a yell of ferocious triumph.
PAGE 288.

on the beach, so wild, so full of frantic grief and rage, that it was plainly heard even at that distance.

The Montenegrin retainers, missing their two young guests, had come forth in quest of them, just in time to witness the last scene of the tragedy; and with them was Danilo Petrovitch, who had hurried back from his hunting expedition to make sure that all was well. But, with all his haste, the brave man arrived too late, and could only clench his hands in powerless desperation as he saw, far beyond the reach of help, his best friends pounced upon by his bitterest foes.

CHAPTER XXXIII.

AN EASTERN ROB ROY.

HEN the Albanians sprang into the boat and seized the two lads, Harry Archer—though his English blood boiled at this rough handling—had the good sense to make no resistance; for, in truth, a struggle between two unarmed boys and four well-armed men could have but one ending.

'Shall we not slay these whelps of the unbeliever?' growled the foremost assailant, laying a hand upon his *yataghan* (short sword). 'Methinks they are hardly worth sparing, for they seem half-dead already.'

'Not so, Ali,' objected the second; 'none but a son of folly would cut down a tree because its fruit is not yet ripe. Surely we will spare them, and sell them for slaves.'

'Nay, let us rather put them to ransom,' broke in the third; 'for it may well be that they are kinsmen of this great Russian chief who hath lately come among these wolves of the Black Mountain (may a pestilence consume them all!). The smaller youth should be a Russian by his face, and he with the blood on his brow hath a bold and free bearing, such as a chief's son should have.'

'It is well spoken, brother Reshid,' cried the fourth; 'and, in any wise, we may not harm them ere we have brought them to the presence of our chief, even Iskander Beg, and have heard how *he* would have us deal with them.'

Though Harry could not understand a word of this debate, he saw, by the loud tones and excited gestures of the speakers, that they were engaged in a hot dispute, and began to hope that they might get up a fight among themselves (which would be quite in the Albanian style), and thus give him and his comrade a chance of slipping away after all. But this hope was instantly quenched by the sudden appearance of a dozen more Albanians from the thicket, all well armed.

It did not, however, escape the keen-eyed English lad that his friend Yury (who had picked up a smattering of Turkish in the Caucasus) had started slightly at the name of Iskander Beg, and appeared to listen with close attention to what followed, his face brightening visibly as he did so. Harry was just about to ask the meaning of this strange satisfaction at a moment when death was staring them both in the face, when they were roughly forced apart, and dragged out of the boat on to the beach, while a harsh voice from the larger group shouted impatiently:

'Bring up the captives quickly, and let us be gone ere yon dogs of the Black Mountain come down upon us, for they seem already preparing to attack.'

Such was indeed the case; for as soon as Danilo Petrovitch saw that the boys had been made captive instead of being killed, he gathered in hot haste every man of the household, and lost not an instant in moving forward to cut off the Albanians from the hills above them.

But the boys saw nothing of all this, for they had been instantly bound and blindfolded, and hurried away at a prodigious rate, their captors half-leading and half-dragging them over the level ground along the lake, while the rest of the Albanians faced round to meet the threatened attack. Presently the footing seemed to grow steeper and more broken, and our heroes suddenly felt themselves lifted from the ground and carried forward at an even more rapid pace than before—a haste fully explained by the dropping shots which rang out in quick succession from the plain below, thrilling the hearts of the two captives with a hope of speedy rescue.

But it was not to be. The firing ceased as suddenly as it had begun, and the steps and voices that were presently heard behind them were those of the Albanians who had covered the retreat. From the few words which they exchanged with their comrades, Yury, listening intently, managed to gather that two Montenegrins and three Albanians had fallen in the skirmish, but that the band was now safe from all further pursuit. It was indeed so, and thus the forlorn lads were left at the mercy of a gang of savages to whom the very name of mercy was unknown.

On his return from this fruitless chase, Danilo, wounded as he was, at once sent off a courier to Tsettinje with the news of what had happened. As may be supposed, Prince Nikeeta and his chiefs were greatly enraged at this daring outrage almost within sight of their capital; but General Naprashkin (whose one object just then was to find Russia a good cause of quarrel with Turkey) seemed rather pleased than otherwise to learn that his own nephew and one of his most intimate friends were prisoners among the fiercest cut-throats of Eastern Europe, and he lost no time in telegraphing to St Petersburg the news of the catastrophe, which, transmitted thence to Central Asia, came (as we have seen) just in time to blast the triumph of Count

Bulatoff and his brother-explorer in the very moment of its completion.

Hurried away into a pathless wilderness by brutal and ferocious robbers, with every step carrying them farther and farther away from all hope of escape, and nothing but death or the worst form of slavery before them, these untried lads might well have given way to despair. But they did nothing of the kind. Harry's native hardihood and simple English creed of 'doing his best and trusting God for the rest' bore him up even under this fearful trial; and Yury's quick brain was already busy with a plan which, with its subtle devices for turning to their advantage the very calamity that now threatened them with destruction, was worthy of his renowned father.

At length, after this strange journey in utter darkness (for their mufflings kept them from seeing anything whatever) had gone on for a time that seemed endless to Harry's impatience, the party came to a sudden halt. There was a clamour of hoarse voices and a quick trampling of feet, and then the boys felt their bonds cast off and their eyes unbandaged, and found themselves in the midst of a very startling scene; for, though the plain below was already in darkness, there was still light enough up here on the hill-top to show our heroes every detail of the wild and striking picture before them.

A huge dark cliff, crested with gloomy pines and shadowy thickets, projected so far over the rocky plateau in front of them as to produce quite the effect of the mouth of a cavern. Beneath this natural vault blazed and crackled a large fire of dry wood, the red glare of which played fitfully on the wild forms and barbaric dress of several scores of Albanian warriors, whose white kilts, grim faces, and glittering eyes, half-seen through the rolling smoke, had a very weird and unearthly effect. At the far end of the plateau two long hunting-spears stood upright, bearing on their points two freshly-severed human heads, to the rayless eyes and distorted features of which the leaping flames gave a horrible semblance of life; and, by the Montenegrin caps, the doomed lads at once knew these ghastly trophies to be the heads of the two brave fellows who had fallen in vainly striving to rescue them.

Close to the fire, with his back propped against a huge boulder, sat cross-legged a stately old graybeard, with a gold-fringed scarf wound turban-wise round his head, and beside him a big wooden bowl of mutton-pilaff, into which he dipped his hand from time to time; and the boys rightly guessed him to be the chief of this savage gang—the redoubtable Iskander Beg himself.

As the old warrior turned his head and his features became fully visible, something in them struck Harry Archer as strangely familiar to him. Where *had* he seen that long, gray, silky beard; that keen blue eye; that fair complexion; that stern, high-cheeked, aquiline face, rendered doubly grim by the fearful scar that ran right across it from side to side? Try as he might, he could not recollect.

But Yury could, as was plain from the look of joyful recognition which lighted up his face the moment that of the chief was disclosed to him. Ere any one could check him, the young Russian stepped briskly up to Iskander, and deliberately helped himself to a handful of food from the old chief's dish (the most sacred bond of brotherhood among all Eastern races), saying in Turkish as he did so:

'Peace be with thee, Iskander Beg.'

'With thee be peace,' replied the Beg, with a look of displeased surprise at this liberty, which was certainly not uncalled for; 'but who art thou who callest me by name and makest thyself my guest unbidden?'

And then Yury, eking out with signs his few words of Turkish (for of the Albanian dialects he knew nothing),* explained that he was the nephew of the great Russian chief who was now visiting that district, and a friend of Danilo Petrovitch, in whose company he had been when they first met the chief himself, and that he claimed Iskander's protection for himself and his comrade, both on that score and as one who had eaten food out of the chief's own dish.

At the name of Danilo Petrovitch the old warrior's keen eyes sparkled.

'Art thou a friend of Danilo of the Black Mountain?' cried he eagerly. 'He is indeed a good warrior, as I can bear witness' (and he touched, with a grim smile, the frightful gash that seamed his weather-beaten face). 'I remember thee now; thou wert with him on the Frank fire-boat that carried me from Corfu to Durazzo,† and with thee was a lad who was the son of a great chief from the West. Is it he who is with thee now?'

'It is,' said Yury promptly; and beckoning Harry forward, he introduced him to the Beg as coolly as if the latter had been his oldest friend. Then, bending toward the chief as if fearful that some one might overhear him, he said in a low, impressive tone:

'Hear me, O Iskander Beg! When my uncle hath spoken

* The various dialects of Albania have the same kind of resemblance to each other as Dutch, German, and Danish; but all alike differ widely from Turkish, Greek, and the speech of the Danube Slavs.
† See chapter xxii.

T

with the chiefs of the Black Mountain, it may be that he will have somewhat to say to *thee!*'

The old man shot a quick glance of intelligence at him, and replied in the same cautious tone:

'We will speak more of this hereafter.'

Then, turning to the thunderstruck Albanians (who were standing mute with amazement at this sudden turning of the tables), he said, with a commanding air:

'Hearken unto me, O my children! These youths are my friends, and he who touches them touches me. Let them be well cared for; on the morrow I will speak with them again.'

'I say, Yury,' cried Harry Archer as soon as they were alone again, 'you mayn't be as strong as me, or as well used to roughing it, but when it comes to getting over anybody, you lick me out of sight. How on earth did you manage to twist that old rogue round your finger like that?'

'Simply enough,' said the young count, with a quiet smile. 'In the first place, I am Danilo's friend'——

'Danilo's friend!' echoed Harry. 'Well, this is a funny sort of country, upon my word, where one's best introduction to a man is to be the friend of his greatest enemy! But what more?'

'Well, my uncle and Danilo have told me a good deal about this man, and I know he's longing to rebel against the Sultan, if he can find any one to back him; and, knowing my uncle to be an agent of our government, very likely he hopes for some help from *him.* It would be very handy for us, you know, the next time we have a war with Turkey (as we are sure to do soon), to have a lot of these Albanian chiefs in rebellion, and keeping a whole Turkish army busy on this side, while we march down into the heart of the country on the other.'

'Well, you *are* a queer fellow, and no mistake!' cried Harry; 'the minute you get into the claws of a murdering old brigand who wants to chop your head off, you're at work planning how to use him as an ally next year or the year after, and talking it over with him as gaily as the Troubadour touched his guitar! After that I may as well hang up *my* fiddle—I'm nowhere at all!'

But Master Harry was destined to witness, not many days later, another triumph of diplomacy even more astounding than this.

CHAPTER XXXIV.

THE OLD MAN OF THE MOUNTAIN.

THUS secured from present danger by Iskander's protection, Harry Archer was now chiefly anxious lest some exaggerated version of this misadventure should by any chance reach his father; for he little dreamed, as day after day went by in this wild mountain solitude (where they were as utterly cut off from the outer world as Robinson Crusoe on his desert island), that the news of their mishap had not only reached his father already, but was the common talk of every capital in Europe. Harry's secret ambition had long been to 'make as big a name as his father;' and now he had done so without knowing it.

At a time when the eyes of all Europe were turned to the East—when the troubles in Egypt and Asia Minor, the anti-Turkish rebellion in Southern Arabia, and the disturbed state of the Danube provinces seemed to presage a speedy collapse of the Sultan's power, and a reopening of the Eastern Question that might set the whole world in a blaze—such an event as the kidnapping of an English and a Russian subject on Turkish soil could not fail to ring from one end of Europe to the other. In cabinet-councils and court drawing-rooms the names of our young heroes were as familiar as those of their renowned fathers; and while the excitement lasted one could hardly open a newspaper without seeing the 'latest particulars of the Albanian outrage' figuring beneath the most sensational heading which editorial skill could devise.

The Russian papers proclaimed that it was time to end a state of things worthy of the darkest ages of barbarism, and that Turkey must choose between prompt amends and instant war. The German press hinted that this was not the first time that Russia's anti-Turkish intrigues had recoiled upon herself, and the great Shakespeare had truly said that it is sport to see the engineer 'hoist with his own petard.' The French journals unanimously pronounced the whole affair a fresh proof of the bad faith of 'perfidious Albion,' and declared that the calamity which had overtaken M. Livingstone Archer was a just punishment for his insidious explorations in Central Africa, which had been uniformly designed to cripple the spread of French influence in that region.

Nor were the English newspapers behind those of the Continent in the fluent ignorance with which, according to custom, they laid down the law on a subject of which they knew nothing whatever. The *British Oracle* ended its wonted flow of smooth and shining commonplaces by observing that the incident was a gratifying proof how staunchly England and Russia, so lately foes, now stood shoulder to shoulder, and that any government would merit the censure of every right-minded man which should, by an ill-judged intervention, balk the two greatest living explorers of the glory which they would gain ere long by extricating their sons from the difficulty into which a hereditary spirit of adventure had led them.

The *Daily Patriot*, on the other hand, called loudly for the full and speedy avenging of the insult offered to the outraged majesty of Britain in the person of a British subject. The *Tory Banner* declared the whole affair to be entirely due to the unprincipled policy of Mr Gladstone— a fresh warning to all true Englishmen (if any such warning were needed) of the danger of again entrusting power to a man who, &c., &c., &c.; and the *Billingsgate Freeman*, with its usual polished courtesy, asserted that 'the safety secured to every Englishman abroad by Cromwell, the man of the English people, would never again be enjoyed till the righteous wrath of a too long oppressed nation had shattered to pieces that gilded cage of unclean birds, that hotbed of tyranny, uselessness, and corruption, which called itself the House of Lords.' And meanwhile, amid all this uproar of excitement and hysterical crowing of journalistic bantam-cocks, the persons about whom all this fuss was made knew nothing about it.

In fact—newspapers and reading-rooms not being abundant in Albania—the two captives knew as little of their sudden celebrity as Alexander Selkirk himself; and as day after day passed they began to find their captivity not so very frightful after all. Harry, in particular—with an English schoolboy's wonderful power of making himself at home anywhere—was soon quite domesticated among these savage cut-throats, sharing their daily sports and occupations, winning golden opinions from them by his brilliant shots when out hunting, and displaying a courage and endurance which they were not slow to appreciate; and to crown all, when the chief's favourite dagger slipped over the edge of a precipice and caught in a thorn-bush too weak to bear the weight of a man, the young Wykehamist scrambled boldly down the face of the cliff, and brought back the cherished weapon in safety.

So delighted was the old 'Rob Roy' with such a promising pupil that he one day announced point-blank his gracious intention of enrolling the English boy as one of his band; and when poor Harry, anxious to evade the alarming compliment of being made an honorary member of a club of robbers, ventured to suggest (through an interpreter) that perhaps his father might not like to part with him, Iskander replied, with the genial smile of a man willing to strain a point in order to make every one happy, that his father was quite welcome to come and join them too!

The only man in the whole band whose enmity to the two lads seemed unsoftened was Iskander's nephew Moukhtar, a surly and ill-looking fellow, who had more than once shown them plainly that, had they not been under his uncle's protection, he would have made short work of them. But this was all he could do—*for the present.*

Harry, ever eager to learn something new, kept picking up all the information he could about the strange people among whom he had been so suddenly thrown; and what he heard fully explained to him why Albania was so troublesome a part of the Sultan's dominions, and why Russian statesmen took so much interest in its incessant quarrels with Montenegro. He learned that the Albanians, over and above their division into 'Ghegs,' or Northerners, and 'Tosks,' or Southerners, were split up into a host of small clans, all at constant feud with each other; and, as if this were not enough, the population contained almost as many Christians as Mohammedans, and the former were subdivided in turn into Roman Catholics and members of the Greek Church, who were bitterly hostile to one another. Hence, what with the two sects of Christian Albanians hating each other, the Mohammedan Albanians detesting both, the Turks abhorring all three, and the Greeks and Slavs cherishing a good, solid, thorough-going hatred of all alike, Albania certainly offered first-rate material to any one wishing to fan the flame of internal strife in Turkey—and there were a good many who did so just then.

Thus matters stood when Iskander Beg, while awaiting the fulfilment of the hopes excited by Yury's mysterious hints, decided to amuse himself with a foray against the Miridites, one of the boldest and fiercest tribes of Albania, who lay not far to the south-east of him, and, being Christians, were a natural object of attack for so zealous a Moslem.

The old chief went gallantly forth to battle, with his best warriors at his back, and his right arm encircled with a linen fillet inscribed with a text of the Koran. But the older men, who were left behind to guard the village, noted with superstitious dismay that the bright morning sun clouded over at the very moment of his setting out, and that a dead bough from a tree above him dropped at his very feet!

'See what a superstitious set they are!' said Yury. 'Now, if any harm happens to the chief, of course they'll all say it was because he would not wait for the blessing of the Old Man of the Mountain.'

'And who is *he*, when he's at home?' asked Harry. 'I remember a gentleman of that name in Gibbon, who kept a boarding-school of assassins, and murdered every one he didn't like; but *he* lived several hundred years ago, and so I suppose it can't be the same man.'

'No,' laughed Yury; 'he's a hermit of special holiness, who lives in a cave near here, and makes a "progress" among the different tribes every now and then, to settle disputes and to bless plundering expeditions and other good works. He's absent just now, and therefore these fellows wished to defer this raid till he came to bless it; and besides that they have an important question to ask him which concerns *us* as well.'

'Indeed? What is it?'

'Well, it seems that one of the favourite haunts of this clan was an old ruined tower near the lake, whence they used to plunder the whole country round; but at last a clansman of theirs, named Mehemet, did some shocking rascality there (I can't find out what), and they, having some reason for not killing him, drove him out of the tribe in disgrace, and forbade him ever to come back. Well, since then they have never been near the old tower again, for it was foretold them that if they went back there while this Mehemet lived some great disaster would befall them, and *he* would be the cause of it!'

'Just like a yarn out of Walter Scott,' cried Harry, who had listened with great interest, though far from guessing that he was hearing the story of the very man whose crafty aid had so lately saved his own father, and Yury's father likewise. 'But how does all that concern *us?*'

'Well, if they do go down there, close to the Montenegrin border, we shall have a far better chance of escaping; but they can't go till they find out if Mehemet is still living (which is easier said than done, for he is supposed to have gone off to Persia or Central Asia), so they want the Old Man of the Mountain (whom they believe to be a prophet) to settle the point for them. I hope he'll settle it in favour of their going; and I hope, too, the Beg will come back safe, for if he don't, Master Moukhtar will be likely to chop our heads off!'

Several days passed without any news of Iskander or his men; but just at sunset on Christmas Day (a strange Christmas indeed for the two boy-captives) our heroes were startled by a long, wild, wailing cry; and hurrying out with a too true foreboding of evil, they beheld, struggling wearily up the mountain-side, through the fast-falling shadows of night, thirty haggard, blood-stained, ghastly-looking men, the sole survivors of the hundred bold warriors who had gone forth so proudly but a few days before. Worse still, the two lads saw at once, with secret dismay, that their enemy Moukhtar was with the diminished band, and that their friend Iskander was *not!*

'Where is our chief?' cried a dozen voices at once.

'His soul is in the gardens of Paradise,' said Moukhtar gloomily; 'his head I bring with me, to save it from the profaning hands of the accursed.'

And he held up his uncle's head, which, in accordance with a custom common alike to Albania and Montenegro, he had cut off to keep it from being used as a trophy by the enemy!

At sight of the well-known features another cry arose, so wild, so piercing, so filled with frantic rage and despair, that both boys started. The movement drew upon them the attention of the new chief, who instantly unsheathed his sword and sprang at them, yelling hoarsely:

'Shall these unbelieving dogs live, when our chief hath died?'

Half-a-dozen of his men echoed the shout, and all seemed over with the poor lads, when a number of the elders of the tribe (the only men living whom these savages reverenced) threw themselves between Moukhtar and his prey—some bidding him remember that their dead chief's last order had been a charge for the safety of the boys, others diplomatically hinting that it was a pity to throw away the chance of a rich ransom, and a few stoutly declaring that these youths were warriors and sons of warriors, and that no man should lay a hand on them.

Then was heard suddenly the voice of the oldest man present, an aged warrior whose consequence in the eyes of the tribe was second only to that of Iskander himself:

'Children! shall true believers quarrel for the sake of infidels? The Old Man of the Mountain will be here ere long; let *him* decide the matter.'

And this struck every one as such a good idea that they all agreed to it on the spot.

Two days later the Old Man of the Mountain came. In one way his arrival was a relief to the captive boys, who had been so closely guarded in the interval that they were hardly allowed to stir out of doors and never left alone for an instant; but, on the other hand, the thought that this man brought with him the decision of life or death to them both, and that, were this decision adverse, a few minutes more would see them hacked to pieces by these brutal savages, was not to be faced unmoved, even by *them*.

When the local saint arrived they were in their hut, guarded by Reshid, one of the four men who had captured them, but now among their chief friends. Through the cracks in the ill-built walls they could see that the famous hermit was a man of middle stature, wrapped in a long gray mantle, with his face half-hidden by his snow-white hair and beard, through which his small, deep-set eyes glittered with a restless, sinister gleam.

The first thing to be done was, of course, to set food before the holy man, and wait till he had despatched it; and then the consultation began. Presently the hermit was seen to turn over the leaves of the Koran that hung at his side, as if consulting an oracle of his own. Then he looked up and spoke a few words, which were greeted with a general shout of joy.

'All is well,' said the listening Reshid to the two boys. 'He hath divined on the Koran, and saith that Mehemet the traitor is dead, and that we may safely go back to our old tower by the lake, where we were wont to gather so much spoil; and there shall we find far more than we expected.'

At any other time the hope of escape offered by this move toward the Montenegrin border would have been a cordial to the prisoners; but now their consciousness that the next question asked would be whether *they* should live or die blotted out every other thought.

'Where are these whelps of a vile race?' shouted the Old Man of the Mountain. 'Bring them before me, that I may see them!'

And as the boys were led forth he looked fixedly at them, and said sternly:

'Death is written on their foreheads—they must die! Carry them with you, on the third day hence, down to the old tower by the lake; and thither will I come to bless your guns and swords, that they may be mighty to take the spoil which cometh to you; and when it *is* come, then slay these sons of mischief, even as they deserve—— Ha, infidels! do ye dare to mock my words?'

As he spoke he turned fiercely on Yury with uplifted arm, as if about to strike him; and as the boy raised *his* arm to ward off the expected blow, the two hands touched each other for a moment.

As they did so Yury felt a *small slip of paper* thrust into his fingers, which instantly closed upon it; and when the boys found an opportunity of examining it unwatched, they saw written on it, in a hand well known to both:

'Be on the lookout; we are at hand.

L. ARCHER.'

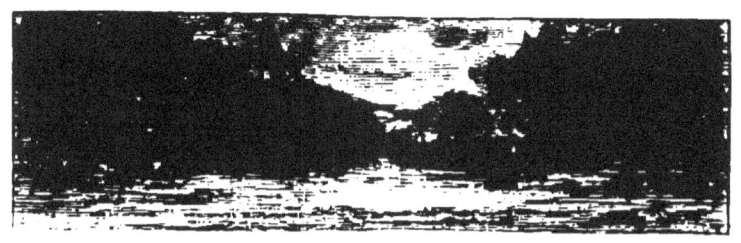

CHAPTER XXXV.

THE LAST NIGHT OF THE YEAR.

EW Year's Eve had come at last. Yet a few hours more and that eventful year would have run its course; and through the narrow, weed-grown loopholes of the old tower by the lake, the doomed lads were watching the fading glow of what was to be (unless help came speedily) the last sunset that they would ever see.

Bound hand and foot, they lay side by side on the floor of an upper chamber of the ruined castle, shivering as the keen winter wind whistled through the chinks of the mouldering walls, and listening to the savage shouts and brutal laughter of the murderous gang below.

The Old Man of the Mountain had kept his promise to bless the weapons of the Albanians; but he had come and gone without the prisoners being allowed to see him, and they had thus had no chance of an explanation of the mysterious letter conveyed to them by his hands—a mystery deepened tenfold by its having reached them through such a postman.

Meanwhile the robbers, in high glee at finding themselves once more in their favourite haunt, and at having a sure prospect of fresh plunder and bloodshed, laughed and shouted like children.

'May our holy hermit's favour increase!' cried Ali. 'When we divide the spoil that he hath promised us, assuredly he shall not lack his share. "Up the Alessio Valley," said he, "comes a traveller with his train; be on the watch for him!" Doubtless it is some knavish Greek trader, who would sell his own father for an *asper* (halfpenny). May dogs defile the graves of the whole generation.'

'Or perchance,' said Reshid, 'it may be one of those crack-brained infidels from Inglistan (England) who wander to other lands because in their own it is always dark and the rain falleth night and day. But the madmen are exceeding rich, and can pay a goodly ransom.'

'It is well spoken!' shouted Moukhtár himself; and 'when we have taken the spoil, then shall these two wolf-cubs whom we hold captive be slain with the sword, that Allah may be pleased with the sacrifice, and send His favour upon us when we go forth to smite the Miridite dogs, who have slain my uncle and the best of his warriors.'

But the ruffians might have been less gleeful could they have heard the conference which was being held, at that very moment, within a few miles of them.

'Is it not time to start yet, Danilo Petrovitch?'

'Patience for a few minutes more, Monsieur Archer; we must not start till it is quite dark. We have to go right down the lake, you know, and a boat can be seen on it miles away.'

'You are the most impatient of us all this time, Lyoff; but *I*, for one, cannot blame you.'

'No, I should hope not, Feodor; but I can tell you that nothing less than the saving of my only son's life should ever have made me associate myself, even for a moment, with a creature like *that!*'

'Well, say what you will,' replied Count Bulatoff, following with his eyes Archer's scornful glance at the Albanian renegade, Mehemet, who stood a little apart from them, 'no one else could have played as *he* did the part of the Old Man of the Mountain.'

'Yes, I can warrant him skilled in every crime that does not require courage,' said the brave Englishman, with blasting contempt; 'but to murder that poor old hermit in cold blood, and then actually cut off his white hair and beard to wear as a disguise—ugh! it makes me sick to think of it!'

'My dear fellow, you are really *too* fastidious!' cried the count, with a quiet smile of indulgent superiority. 'Medicine is nasty, but one has to take it all the same; and such rogues are like medicine—not nice themselves, but very useful to other people. I must own that you were quite right not to let us hang him that time on the Ili; though, of course, we could not foresee *then* what good service he was to do later on. But here comes Danilo to tell us that the boats are ready.'

The night was far spent and dawn was already at hand, when one of the two scouts sent forth by Moukhtar came in hot haste up the valley, with the news that two travellers in Frank dress were approaching, with eight attendants clothed like Greeks and a mule carrying baggage.

'Assuredly this is what the holy hermit promised us,' cried Moukhtar, with a grin of ferocious joy. 'Follow me, children, to the spoil!'

Out trooped the savage gang with muttered exclamations of brutal glee; and even the three or four men left behind to guard the prisoners, deeming the latter too securely bound to have any chance of escape, at length forsook their post and hurried after their comrades.

Meanwhile Harry Archer, bound as he was, had contrived, though with great difficulty, to drag himself up on to his feet and shuffle across the floor of his dungeon to a loophole commanding a view of the valley.

'There must be some travellers coming, whom they mean to rob,' said he; 'but when they come near enough I'll give 'em a shout to warn them, if I die for it!'

But Yury, who was already beside him, shook his head, and, bending close to his comrade's ear, said something in a whisper as low as if he feared that the very walls might overhear him; for he was still ignorant that their jailers had departed with the rest.

Whatever that whisper conveyed, it seemed to startle Harry beyond measure.

'Do you really think so?' asked he in the same cautious tone.

'I'm sure of it,' replied the young Russian; 'just wait and see.'

Through the cold gray mist of early morning a shadowy mass began to loom out, plainer and plainer every moment, till the approaching figures of several men on foot were dimly seen. Then the Albanians, not wishing to fire lest they should kill the very travellers whom they hoped to put to ransom, rushed upon them sword in hand with a wolfish yell.

Quick as thought, every man of the strangers levelled a gun or a revolver, and the report mingled with the death-cry of nearly a dozen of the over-boastful cut-throats; while a second volley, equally fatal, flashed among them from the thickets on the right.

The startled robbers attempted to return the fire; but their pieces snapped without going off, for the pretended hermit had indeed 'blessed' the guns to good purpose, by wetting the priming of one and all! In that moment of confusion and dismay the terrible Montenegrin war-cry made the air ring, and the thunderstruck assailants were themselves assailed on both sides at once.

'There goes Danilo into the thick of it!' cried Harry joyfully; for by this time the firing had begun to scatter the mist, and the struggle was plainly visible. 'Well done, old fellow! Keep it up!'

'I was right, you see,' chuckled Yury; 'and this time the sheep are hunting the wolves!'

At that very moment they saw the cruel Moukhtar himself fall beneath the sword of Danilo Petrovitch, who, looking down upon him, murmured sadly:

'If it had only been his uncle Iskander! It is grievous to think that that brave old fellow should have been killed by *some one else* after all!'

Surprised, outnumbered, and cut off from retreat, the ruffianly Albanians perished to a man, though they did not fall unavenged, for with them fell the arch-traitor Mehemet, whom one of them, recognising the renegade among their assailants, despatched with a single blow.

A few minutes later the ruined tower was filled with the victorious Montenegrins, and the captive boys were freed from their bonds by the hands of their own fathers.

The following day saw rescuers and rescued safe back at Tsettinje, whence Mr Archer and his son lost no time in starting to catch the Trieste steamer at Cattaro, on their way home to England, having had for the present quite enough of foreign travel.

Not without regret did they take leave of General Naprashkin and Danilo Petrovitch; and they parted even more unwillingly from Yury Bulatoff and his father, little guessing that they were destined to meet again with all four, only a few years later, in the thick of the great Russo-Turkish war of 1877. But the story of that strange meeting, and of the startling adventures that followed it, must be told in another place.

THE END.

Edinburgh:
Printed by W. & R. Chambers, Limited.

BOOKS by DAVID KER
PUBLISHED BY
W. & R. CHAMBERS, Limited.

SWEPT OUT TO SEA. Six Illustrations by J. Ayton Symington 3/6

THE WIZARD KING: A Story of the Last Moslem Invasion of Europe. Six Illustrations by W. S. Stacey..3/6

PRISONER AMONG PIRATES. Six Illustrations by W. S. Stacey.......................................3/6

VANISHED; or, The Strange Adventures of Arthur Hawkesleigh. Illustrated by W. Boucher..........2/6

COSSACK AND CZAR. Illustrated by W. S. Stacey..2/6

W. & R. CHAMBERS, LTD., LONDON AND EDINBURGH.

Books by G. Manville Fenn

PUBLISHED BY

W. & R. CHAMBERS, Limited.

VINCE THE REBEL; or, The Sanctuary in the Bog. With Eight Illustrations by W. H. C. Groome...5/

THE BLACK TOR: A Tale of the Reign of James I. Eight Illustrations by W. S. Stacey....................5/

ROY ROYLAND; or, The Young Castellan. Eight Illustrations by W. Boucher........................5/

DIAMOND DYKE; or, The Lone Farm on the Veldt. Eight Illustrations by W. Boucher............5/

REAL GOLD: A Story of Adventure. Eight Illustrations by W. S. Stacey..............................5/

THE RAJAH OF DAH. Six Illustrations by W. S. Stacey...3/6

THE DINGO BOYS; or, The Squatters of Wallaby Range. Six Illustrations by W. S. Stacey...........3/6

BEGUMBAGH: A Tale of the Indian Mutiny; and Other Stories. Illustrated.......................1/6

W. & R. CHAMBERS, Ltd., LONDON AND EDINBURGH.

BOOKS

SUITABLE FOR PRIZES AND PRESENTATION.

Price 5s.

MEG LANGHOLME, or the Day after To-morrow. By Mrs MOLESWORTH, author of *Philippa, Olivia, Blanche, Carrots, Imogen,* &c. With eight Illustrations by W. Rainey.   5/

Mrs Molesworth with her usual charm of manner, and easy natural grace, traces the development of Meg Langholme from early girlhood to young womanhood, with her friends and companions in the home of Bray Weald, where she is like an adopted daughter, until mysterious warnings bode the disaster of her life; for certain reasons she is kidnapped and concealed until cleverly rescued, and happily married to a lifelong friend then home from India.

VINCE THE REBEL, or the Sanctuary in the Bog. By GEORGE MANVILLE FENN, author of *The Black Tor, Roy Royland, Diamond Dyke, The Rajah of Dah, Real Gold,* &c. With eight Illustrations by W. H. C. Groome.   5/

Relates the troubles at Mere Abbey, a fine South-of-England mansion, surrounded by bogs and woodlands, during the reign of James II. of England, and how Vince the Rebel lay in hiding here after Sedgemoor, and escaped the soldiers sent in pursuit. The free and healthy country life enjoyed by Walter Heron and his cousin Vince, along with Sol Bogg, the man-servant, who aids in all the fishing, hunting, and woodland adventures, form a fascinating and enjoyable narrative for readers of all ages.

W. & R. Chambers, Limited, London and Edinburgh.

WILD KITTY. By L. T. MEADE, author of *Catalina*, &c. With eight Illustrations by J. Ayton Symington. 5/

> Mrs Meade again gives a picture of school-girl life, in which many varied characters play a part, the most interesting and original being Kitty Malone from Castle Malone in Ireland, who earns the nickname of Wild Kitty because of her love of mischief and unconventional manners. Mrs Meade is herself a native of Ireland and quite at home in sketching such a character, and she does not fail to weave a fascinating narrative, and one which she herself believes will rank amongst her best efforts.

PHILIPPA. By Mrs MOLESWORTH, author of *Olivia, Blanche, Robin Redbreast, Carrots, Imogen*, &c. With eight Illustrations by J. Finnemore. 5/

> 'Very clever, very fantastic, and very enjoyable.'—*Spectator.*
> 'One of Mrs Molesworth's best stories for girls.'—*The Queen.*
> 'Fully maintains her charm of style and narration.'—*Leeds Mercury.*

THE GIRL AT THE DOWER HOUSE, AND AFTERWARD. By AGNES GIBERNE, author of *Sun, Moon, and Stars; A Lady of England*, &c. With eight Illustrations by J. Finnemore. 5/

> 'An absorbing story.'—*Daily Free Press.*
> 'A charming love-tale.'—*Westminster Review.*

CATALINA: Art Student. By L. T. MEADE, author of *Betty, Four on an Island, Wilton Chase*, &c. With eight Illustrations by W. Boucher. 5/

> 'The story is managed with great skill.'—*Daily Free Press.*
> 'Unquestionably one of Mrs Meade's best books.'—*Evening News.*
> 'Very brightly told.'—*Punch.*

THE BLACK TOR: A Tale of the Reign of James I. By GEORGE MANVILLE FENN, author of *Roy Royland, Diamond Dyke, The Rajah of Dah, Real Gold*, &c. With eight Illustrations by W. S. Stacey. 5/

> 'A capital story . . . full of incident and adventure.'—*The Standard.*
> 'There is a fine manly tone about the book, which makes it particularly appropriate for youth.'—*Sheffield Daily Telegraph.*

W. & R. Chambers, Limited, London and Edinburgh.

From MEG LANGHOLME, by *Mrs Molesworth*; price 5s.

The quaint, trim figure, the snuff-coloured wig and coat to match . . . made up a personality like no other I have ever seen.

PAGE 173.

ROY ROYLAND, or the Young Castellan. By GEORGE MANVILLE FENN. With eight Illustrations by W. Boucher. 5/
    'Fascinating from beginning to end . . . is told with much spirit and go.'—*Birmingham Gazette.*

THE BROTHERHOOD OF THE COAST. By DAVID LAWSON JOHNSTONE. With twenty-one Illustrations by W. Boucher. Large crown 8vo, antique cloth gilt. 5/
    'There is fascination for every healthily-minded boy in the very name of the Buccaneers. . . . Mr D. Lawson Johnstone's new story of adventure is already sure of a warm welcome.'—*Manchester Guardian.*

GIRLS NEW AND OLD. By L. T. MEADE. With eight Illustrations by J. Williamson. 5/
    'A sound as well as entertaining romance.'—*Yorkshire Daily Post.*
    'It is a fine, bright, wholesome book, well bound and illustrated.'—*Saturday Review.*

DON. By the author of *Laddie,* &c. With eight Illustrations by J. Finnemore. Large crown 8vo, antique cloth gilt. 5/
    'A fresh and happy story . : . told with great spirit . . . it is as pure as spring air.'—*Glasgow Herald.*

OLIVIA. By Mrs MOLESWORTH. With eight Illustrations by Robert Barnes. 5/
    'A beautiful story, an ideal gift-book for girls.'—*British Weekly.*

BETTY: a School Girl. By L. T. MEADE. With eight Illustrations by Everard Hopkins. 5/
    'This is an admirable tale of school-girl life : her history involves an excellent moral skilfully conveyed.'—*Glasgow Herald.*

WESTERN STORIES. By WILLIAM ATKINSON. With Frontispiece. 5/
    'These stories touch a very high point of excellence. They are natural, vivid, and thoroughly interesting.'—*Speaker.*

BLANCHE. By Mrs MOLESWORTH, author of *Robin Redbreast, The Next-Door House,* &c. With eight Illustrations by Robert Barnes. 5/
    'Eminently healthy . . . pretty and interesting, free from sentimentality.'—*Queen.*

From VINCE THE REBEL, *by G. Manville Fenn ; price 5s.*

'Hunting me night and day.'

PAGE 240.

DIAMOND DYKE, or the Lone Farm on the Veldt: a Story of South African Adventure. By GEORGE MANVILLE FENN, author of *The Rajah of Dah, Dingo Boys,* &c. With eight Illustrations by W. Boucher. **5/**
  'There is not a dull page in the book.'—*Aberdeen Free Press.*

REAL GOLD: a Story of Adventure. By GEORGE MANVILLE FENN. With eight Illustrations by W. S. Stacey. **5/**
  'In the author's best style, and brimful of life and adventure.... Equal to any of the tales of adventure Mr Fenn has yet written.'—*Standard.*

POMONA. By the author of *Laddie, Rose and Lavender, Zoe, Baby John,* &c. With eight Illustrations by Robert Barnes. **5/**
  'A bright, healthy story for girls.'—*Bookseller.*

DOMESTIC ANNALS OF SCOTLAND, from the Reformation to the Rebellion of 1745. By ROBERT CHAMBERS, LL.D. Abridged from the original octavo edition in three volumes. **5/**

ALL ROUND THE YEAR. A Monthly Garland by THOMAS MILLER, author of *English Country Life,* &c. And Key to the Calendar. With Twelve Allegorical Designs by John Leighton, F.S.A., and other Illustrations. **5/**

Price 3s. 6d.

HUNTED THROUGH FIJI, or 'Twixt Convict and Cannibal. By REGINALD HORSLEY, author of *The Yellow God, The Blue Balloon,* &c. With six Illustrations by J. Ayton Symington.
3/6

  Dr Horsley is here at his best in following the fortunes of three young lads pursued by convicts and natives through Fiji in the cannibal days. The pages are crowded with adventures and hairbreadth escapes, sufficient to carry any reader from beginning to close without abatement of interest.

W. & R. Chambers, Limited, London and Edinburgh.

HOODIE. By Mrs MOLESWORTH. With seventeen Illustrations by Lewis Baumer. 3/6

The story, very simply and naturally told, is of a rather naughty little girl who at first has a mistaken idea that she is out of favour with everybody, but who gets brought to a better mind by an illness. The little heroine displays great character.

THE 'ROVER'S' QUEST: a Story of Foam, Fire, and Fight. By HUGH ST LEGER, author of *Sou'wester and Sword*, &c. With six Illustrations by J. AYTON SYMINGTON. 3/6

A tough yarn, which relates how Noel Hamilton is picked up from a boat in the Channel by a passing merchant ship and carried into eastern seas, where he encounters all the horrors of a mutiny, a sea-quake, and shipwreck, his loneliness on a barren island being shared by two fine old salts named Sam Port and Eli Grouse. How they are rescued by the *Rover*, out on a strange quest, and how this quest is accomplished, form the thread of an interesting narrative of sea life.

A DAUGHTER OF THE KLEPHTS, or A Girl of Modern Greece. By ISABELLA FYVIE MAYO (Edward Garrett), author of *Occupations of a Retired Life, By Still Waters*, &c. Crown 8vo, art linen, gilt. With six Illustrations by W. Boucher. 3/6

'A well-written, sensible piece of work, likely to please educated and thoughtful girls.'—*The Globe.*
'The book is interesting as a dramatic representation of incidents both tragical and heroic.'—*Inverness Courier.*
'The numerous characters in the story are vivid portraitures, the very humblest has nothing of the puppet in him or her, and the story from the first page to the last is highly interesting, realistic, and natural.'—*Scotsman.*

YOUNG DENYS: a Story of the Days of Napoleon. By ELEANOR C. PRICE, author of *In the Lion's Mouth, Miss Latimer of Bryans, The Little One, A Lost Battle*, &c. With six Illustrations by G. Nicolet. 3/6

'An interesting tale of the great Napoleon.'—*Punch.*
'Children of any age can enjoy its quiet vigour and character sketches.'—*Spectator.*

W. & R. Chambers, Limited, London and Edinburgh.

A SOLDIER OF THE LEGION: a Romance. By DAVID LAWSON JOHNSTONE, author of *The Brotherhood of the Coast, The Rebel Commodore*, &c. With seventeen Illustrations by W. Boucher. **3/6**

> 'A spirited romance of adventure ... which follows the career of a young Englishman in the Carlist wars.'—*Scotsman.*
> 'Distinguished alike for accuracy in detail and for vivid imagination.'—*The Standard.*

SWEPT OUT TO SEA. By DAVID KER, author of *Prisoner among Pirates, Cossack and Czar, Vanished, The Wizard King*, &c. With six Illustrations by J. Ayton Symington. **3/6**

> 'A fine stirring story of adventure on sea and land. ... The local colour of the West Indies is laid on delicately and truthfully.' —*Birmingham Gazette.*
> 'Crowded with adventure and excitement.'—*Black and White.*

TWO BOY TRAMPS. By J. MACDONALD OXLEY, author of *Bert Lloyd's Boyhood, Fergus Mactavish*, &c. With six Illustrations by H. Sandham. **3/6**

> 'An uncommonly good tale.'—*School Board Chronicle.*
> 'There is plenty of incident, and the interest is throughout well kept up.'—*Spectator.*

THE BLUE BALLOON: a Tale of the Shenandoah Valley. By REGINALD HORSLEY. With six Illustrations by W. S. Stacey. **3/6**

> 'We have seldom read a finer tale. It is a kind of masterpiece.'— *Methodist Times.*

THE WIZARD KING: a Story of the Last Moslem Invasion of Europe. By DAVID KER. With six Illustrations by W. S. Stacey. **3/6**

> 'This volume ought to find an army of admiring readers.'— *Liverpool Mercury.*

THE REBEL COMMODORE (Paul Jones); being Memoirs of the Earlier Adventures of Sir Ascott Dalrymple. By D. LAWSON JOHNSTONE. With six Illustrations by W. Boucher. **3/6**

> 'It is a good story, full of hairbreadth escapes and perilous adventures.'—*To-day.*

W. & R. Chambers, Limited, London and Edinburgh.

From HUNTED THROUGH FIJI, *by Reginald Horsley: price 3s. 6d.*

'My land, William, I've got the drop on you.'

ROBIN REDBREAST. By Mrs Molesworth, author of *Imogen, Next-Door House, The Cuckoo Clock*, &c. With six original Illustrations by Robert Barnes. 3/6

> 'It is a long time since we read a story for girls more simple, natural, or interesting.'—*Publishers' Circular.*

THE WHITE KAID OF THE ATLAS. By J. Maclaren Cobban. With six Illustrations by W. S. Stacey. 3/6

> 'A well-told tale of adventure and daring in Morocco, in which the late and the present Sultan both figure. . . . A very pleasant book to read.'—*Imperial and Asiatic Quarterly Review.*

THE YELLOW GOD: a Tale of some Strange Adventures. By Reginald Horsley. With six Illustrations by W. S. Stacey. 3/6

> 'Admirably designed, and set forth with life-like force. . . . A first-rate book for boys.'—*Saturday Review.*

PRISONER AMONG PIRATES. By David Ker, author of *Cossack and Czar, The Wild Horseman of the Pampas,* &c. With six Illustrations by W. S. Stacey. 3/6

> 'A singularly good story, calculated to encourage what is noble and manly in boys.'—*Athenæum.*

JOSIAH MASON: A BIOGRAPHY. With Sketches of the History of the Steel Pen and Electroplating Trades. By John Thackray Bunce. With Portrait and Illustrations. 3/6

FOUR ON AN ISLAND: a Story of Adventure. By L. T. Meade, author of *Daddy's Boy, Scamp and I, Wilton Chase,* &c. With six original Illustrations by W. Rainey. 3/6

> 'This is a very bright description of modern Crusoes.'—*Graphic.*

IN THE LAND OF THE GOLDEN PLUME: a Tale of Adventure. By David Lawson Johnstone, author of *The Paradise of the North, The Mountain Kingdom,* &c. With six Illustrations by W. S. Stacey. 3/6

> 'Most thrilling, and excellently worked out.'—*Graphic.*

W. & R. Chambers, Limited, London and Edinburgh.

THE DINGO BOYS; or the Squatters of Wallaby Range. By GEORGE MANVILLE FENN, author of *The Rajah of Dah*, *In the King's Name*, &c. With six original Illustrations by W. S. Stacey. 3/6

THE CHILDREN OF WILTON CHASE. By L. T. MEADE, author of *Four on an Island*, *Scamp and I*, &c. With six Illustrations by Everard Hopkins. 3/6

'Both entertaining and instructive.'—*Spectator*.

THE PARADISE OF THE NORTH: a Story of Discovery and Adventure around the Pole. By D. LAWSON JOHNSTONE, author of *Richard Treyellas*, *The Mountain Kingdom*, &c. With fifteen Illustrations by W. Boucher. 3/6

'Marked by a Verne-like fertility of fancy.'—*Saturday Review*.

THE RAJAH OF DAH. By GEORGE MANVILLE FENN, author of *In the King's Name*, &c. With six Illustrations by W. S. Stacey. 3/6

Price 2s. 6d.

ANIMAL STORIES. Selected and edited by ROBERT COCHRANE, editor of *Great Thinkers and Workers*, *Romance of Industry and Invention*, &c. Profusely Illustrated. 2/6

A selection of varied true stories of animal life, illustrating sagacity, instinct, the almost human traits of monkeys, speaking powers of parrots, the usefulness and cleverness of many dogs, horses, elephants, and hairbreadth escapes from lions, tigers, bears, and snakes. The examples are drawn from a wide field, and the narratives are brightly written.

ELSIE'S MAGICIAN. By FRED WHISHAW, author of *Boris the Bear Hunter*, *A Tsar's Gratitude*, &c. With ten Illustrations by Lewis Baumer. 2/6

A pretty story told with real humour and vivacity of how a little London girl managed to provide for her mother a much-needed holiday abroad, and brought together a father and daughter who had been alienated for many years to the sorrow and misfortune of both.

W. & R. Chambers, Limited, London and Edinburgh.

THE ROMANCE OF COMMERCE. By J. MACDONALD OXLEY, LL.B., B.A. With fifteen Illustrations. 2/6

'Sure to fascinate young lads fond of tales of adventure and daring.'—*Evening News.*

ABIGAIL TEMPLETON; or Brave Efforts. A Story of To-day. By EMMA MARSHALL, author of *Under Salisbury Spire*, &c. With four Illustrations by J. Finnemore. 2/6

'A bright and happy narrative. . . . Told with great spirit.'—*Birmingham Gazette.*

THE ROMANCE OF INDUSTRY AND INVENTION. Selected by ROBERT COCHRANE, editor of *Great Thinkers and Workers, Beneficent and Useful Lives, Adventure and Adventurers, Recent Travel and Adventure, Good and Great Women, Heroic Lives,* &c. With 34 process and woodcut Illustrations. 2/6

'It is hard to say which chapter is the best, for each seems more interesting than the last.'—*The Queen.*
'A most interesting and inspiring book.'—*Colliery Guardian.*
'We can recommend this work as at once instructive and interesting.'—*New Age.*

THROUGH THICK AND THIN: The Story of a School Campaign. By ANDREW HOME, author of *From Fag to Monitor, Disturbers of the Peace,* &c. With four Illustrations by W. Rainey. 2/6

'This is just the kind of book for boys to rave over; it does not cram moral axioms down their throats, the characters act them instead.'—*Glasgow Daily Mail.*

PLAYMATES: A Story for Boys and Girls. By L. T. MEADE. With six Illustrations by G. Nicolet. 2/6

'The charm of Mrs Meade's stories for children is well sustained in this pretty and instructive tale.'—*Liverpool Mercury.*

OUTSKERRY: The Story of an Island. By HELEN WATERS. With four Illustrations by R. Burns. 2/6

'The diversion provided is varied beyond expectation (and indeed belief). We read of an "Arabian Night's Entertainment," but here is enough for an Arctic night.'—*The Times.*

W. & R. Chambers, Limited, London and Edinburgh.

From THE 'ROVER'S' QUEST, *by Hugh St Leger ; price 3s. 6d.*

'There'll be more than one dead corpse amongst you afore you can say knife, mark me!'—Page 91.

WHITE TURRETS. By Mrs MOLESWORTH, author of *Carrots, Olivia,* &c. With four Illustrations by W. Rainey. 2/6

'A charming story. . . . A capital antidote to the unrest that inspires young folks that seek for some great thing to do, while the great thing for them is at their hand and at their home.'—*Scotsman.*

HUGH MELVILLE'S QUEST: a Boy's Adventures in the Days of the Armada. By F. M. HOLMES. With four Illustrations by W. Boucher. 2/6

'A refreshing, stirring story . . . and one sure to delight young boys and young girls too.'—*Spectator.*

ELOCUTION, a Book for Reciters and Readers. Edited by R. C. H. MORISON. 2/6

'No elocutionist's library can be said to be complete without this neatly bound volume of 500 pages. . . . An introduction on the art of elocution is a gem of conciseness and intellectual teaching.'—*Era.*

'One of the best books of its kind in the English language.'—*Glasgow Citizen.*

VANISHED, or the Strange Adventures of Arthur Hawkesleigh. By DAVID KER. Illustrated by W. Boucher. 2/6

'It must be ranked high amongst its kind.'—*Spectator.*
'A quite entrancing tale of adventure.'—*Athenæum.*

THISTLE AND ROSE. By AMY WALTON. Illustrated by Robert Barnes. 2/6

'Is as desirable a present to make to a girl as any one could wish.'—*Sheffield Daily Telegraph.*

ADVENTURE AND ADVENTURERS; being True Tales of Daring, Peril, and Heroism. With Illustrations. 2/6

'The narratives are as fascinating as fiction.'—*British Weekly.*

BLACK, WHITE, AND GRAY: a Story of Three Homes. By AMY WALTON, author of *White Lilac, A Pair of Clogs,* &c. With four Illustrations by Robert Barnes. 2/6

W. & R. Chambers, Limited, London and Edinburgh.

OUT OF REACH: a Story. By ESMÈ STUART, author of *Through the Flood, A Little Brown Girl,* &c. With four Illustrations by Robert Barnes.   2/6

'The story is a very good one, and the book can be recommended for girls' reading.'—*Standard.*

IMOGEN, or Only Eighteen. By Mrs MOLESWORTH. With four Illustrations by H. A. Bone.   2/6

'The book is an extremely clever one.'—*Daily Chronicle.*
'A readable and very pretty story.'—*Black and White.*

THE LOST TRADER, or the Mystery of the *Lombardy.* By HENRY FRITH, author of *The Cruise of the 'Wasp,' The Log of the 'Bombastes,'* &c. With four Illustrations by W. Boucher.   2/6

'Mr Frith writes good sea-stories, and this is the best of them that we have read.'—*Academy.*

BASIL WOOLLCOMBE, MIDSHIPMAN. By ARTHUR LEE KNIGHT, author of *The Adventures of a Midshipmite,* &c. With Frontispiece by W. S. Stacey, and other Illustrations.   2/6

THE NEXT-DOOR HOUSE. By Mrs MOLESWORTH. With six Illustrations by W. Hatherell.   2/6

'I venture to predict for it as loving a welcome as that received by the inimitable *Carrots.'—Manchester Courier.*

COSSACK AND CZAR. By DAVID KER, author of *The Boy Slave in Bokhara, The Wild Horseman of the Pampas,* &c. With original Illustrations by W. S. Stacey.   2/6

'There is not an uninteresting line in it.'—*Spectator.*

THROUGH THE FLOOD, the Story of an Out-of-the-way Place. By ESMÈ STUART. With Illustrations.   2/6

'A bright story of two girls, and shows how goodness rather than beauty in a face can heal old strifes.'—*Friendly Leaves.*

W. & R. Chambers, Limited, London and Edinburgh.

WHEN WE WERE YOUNG. By Mrs O'Reilly, author of *Joan and Jerry*, *Phœbe's Fortunes*, &c. With four Illustrations by H. A. Bone. 2/6

'A delightfully natural and attractive story.'—*Journal of Education.*

ROSE AND LAVENDER. By the author of *Laddie*, *Miss Toosey's Mission*, &c. With four original Illustrations by Herbert A. Bone. 2/6

'A brightly-written tale, the characters in which, taken from humble life, are sketched with lifelike naturalness.'—*Manchester Examiner.*

JOAN AND JERRY. By Mrs O'Reilly, author of *Sussex Stories*, &c. With four original Illustrations by Herbert A. Bone. 2/6

'An unusually satisfactory story for girls.'—*Manchester Guardian.*

THE YOUNG RANCHMEN, or Perils of Pioneering in the Wild West. By Charles R. Kenyon. With four original Illustrations by W. S. Stacey, and other Illustrations. 2/6

MEMOIR OF WILLIAM AND ROBERT CHAMBERS. With Autobiographic Reminiscences of William Chambers, and Supplemental Chapter. 15th edition. With Portraits and Illustrations. 2/6

POPULAR RHYMES OF SCOTLAND. By Robert Chambers. 2/6

TRADITIONS OF EDINBURGH. By Robert Chambers. *New Edition.* With Illustrations. 2/6

GOOD AND GREAT WOMEN: a Book for Girls. Comprises brief lives of Queen Victoria, Florence Nightingale, Baroness Burdett-Coutts, Mrs Beecher-Stowe, Jenny Lind, Charlotte Brontë, Mrs Hemans, Dorothy Pattison. Numerous Illustrations. 2/6

'A brightly written volume, full to the brim of interesting and instructive matter; and either as reader, reward, or library book, is equally suitable.'—*Teachers' Aid.*

W. & R. Chambers, Limited, London and Edinburgh.

LIVES OF LEADING NATURALISTS. By H. ALLEYNE NICHOLSON, Professor of Natural History in the University of Aberdeen. Illustrated. 2/6

'Popular and interesting by the skilful manner in which notices of the lives of distinguished naturalists, from John Ray and Francis Willoughby to Charles Darwin, are interwoven with the methodical exposition of the progress of the science to which they are devoted.' —*Scotsman.*

HISTORY OF THE REBELLION OF 1745-6. By ROBERT CHAMBERS. *New Edition*, with Index and Illustrations. 2/6

'There is not to be found anywhere a better account of the events of '45 than that given here.'—*Newcastle Chronicle.*

BENEFICENT AND USEFUL LIVES. Comprising Lord Shaftesbury, George Peabody, Andrew Carnegie, Walter Besant, Samuel Morley, Sir James Y. Simpson, Dr Arnold of Rugby, &c. By R. COCHRANE. With numerous Illustrations. 2/6

'Nothing could be better than the author's selection of facts setting forth the beneficent lives of those generous men in the narrow compass which the capacity of the volume allows.'—*School Board Chronicle.*

GREAT THINKERS AND WORKERS; being the Lives of Thomas Carlyle, Lord Armstrong, Lord Tennyson, Charles Dickens, Sir Titus Salt, W. M. Thackeray, Sir Henry Bessemer, John Ruskin, James Nasmyth, Charles Kingsley, Builders of the Forth Bridge, &c. With numerous Illustrations. 2/6

'One of the most fitting presents for a thoughtful boy that we have come across.'—*Review of Reviews.*

RECENT TRAVEL AND ADVENTURE. Comprising Stanley and the Congo, Lieutenant Greely, Joseph Thomson, Livingstone, Lady Brassey, Vambéry, Burton, &c. Illustrated. Cloth. 2/6

'It is wonderful how much that is of absorbing interest has been packed into this small volume.'—*Scotsman.*

LITERARY CELEBRITIES; being brief biographies of Wordsworth, Campbell, Moore, Jeffrey, and Macaulay. Illustrated. 2/6

W. & R. Chambers, Limited, London and Edinburgh.

SONGS OF SCOTLAND prior to Burns, with the Tunes, edited by ROBERT CHAMBERS, LL.D. With Illustrations. 2/6

    This volume embodies the whole of the pre-Burnsian songs of Scotland that possess merit and are presentable, along with the music; each accompanied by its own history.

GREAT HISTORIC EVENTS. The Conquest of India, Indian Mutiny, French Revolution, the Crusades, the Conquest of Mexico, Napoleon's Russian Campaign. Illustrated. 2/6

HISTORICAL CELEBRITIES. Comprising lives of Oliver Cromwell, Washington, Napoleon Bonaparte, Duke of Wellington. Illustrated. 2/6

    'The story of their life-work is told in such a way as to teach important historical, as well as personal, lessons bearing upon the political history of this country.'—*Schoolmaster.*

STORIES OF REMARKABLE PERSONS. The Herschels, Mary Somerville, Sir Walter Scott, A. T. Stewart, &c. By WILLIAM CHAMBERS, LL.D. 2/6

    Embraces about two dozen lives, and the biographical sketches are freely interspersed with anecdotes, so as to make it popular and stimulating reading for both young and old.

STORIES OF OLD FAMILIES. By W. CHAMBERS, LL.D. 2/6

    The Setons—Lady Jean Gordon—Countess of Nithsdale—Lady Grisell Baillie—Grisell Cochrane—the Keiths—Lady Grange—Lady Jane Douglas—Story of Wedderburn—Story of Erskine—Countess of Eglintoun—Lady Forbes—the Dalrymples—Montrose—Buccleuch Family—Argyll Family, &c.

YOUTH'S COMPANION AND COUNSELLOR. By WILLIAM CHAMBERS, LL.D. 2/6

TALES FOR TRAVELLERS. Selected from Chambers's *Papers for the People.* 2 volumes, each 2/6

    Containing twelve tales by the author of *John Halifax, Gentleman,* George Cupples, and other well-known writers.

Price 2s.

BUNYAN'S PILGRIM'S PROGRESS. With Index; and Prefatory Memoir by Rev. JOHN BROWN, D.D., Bedford. Illustrated by J. D. Watson. 2/

A careful reprint, giving the best text of Bunyan's masterpiece, with a useful index for ready reference.

BRUCE'S TRAVELS. Travels of James Bruce through part of Africa, Syria, Egypt, and Arabia, into Abyssinia, to discover the source of the Nile. Illustrated. 2/

'An ideal volume for a school prize.'—*Publishers' Circular.*
'The record of his journey in this volume is full of fascination and freshness. Few travellers have followed in Bruce's footsteps; none have seen with a clearer eye or left more vivid impressions of what he saw.'—*Aberdeen Free Press.*
'A healthier or more entertaining book it would be impossible to place in the hands of any youth. When we look to the 358 pages of clear letterpress, the capital illustrations, and the pretty binding, the book seems a marvel of cheapness.'—*Perthshire Courier.*

THE HALF-CASTE: an Old Governess's Story, and other Tales. By the author of *John Halifax, Gentleman.* 2/

'Cannot but edify, while it must of necessity gratify and please the fortunate reader.'—*Liverpool Mercury.*
'The volume contains six short stories, which may be unhesitatingly recommended to such as relish fiction that is free from all morbidness, and is at the same time interesting.'—*Publishers' Circular.*

THE LIFE AND TRAVELS OF MUNGO PARK IN AFRICA. With Illustrations, Introduction, and concluding chapter on the Present Position of Affairs in the Niger Territory. 2/

'Few books of travel have acquired so speedy and extensive a reputation as this of Park's.'—THOMAS CARLYLE.
'A notable work well worthy of recommendation.'—*Birmingham Gazette.*

W. & R. Chambers, Limited, London and Edinburgh.

TWO ROYAL LIVES: Queen Victoria, William I., German Emperor. 2/

FOUR GREAT PHILANTHROPISTS: Lord Shaftesbury, George Peabody, John Howard, J. F. Oberlin. Illustrated. 2/
> Shows the good accomplished through the agency of the lives and labours of a noble Earl, a millionaire, a prison reformer, and the humble pastor of the remote Ban de la Roche.

TWO GREAT AUTHORS. Lives of Scott and Carlyle. 2/
> 'Youthful readers will find these accounts of the boyhood and youth of two of the three Scotch literary giants full of interest.'—*Schoolmaster.*

EMINENT ENGINEERS. Lives of Watt, Stephenson, Telford, and Brindley. 2/
> 'All young persons should read it, for it is in an excellent sense educational. It were devoutly to be wished that young people would take delight in such biographies.'—*Indian Engineer.*

TALES OF THE GREAT AND BRAVE. By MARGARET FRASER TYTLER. 2/
> A collection of interesting biographies and anecdotes of great men and women of history, in the style of Scott's *Tales of a Grandfather,* written by a niece of the historian of Scotland.

THROUGH STORM AND STRESS. By J. S. FLETCHER. With Frontispiece by W. S. Stacey. 2/
> 'Full of excitement and incident.'—*Dundee Advertiser.*

GREAT WARRIORS: Nelson, Wellington, Napoleon. 2/
> 'One of the most instructive books published this season.'—*Liverpool Mercury.*

HEROIC LIVES: Livingstone, Stanley, General Gordon, Lord Dundonald. 2/
> 'It would be difficult to name four other lives in which we find more enterprise, adventure, achievement. . . . The book is sure to please.'—*Leeds Mercury.*

W. & R. Chambers, Limited, London and Edinburgh.

BOOKS FOR PRIZES AND PRESENTATION. 21

THE REMARKABLE ADVENTURES OF WALTER TRELAWNEY, Parish 'Prentice of Plymouth, in the year of the Great Armada. Re-told by J. S. FLETCHER, author of *Through Storm and Stress*, &c. With Frontispiece by W. S. Stacey. 2/

'A wonderfully vivid story of the year of the Great Armada; far more effective than the unwholesome trash which so often does duty for boys' books nowadays.'—*Idler.*

FIVE VICTIMS: a School-room Story. By M. BRAMSTON, author of *Boys and Girls, Uncle Ivan*, &c. With Frontispiece by H. A. Bone. 2/

'A delightful book for children. Miss Bramston has told her simple story extremely well.'—*Associates' Journal.*

SOME BRAVE BOYS AND GIRLS. By EDITH C. KENYON, author of *The Little Knight, Wilfrid Clifford*, &c. 2/

'A capital book : will be read with delight by both boys and girls.'—*Manchester Examiner.*

ELIZABETH, or Cloud and Sunshine. By HENLEY I. ARDEN, author of *Leather Mill Farm, Aunt Bell*, &c. With Frontispiece by Herbert A. Bone. 2/

'This is a charming story, and in every way suitable as a gift-book or prize for girls.'—*Schoolmaster.*

HEROES OF ROMANTIC ADVENTURE, being Biographical Sketches of Lord Clive, founder of British supremacy in India ; Captain John Smith, founder of the colony of Virginia; the Good Knight Bayard; and Garibaldi, the Italian patriot. Illustrated. 2/

FAMOUS MEN. Illustrated. 2/

Biographical Sketches of Lord Dundonald, George Stephenson, Lord Nelson, Louis Napoleon, Captain Cook, George Washington, Sir Walter Scott, Peter the Great, &c.

LIFE OF BENJAMIN FRANKLIN. Illustrated. 2/

'A fine example of attractive biographical writing. . . . A short address, "The Way to Wealth," should be read by every young man in the kingdom.'—*Teachers' Aid.*

W. & R. Chambers, Limited, London and Edinburgh.

EMINENT WOMEN, and Tales for Girls. Illustrated. 2/

'The lives include those of Grace Darling, Joan of Arc, Flora Macdonald, Helen Gray, Madame Roland, and others.'—*Teachers' Aid.*

TALES FROM CHAMBERS'S JOURNAL. 4 vols., each 2/

Comprise interesting short stories by James Payn, Hugh Conway, D. Christie Murray, Walter Thornbury, G. Manville Fenn, Dutton Cook, J. B. Harwood, and other popular writers.

BIOGRAPHY, EXEMPLARY AND INSTRUCTIVE. Edited by W. CHAMBERS, LL.D. 2/

The Editor gives in this volume a selection of biographies of those who, while exemplary in their private lives, became the benefactors of their species by the still more exemplary efforts of their intellect.

OUR ANIMAL FRIENDS—the Dog, Cat, Horse, and Elephant. With numerous Illustrations. 2/

AILIE GILROY. By W. CHAMBERS, LL.D. 2/

'The life of a poor Scotch lassie . . . a book that will be highly esteemed for its goodness as well as for its attractiveness.'—*Teachers' Aid.*

ESSAYS, FAMILIAR AND HUMOROUS. By ROBERT CHAMBERS, LL.D. 2 vols., each 2/

Contains some of the finest essays, tales, and social sketches of the author of *Traditions of Edinburgh*, reprinted from *Chambers's Journal*.

MARITIME DISCOVERY AND ADVENTURE. Illustrated. 2/

Columbus—Balboa—Richard Falconer—North-east Passage—South Sea Marauders—Alexander Selkirk—Crossing the Line—Genuine Crusoes—Castaway—Scene with a Pirate, &c.

SHIPWRECKS AND TALES OF THE SEA. Illustrated. 2/

'A collection of narratives of many famous shipwrecks, with other tales of the sea. . . . The tales of fortitude under difficulties, and in times of extreme peril, as well as the records of adherence to duty, contained in this volume, cannot but be of service.'—*Practical Teacher.*

SKETCHES, LIGHT AND DESCRIPTIVE. By W. CHAMBERS, LL.D.
2/

A selection from contributions to *Chambers's Journal*, ranging over a period of thirty years.

MISCELLANY OF INSTRUCTIVE AND ENTERTAINING TRACTS.
Each 2/

These Tracts comprise Tales, Poetry, Ballads, Remarkable Episodes in History, Papers on Social Economy, Domestic Management, Science, Travel, &c. The articles contain wholesome and attractive reading for Mechanics', Parish, School, and Cottage Libraries.

	s.	d.		s.	d.
20 Vols. cloth	20	0	10 Vols. half-calf	45	0
10 Vols. cloth	20	0	160 Nos. ....each	0	1
10 Vols. cloth, gilt edges	25	0	Which may be had separately.		

Price 1s. 6d.
With Illustrations.

SWISS FAMILY ROBINSON. Their Life and Adventures on a Desert Island. 1/6

SKETCHES OF ANIMAL LIFE AND HABITS. By ANDREW WILSON, Ph.D., &c. 1/6

A popular natural history text-book, and a guide to the use of the observing powers. Compiled with a view of affording the young and the general reader trustworthy ideas of the animal world.

RAILWAYS AND RAILWAY MEN. 1/6
'A readable and entertaining book.'—*Manchester Guardian.*

EXPERIENCES OF A BARRISTER. 1/6
Eleven tales embracing experiences of a barrister and attorney.

BEGUMBAGH, a Tale of the Indian Mutiny. 1/6
A thrilling tale by GEORGE MANVILLE FENN.

BOOKS FOR PRIZES AND PRESENTATION.

THE BUFFALO HUNTERS, and other Tales.   1/6
Fourteen short stories reprinted from *Chambers's Journal*.

TALES OF THE COASTGUARD, and other Stories.   1/6
Fifteen interesting stories from *Chambers's Journal*.

THE CONSCRIPT, and other Tales.   1,6
Twenty-two short stories specially adapted for perusal by the young.

THE DETECTIVE OFFICER, by 'WATERS;' and other Tales.   1/6
Nine entertaining detective stories, with three others.

FIRESIDE TALES AND SKETCHES.   1/6
Contains eighteen tales and sketches by R. Chambers, LL.D., and others by P. B. St John, A. M. Sargeant, &c.

THE GOLD-SEEKERS, and other Tales.   1/6
Seventeen interesting tales from *Chambers's Journal*.

THE HOPE OF LEASCOMBE, and other Stories.   1/6
The principal tale inculcates the lesson that we cannot have everything our own way, and that passion and impulse are not reliable counsellors.

THE ITALIAN'S CHILD, and other Tales.   1/6
Fifteen short stories from *Chambers's Journal*.

JURY-ROOM TALES.   1/6
Entertaining stories by James Payn, G. M. Fenn, and others.

KINDNESS TO ANIMALS. By W. CHAMBERS, LL.D.   1/6
'Illustrates, by means of a series of anecdotes, the intelligence, gentleness, and docility of the brute creation.'—*Sunday Times*.

THE MIDNIGHT JOURNEY. By LEITCH RITCHIE; and other Tales.   1/6
Sixteen short stories from *Chambers's Journal*.

OLDEN STORIES.   1/6
Sixteen short stories from *Chambers's Journal*.

W. & R. Chambers, Limited, London and Edinburgh.

From A DAUGHTER OF THE KLEPHTS, *by Mrs Isabella Fyvie Mayo;* price 3s. 6d.

Patience was sitting idly crooning a monotonous wailing sound to which she put no words.

P. 148

THE RIVAL CLERKS, and other Tales. 1/6

The first tale shows how dishonesty and roguery are punished, and virtue triumphs in the end.

ROBINSON CRUSOE. By DANIEL DEFOE. 1/6

A handy edition, profusely illustrated.

PARLOUR TALES AND STORIES. 1/6

Seventeen short tales from the old series of *Chambers's Journal*, by Anna Maria Sargeant, Mrs Crowe, Percy B. St John, Leitch Ritchie, &c.

THE SQUIRE'S DAUGHTER, and other Tales. 1/6

Fifteen short stories from *Chambers's Journal*.

TALES FOR HOME READING. 1/6

Sixteen short stories from the old series of *Chambers's Journal*, by A. M. Sargeant, Frances Brown, Percy B. St John, Mrs Crowe, and others.

TALES FOR YOUNG AND OLD. 1/6

Fourteen short stories from *Chambers's Journal*, by Mrs Crowe, Miss Sargeant, Percy B. St John, &c.

TALES OF ADVENTURE. 1/6

Twenty-one tales, comprising wonderful escapes from wolves and bears, American Indians, and pirates; life on a desert island; extraordinary swimming adventures, &c.

TALES OF THE SEA. 1/6

Five thrilling sea tales, by G. Manville Fenn, J. B. Harwood, and others.

TALES AND STORIES TO SHORTEN THE WAY. 1/6

Fifteen interesting tales from *Chambers's Journal*.

TALES FOR TOWN AND COUNTRY. 1/6

Twenty-two tales and sketches, by R. Chambers, LL.D., and other writers.

HOME-NURSING. By RACHEL A. NEUMAN. Paper, 1/; cloth, 1/6

A work intended to help the inexperienced and those who in a sudden emergency are called upon to do the work of home-nursing.

W. & R. Chambers, Limited, London and Edinburgh.

Price 1s.

COOKERY FOR YOUNG HOUSEWIVES. By ANNIE M. GRIGGS. 1/

A book of practical utility, showing how tasteful and nutritious dishes may be prepared at little expense.

NEW SERIES OF CHAMBERS'S LIBRARY FOR YOUNG PEOPLE.

ILLUSTRATED.

Price 1s.

'Excellent popular biographies.'—*British Weekly.*

POPULAR BIOGRAPHIES.

WALLACE AND BRUCE: Heroes of Scotland. By MARY COCHRANE, L.L.A. Illustrated. 1/

This little book gives the main outlines of the lives of the founders of Scottish political freedom. In its preparation the best authorities have been consulted, and here is given in small bulk the results of research only to be found in larger volumes more difficult of access.

WILLIAM SHAKESPEARE: the Story of his Life and Times. By EVAN J. CUTHBERTSON. With Portrait and numerous Illustrations. 1/

Gives in brief and compact form what history, tradition, and research are able to tell us of the life-story of the world's greatest dramatist. An attempt is made to picture the England he lived in, the scenes among which he moved, the people he associated with, and the customs that bound him.

QUEEN VICTORIA: the Story of her Life and Reign. 1/

'A sympathetic and popular sketch of the life and rule of our Queen up to the present day.'—*Manchester Guardian.*

W. & R. Chambers, Limited, London and Edinburgh.

LORD SHAFTESBURY AND GEORGE PEABODY. Being the Story of Two Great Public Benefactors. With Portraits. 1/

'Cheap, interesting, and readable biographies.'—*Methodist Times.*
'May be recommended to young readers as being as inspiring as it is interesting.'—*Scotsman.*

WILLIAM I., GERMAN EMPEROR, AND HIS SUCCESSORS. By Mary Cochrane, L.L.A. Illustrated. 1/

'Must take a prominent place among compilations on the same subject. . . . Compact and comprehensive.'—*Daily Chronicle.*

THOMAS CARLYLE: the Story of his Life and Writings. 1/

'We don't know where to find a better biography of any man at the price.'—*Methodist Times.*

THOMAS ALVA EDISON: the Story of his Life and Inventions. By E. C. Kenyon. 1/

'It will repay any one who is interested in Edison's various works to read this little book.'—*Inventions.*

THE STORY OF WATT AND STEPHENSON. 1/

'As a gift-book for boys this is simply first-rate.'—*Schoolmaster.*

THE STORY OF NELSON AND WELLINGTON. 1/

'This book is cheap, artistic, and instructive. It should be in the library of every home and school.'—*Schoolmaster.*

GENERAL GORDON AND LORD DUNDONALD: the Story of Two Heroic Lives. 1/

THOMAS TELFORD AND JAMES BRINDLEY. 1/

'This is a capital book for boys of active and inquiring mind.'—*Saturday Review.*

LIVINGSTONE AND STANLEY: the Story of the opening up of the Dark Continent. 1/

W. & R. Chambers, Limited, London and Edinburgh.

COLUMBUS AND COOK: the Story of their Lives, Voyages, and Discoveries. 1/

'Models of compact biography.'—*Christian World.*
'Is a fascinating and historical account of daring adventure.'—*Bristol Mercury.*

THE STORY OF THE LIFE OF SIR WALTER SCOTT. By ROBERT CHAMBERS, LL.D. Revised, with additions, including the AUTOBIOGRAPHY. 1/

Besides the AUTOBIOGRAPHY, many interesting and characteristic anecdotes of the boyhood of Scott, which challenge the attention of the young reader, have been added; while the whole has been revised and brought up to date.

THE STORY OF HOWARD AND OBERLIN. 1/

The book is equally divided between the lives of Howard the prison reformer, and Oberlin the pastor and philanthropist, who worked such a wonderful reformation amongst the dwellers in a valley of the Vosges Mountains.

THE STORY OF NAPOLEON BONAPARTE. 1/

A brief and graphic life of the first Napoleon, set in a history of his own times: the battle of Waterloo, as of special interest to English readers, being fully narrated.

PERSEVERANCE AND SUCCESS: the Life of William Hutton. 1/

STORY OF A LONG AND BUSY LIFE. By W. CHAMBERS, LL.D. 1/

STORIES FOR YOUNG PEOPLE.

WONDERFUL STORIES FOR CHILDREN. By HANS CHRISTIAN ANDERSEN. Translated by Mary Howitt. Illustrated. 1/

One of the first forms in which these ever-delightful stories of Hans Andersen were given to the British public.

W. & R. Chambers, Limited, London and Edinburgh.

A FAIRY GRANDMOTHER; or, Madge Ridd, a Little London Waif. By L. E. TIDDEMAN, author of *A Humble Heroine.* 1/

A realistic story of a London waif, who runs off from a drunken mother, and who after many adventures is adopted by a good old lady in the country, who proves herself a fairy grandmother indeed.

THE CHILDREN OF MELBY HALL. By M. and J. M'KEAN. Illustrated. 1/

These talks and stories of plant and animal life afford simple lessons on the importance of 'Eyes and No Eyes,' and show what an immense interest the study of natural history, even in its simplest forms, will produce in the minds of young folks.

MARK WESTCROFT, CORDWAINER: a Village Story. By F. SCARLETT POTTER. 1/

A HUMBLE HEROINE. By L. E. TIDDEMAN. 1/

BABY JOHN. By the author of *Laddie, Tip-Cat, Rose and Lavender,* &c. With Frontispiece by H. A. Bone. 1/

'Told with quite an unusual amount of pathos.'—*Spectator.*

THE GREEN CASKET; LEO'S POST-OFFICE; BRAVE LITTLE DENIS. By Mrs MOLESWORTH. 1/

Three charming stories by the author of the *Cuckoo Clock*, each teaching an important moral lesson.

JOHN'S ADVENTURES: a Tale of Old England. By THOMAS MILLER, author of *Boy's Country Book*, &c. 1/

THE BEWITCHED LAMP. By Mrs MOLESWORTH. With Frontispiece by Robert Barnes. 1/

ERNEST'S GOLDEN THREAD. 1/

LITTLE MARY, and other Stories. By L. T. MEADE. 1/

THE LITTLE KNIGHT. By EDITH C. KENYON. 1/

'Has an admirable moral. . . . Natural, amusing, pathetic.'—*Manchester Guardian.*

WILFRID CLIFFORD, or The Little Knight Again. By EDITH C. KENYON. With Frontispiece by W. S. Stacey. 1/

W. & R. Chambers, Limited, London and Edinburgh.

ZOE. By the author of *Tip-Cat, Laddie*, &c. 1/
'A charming and touching study of child life.'—*Scotsman*.

UNCLE SAM'S MONEY-BOX. By Mrs S. C. HALL. 1/

THEIR HAPPIEST CHRISTMAS. By EDNA LYALL, author of *Donovan*, &c. 1/

FIRESIDE AMUSEMENTS; a Book of Indoor Games. 1/
'A thoroughly useful work, which should be welcomed by all who have the organisation of children's parties.'—*Review of Reviews*.

THE STEADFAST GABRIEL: a Tale of Wichnor Wood. By MARY HOWITT. 1/

GRANDMAMMA'S POCKETS. By Mrs S. C. HALL. 1/

THE SWAN'S EGG. By Mrs S. C. HALL. 1/

MUTINY OF THE BOUNTY, and LIFE OF A SAILOR BOY. 1/

DUTY AND AFFECTION, or the Drummer-boy. 1/
A thrilling narrative of the wars of the first Napoleon.

FAMOUS POETRY. Being a collection of the best English verse. Illustrated. 1/

Price 9d.

Cloth, Illustrated.

YOUNG KING ARTHUR.
THE LITTLE CAPTIVE KING.
FOUND ON THE BATTLEFIELD.
ALICE ERROL, and other Tales.
THE WHISPERER. By Mrs S. C. HALL.
TRUE HEROISM, and other Stories.
PICCIOLA, and other Tales.

TWELFTH NIGHT KING.
JOE FULWOOD'S TRUST.
PAUL ARNOLD.
CLEVER BOYS.
THE LITTLE ROBINSON.
MIDSUMMER HOLIDAY.
MY BIRTHDAY BOOK.

W. & R. Chambers, Limited, London and Edinburgh.

Price 6d.

Cloth, with Illustrations.

'For good literature at a cheap rate, commend us to a little series published by W. & R. Chambers, which consists of a number of readable stories by good writers.'—*Review of Reviews.*

'One contains three little stories from the pen of Mrs Molesworth, one of the most charming of writers for the little ones; and the name of L. T. Meade is a guarantee of good reading of a kind which children are sure to enjoy.'—*School Board Chronicle.*

CASSIE, and LITTLE MARY. By L. T. MEADE.

A LONELY PUPPY, and THE TAMBOURINE GIRL. By L. T. MEADE.

LEO'S POST-OFFICE, and BRAVE LITTLE DENIS. By Mrs MOLESWORTH.

GERALD AND DOT. By Mrs FAIRBAIRN.

KITTY AND HARRY. By EMMA GELLIBRAND, author of *J. Cole*.

DICKORY DOCK. By L. T. MEADE, author of *Scamp and I*, &c.

FRED STAMFORD'S START IN LIFE. By Mrs FAIRBAIRN.

NESTA; or Fragments of a Little Life. By Mrs MOLESWORTH.

NIGHT-HAWKS. By the Hon. EVA KNATCHBULL-HUGESSEN.

A FARTHINGFUL. By L. T. MEADE.

POOR MISS CAROLINA. By L. T. MEADE.

THE GOLDEN LADY. By L. T. MEADE.

MALCOLM AND DORIS; or Learning to Help. By DAVINA WATERSON.

WILLIE NICHOLLS; or False Shame and True Shame.

SELF-DENIAL. By Miss EDGEWORTH.

W. & R. Chambers, Limited, London and Edinburgh.

www.ingramcontent.com/pod-product-compliance
Lightning Source LLC
Chambersburg PA
CBHW020233240426
43672CB00006B/510